Reading and Responding in the Middle Grades

Approaches for All Classrooms

Lee Galda
University of Minnesota

Michael F. Graves
University of Minnesota

Boston • New York • San Francisco
Mexico City • Montreal • Toronto • London • Madrid • Munich • Paris
Hong Kong • Singapore • Tokyo • Cape Town • Sydney

Executive Editor: *Aurora Martínez Ramos*
Editorial Assistant: *Mekea Harvey*
Executive Marketing Manager: *Krista Clark*
Production Editor: *Janet Domingo*
Editorial Production Service: *Omegatype Typography, Inc.*
Composition Buyer: *Linda Cox*
Manufacturing Buyer: *Linda Morris*
Electronic Composition: *Omegatype Typography, Inc.*
Photo Researcher: *Annie Pickert*
Cover Administrator: *Joel Gendron*

For related titles and support materials, visit our online catalog at www.ablongman.com.

Between the time Website information is gathered and then published, it is not unusual for some sites to have closed. Also, the transcription of URLs can result in typographical errors. The publisher would appreciate notification where these errors occur so that they may be corrected in subsequent editions.

Library of Congress Cataloging-in-Publication Data

Galda, Lee.
  Reading and responding in the middle grades : approaches for all classrooms / Lee Galda, Michael F. Graves.
    p. cm.
  Includes bibliographical references and index.
  ISBN 0-205-49122-7 (pbk.)
  1. Reading (Middle school) 2. Middle school students—Books and reading. 3. Reading comprehension. I. Graves, Michael F. II. Title.

LB1632.G345 2007
428.4071'2—dc22

                                                                                    2005057484

Printed in the United States of America

10 9 8 7 6 5 4 3 2 1   10 09 08 07 06

Photo credits appear on p. 292, which constitutes an extension of the copyright page.

Contents

Preface

Middle-grade teachers occupy many roles and face many responsibilities. Some are reading teachers; others are English and language arts teachers; and still others are science teachers, social studies teachers, health teachers, and so on. No matter their specific role and job title, one thing that all middle-grade teachers share is the need to help their students become increasingly proficient readers. Most middle-grade students know how to read, but many of them are not truly proficient readers. Many cannot fully comprehend the increasingly challenging narrative and expository texts they meet in the middle grades; many don't read widely or respond in the myriad ways possible to the subtleties of the middle-grade literature they encounter; and many don't yet know how to read to learn, how to use their reading abilities to master the important concepts that make up the curricula of science, social studies, mathematics, art, music, and language. This text is meant to help middle-grade teachers help their students hone their reading abilities, learn from what they read, and become increasingly motivated to read and competent in responding to the sophisticated texts they encounter in the middle grades and beyond.

In Chapter 1, the Middle-School Learner, we consider the middle-grade learner and the basic theoretical frameworks of a cognitive approach to reading, a social–constructivist orientation to learning, and a transactional theory of literary response. In Chapter 2, Motivation and Engagement, we discuss the importance of motivation and present key ideas that will help you understand the complexities of motivation and effective strategies for engaging your students in learning literacy. Chapter 3, Literature for Adolescents, explores adolescent literature and some of the excellent, authentic materials—fiction, exposition, and poetry—that have been written for adolescents. In Chapter 4, we present strategies for Scaffolding Students' Comprehension, Learning, and Engagement with Text. Chapter 5 provides additional information on comprehension instruction as we consider Teaching Comprehension and Study Strategies. In Chapter 6, Teaching Literature, we return to adolescent literature and discuss practices that promote reading and responding to literature. Chapter 7 explores Fostering Higher-Order Thinking and Deep Understanding. In Chapter 8, Vocabulary Instruction, we describe a multi-pronged approach to the challenging task of building students' vocabularies. Ongoing assessment is integral to good teaching, and Chapter 9 focuses on Assessment, presenting rationales and strategies for classroom assessments that shape good instructional practice. Finally, in Chapter 10, Organizing Classrooms to Promote Reading and Responding, we discuss some ways to organize your classroom and present several portraits of effective middle-grade classrooms. We hope that when you finish this text you will have a more complete knowledge of effective teaching practices, as well as an understanding of why they are effective, and how the learning that they foster can make a difference in the lives of your students.

Acknowledgments

As in most endeavors in life, this book was not written without the help of others. Cheri Cooke has done a marvelous job with the Instructor's Manual and other ancillaries. We also want to acknowledge the assistance of many teachers we know, people such as David Carberry, Todd Roudabush, and Jessie Dockter, our graduate students including Lauren Liang, and our editor at Allyn and Bacon, Aurora Martínez Ramos. We would also like to thank the reviewers of this book for their helpful comments: Maribelle Betterton, University of Northern Iowa; Maria Ceprano, Buffalo State College; Cheryl Dzuback, Howard Community College; and Kurtis Meredith, University of Northern Iowa.

As always, we are grateful to our spouses and children, to Bonnie, Julie, and Erin Graves and to Tony, Anna, and Adam Pellegrini.

About the Authors

Lee Galda, after teaching in elementary and middle school classrooms for a number of years, received her Ph.D. in English Education from New York University. Formerly at the University of Georgia, she is now a professor at the University of Minnesota where she teaches courses in children's and adolescent literature and language arts. Dr. Galda is a member of the National Reading conference, the National Council of Teachers of English, the International Reading Association, the American Library Association, and the United States Board on Books for Young People and has been on the review boards of many professional journals. She was the Children's Books Department editor for *The Reading Teacher* and a member of the 2003 Newbery Award selection committee. Author of numerous articles and book chapters, Dr. Galda co-authored a chapter on research in children's literature in the *Handbook of Reading Research, Volume III* (2000, Erlbaum), and is the co-author of *Literature and the Child, 6th edition* (2006, Wadsworth).

Michael Graves is Professor of Literacy Education at the University of Minnesota. He received his Ph.D. in Education from Stanford University and his M.A. and B.A. in English from California State College at Long Beach, and he has taught in the Long Beach and Huntington Beach Public Schools. His research and development efforts focus on compre-hension instruction and vocabulary learning and instruction. His recent books include *Teaching Reading in the 21st Century* (4th edition in press, with Connie Juel and Bonnie Graves, Allyn & Bacon), *The Vocabulary Book* (2006, Teachers College Press, IRA, and NCTE), and *Scaffolding Reading Experiences for English-Language Learners* (2004, with Jill Fitzgerald, Christopher-Gordon). He has also published in journals such as *Reading Research Quarterly, Research in the Teaching of English, Journal of Educational Psychology, Journal of Reading Behavior, The Reading Teacher, Journal of Adolescent and Adult Literacy, Elementary School Journal, American Educator,* and *Educational Leadership.* Dr. Graves is the former editor of the *Journal of Reading Behavior* and the former associate editor of *Research in the Teaching of English.*

The Middle-School Learner: Theory and Research That Inform Practice

Middle-grade students display a wide range of physical, emotional, and cognitive maturity.

The fifth graders at Kalen Elementary School are feeling pretty grown-up as they arrive for the first day of school. After all, they're the seniors in the school, the oldest students in the building. About half of them have been at Kalen since kindergarten; the others have arrived in their first through fourth grade years. They come from various parts of the city, including the neighborhood that surrounds the school. Some, including most of the boys, are small and look like young children. Others, including many of the girls, tower above the others, looking exactly like who they are—middle-grade students in transition from childhood to adulthood.

This transition period, called adolescence, is apparent a few miles away in Arthur Middle School as well. Last year's fifth graders at Kalen—the big shots—are this year's sixth graders at Arthur, and in comparison to the eighth graders they look almost as young as the fifth graders at Kalen. These sixth graders are still very different, and the same is true of the seventh and eighth grade students. While some boys have grown tall and are beginning to get muscular, others remain short and skinny, or plump. Almost all of the girls are beginning to look like women, and the mix of boys and girls looks incongruous. They range from kids who don't look old enough to be in middle school to kids who look old enough to be holding down a job, as some of them do.

By the end of the year, these students will have matured in many different ways. Girls generally begin the physical changes of puberty in grades four through eight. Boys generally begin their physical changes between sixth and tenth grade. Along with these physical changes come intellectual and social challenges and changes. Thus the disparity in the way they look; thus the turmoil that marks adolescence in the middle-grade years; thus the joys and challenges of teaching in the middle grades.

What This Book Is About

We write this book out of our own experience with middle-grade students—as teachers and as parents—as well as our more than 50 cumulative years of experience helping middle-grade teachers learn how to teach reading, the English language arts, and reading in the content areas. We also bring to this task our expertise in two complementary areas: literature and reading. Too often, middle-grade teachers have been trained to teach either a subject area, such as English or social studies, or reading as a tool, but not both. Yet in many, many middle-grade classrooms, teachers need to do both. We also write this book out of our conviction that helping middle-grade students engage in reading is vitally important. The middle grades, with their fluctuating attitudes, emotions, skills, interests, and abilities, may be the last good opportunity to engage students as readers, to help them become fully fledged members of a literate community, to develop their practice of literacy, and to form them into thoughtful, critical readers and thinkers ready to assume their roles in our society. It is also a time to bolster students' competence in using reading as a tool for learning.

This book is about how to help middle-grade students learn, specifically how to help them learn how to read with understanding, recognizing and remembering important information; with a critical stance; and with a depth of personal engagement. Thus our focus is on working with printed texts in many genres. While we acknowledge the importance of oral language to reading and thinking about texts, we do not present information about developing oral language except as that relates to reading, as in creating an effective discussion group to talk about texts. Similarly, we do not present information about teaching writing, although we do indicate how writing supports learning about text. There are many fine books on teaching writing, such as Atwell's *In the Middle,* Calkins's *The Art of Teaching Writing,* and others.

The ideas that we explore are appropriate for all students—gifted or struggling, motivated or disengaged, fluent English-language users or English-language learners—with the teacher increasing or decreasing the challenge of the task through the texts that are used, the time allotted, and the way the tasks are framed. Where appropriate, we have noted ideas that are especially important to working with specific students, such as English-language learners.

Although this is a text about reading and responding, it is not just for the reading, English, or language arts classroom. Much of the information presented here is applicable to other content areas, such as social studies and science. The development of skills that allow middle-grade students to read to learn is important across all subject areas.

The content that we present in this and the next nine chapters is rooted in knowledge of middle-grade students, of how students learn, and of effective teaching practices. This knowledge is framed by some basic theoretical frameworks regarding teaching and learning: the cognitive–constructivist view of reading and transactional theory. The ideas that we present are also based on research; there is evidence about the effects of the sound educational practices that we advocate.

In this chapter we discuss the middle-grade learner and the basic theoretical frameworks of a cognitive approach to reading, a social–constructivist orientation to learning, and a transactional theory of literary response. In Chapter 2, Motivation and Engagement, we discuss the importance of motivation and present key ideas that will help you understand the complexities of motivation and effective strategies for engaging your students in learning literacy. Chapter 3, Literature for Adolescents, explores adolescent literature and some of the excellent, authentic materials—fiction, exposition, and poetry—that have been written for adolescents. In Chapter 4, we present strategies for Scaffolding Students' Comprehension, Learning, and Engagement with Text. Chapter 5 extends the focus on comprehension, with an examination of Teaching Comprehension and Study Strategies. In Chapter 6, Teaching Literature, we return to adolescent literature and discuss practices that promote reading and responding to literature. Chapter 7 explores Fostering Higher-Order Thinking and Deep Understanding. Vocabulary study is presented in Chapter 8. Ongoing assessment is integral to good teaching, and Chapter 9, Assessment, presents rationales and strategies for classroom assessments that shape good instructional practice. Finally, we present some ways to organize your classroom in Chapter 10, Organizing Classrooms to Promote Reading and Responding. We hope that when you finish this text you will have a more complete knowledge of effective teaching practices, as well as an understanding of why they are effective, and how the learning that they foster can make a difference in the lives of your students.

The Middle-Grade Learner

Look into any classroom that houses students from fifth through eighth grade and you will understand why these grades are often called the middle grades. They *are* in the middle, between elementary school and high school. Students in these grades are likewise in the middle—between childhood and adulthood, between girl and woman, boy and man. They also exhibit behaviors that reflect their in-between status, veering between kind and cruel, social and self-absorbed, accomplished and struggling. No wonder that Hynds (1997), in her book describing the working life of one middle-grade teacher and her students, uses the metaphor of a skateboarder on the brink of an edge.

When we think of the middle grades we not only think of the disparities among individual children, but also within individual children as they navigate their days. Often these vacillations are evident minute-by-minute as a mature response of "I'm sorry" when bumping into someone might be followed by an immature, shouted "Watch where you're going," when bumped into by someone else. Teachers and parents of middle-grade students need to be ready to support them in either guise, understanding that even those who look mature are still children, and that much of what they do is beyond their immediate control. Indeed, one of the markers of this young adolescent period is gaining increasing control of the physical, psychological, and social aspects of their lives.

This wide range of development across the physical, psychological, and social aspects of life is echoed in the wide range of reading abilities and behaviors that middle-grade students exhibit, both within and across individuals (Liang, 2004). Students might avoid independent reading, yet sit mesmerized as a teacher reads aloud from a picture book. Or the same students who work diligently on a research project might mask their discomfort about being in front of classmates by clowning around during their presentation. Across the typical middle-grade class, readers range from beginning readers to those who read at the twelfth-grade level or beyond. Ivey (2001) points out that even within individual readers there is a wide range of abilities, just as there is a wide range of emotion. For example, while a middle-grade student might be an accomplished reader when working with the adolescent fiction that she loves and is familiar with, this same reader might struggle with expository text. As Liang points out, reading abilities are not very consistent for many middle-school readers, just as behaviors and emotions aren't consistent, either. And to make matters even more complex, the demands of the reading task change as well.

During their elementary school years, students were engaged in learning to read. Now, in the middle grades, they are expected to read to learn. Halliday (1983) pointed out many years ago that people learn language, learn *about* language, and learn *through* language. By the middle grades the focus moves from learning language, in this case learning to read, to continuing to learn about reading and increasingly learn through reading in science, mathematics, social studies, literature, and other domains. This calls for increasingly sophisticated reading skills and strategies, as well as organizational skills and strategies (Alvermann & Moore, 1991). Not only does the focus change from learning to doing, but the texts that middle-grade students read become more complex. Expository texts for these readers contain highly developed concepts and increasingly complex information presented within challenging structures. Narrative fiction for adolescents often contains complex plot structure, ambiguity, and an increased demand for drawing inferences and making judgments. Factors like these help account for the fact that many middle-grade

Teaching Idea 1.1
Finding Issues of Interest

Talk with your students about things that you are interested in and what you like to read. For example, you might mention that you are really interested in reading nonfiction about space because you have always been fascinated by space exploration. Or you might say that you love fiction that explores family relationships. You should stress that you like to read books that help you find out about topics that you are interested in or that let you think about life experiences through someone else's eyes. Then ask your students to write down two or three reading interests that they might have. Compile these interests and take a list of them to your school librarian to enlist his or her help in finding books that might pique the interest of your students. If there are some interests that seem dominant, books that connect with those interests would be a good choice for reading as a class.

students develop negative attitudes toward reading for pleasure and reading instruction (McKenna, Kear, & Ellsworth, 1995). To make matters even worse, many students have less time in school for, and less choice about, independent reading (Stewart, Paradis, Ross, & Lewis, 1996; Worthy & McKool, 1996).

Physical, psychological, and social turmoil, coupled with increasing intellectual demands, make the middle grades a challenge for both teachers and students. Ready or not, most middle-grade students are moving from being in one classroom with one main teacher into an often bewildering array of rooms and teachers. Just as they most need a stable environment led by someone who knows them well, they may move among teachers who may have 150 other students each day. Even with that many students each day, teachers have many opportunities to get to know their students as they teach them to become increasingly sophisticated in their use of language to learn. Helping students learn to read, write, speak, and listen with increasing fluency and control involves giving them opportunities to develop the tools of literacy that will enable them to make sense of and shape their worlds. As they learn to read and write to learn in science, social studies, or literature, they also learn to read and write to discover themselves and their world. The opportunity to guide middle-grade students as they grapple with ideas, issues, and conflicts in both life and literature is as exciting as it is challenging. One way to find out about students' passions is described in Teaching Idea 1.1.

Discovering your students' passions is also a way to help you learn about the varied cultural contexts that they inhabit, many of which might be quite different from your own. Schools today are increasingly diverse, with students representing an increasing number of different cultural groups in many classrooms. Understanding the values, attitudes, customs, beliefs, and ethics of those groups is important if you want to connect what you do in school with the lives of students outside of school. As Moll and Greenberg (1990) point out, all cultures, families, and communities have a wealth of knowledge and skills that help them function in society. It is to your advantage to understand this and try to honor that knowledge in your classroom. Many teachers are successful at bringing parents and community leaders into their classrooms as experts on various topics that the class will consider. Other teachers help students connect across school and home cultures by being sure that the material they read is diverse. Given the increasingly global nature of our society, it is vital that all students learn to consider ideas and opinions that differ from their own. Many teachers incorporate the principles suggested by Banks (1996) and work to not only include diverse material, but to transform their curriculum into one that considers basic questions from a variety of perspectives. This can, in turn, lead to students' valuing the work they do in school as a way of learning about and affecting their lives, and the lives of others, at home.

Another aspect of the challenge of teaching the middle grades is the amount of intellectual growth that occurs during these years. Students begin to develop their analytical thinking skills in these grades, moving from a reliance on connecting their learning to their lived experience and seeing the world in terms of predefined categories, to being able to think abstractly and consider many possibilities. They begin to learn to think about what they know analytically, and to consider the possibility that they might be wrong, even as they fight passionately for their own ideas. They have an increased knowledge about and interest in a variety of topics. Perhaps most of all, they are passionate about many things, and good teachers learn how to help students harness this passion and bring it to the task of learning.

In addition to understanding middle-grade students as developing adolescents, it is important to have some general knowledge about their reading proficiency. The best source of such knowledge comes from large-scale assessments conducted by the National Assessment of Educational Progress (NAEP). Established by the federal government 35 years ago, NAEP provides a periodic report card on students' achievements in reading and other academic areas. In other words, it was established to do exactly the job we are trying to do here—communicate about how U.S. students are doing in school. NAEP typically tests about every 4 years, and reports data for 9-, 14-, and 17-year-olds, or students in grades 4, 8, and 12. The NAEP data clearly reveal two facts. First, students' average reading proficiency has remained virtually the same over the past 30 years, as shown in Figure 1.1 (Campbell, Hombo, & Mazzeo, 2000; Donahue, Finnegan, Lutkus, Allen, & Campbell, 2001; Donahue, Voelkl, Campbell, & Mazzeo, 1999). The most important feature of the graph to recognize is the slope, or rather the lack of slope, of the trend lines for each age level. For all practical purposes, the lines are flat. In 2000, U.S. students read very much like U.S. students did in 1971. Comparisons with even earlier times, though difficult to make because comparable data are in short supply, show very similar results (Anderson, Hiebert, Scott, & Wilkinson, 1985). This is not good news, because while students' proficiency is remaining the same, the demands for more sophisticated literacy continue to rise.

The second fact clearly revealed by NAEP data is that many middle-grade students do not read very well. The 2002 assessment (Grigg, Daane, Jin, & Campbell, 2003) showed that 37 percent of fourth graders and 26 percent of eighth graders performed below the basic level. As noted in a recent Department of Education report (Institute of Educational Sciences, 2004), this means that "when reading grade-appropriate text these students cannot abstract the general meaning or make obvious connections be-

Figure 1.1 **U.S. Students' Reading Proficiency, 1971–2003**

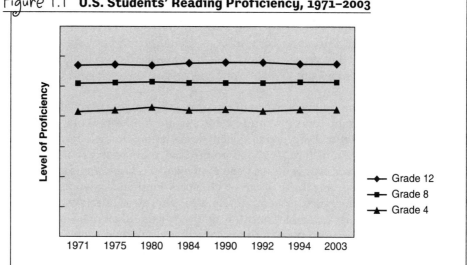

tween the text and their own experiences or make simple inferences from the text. In other words, they cannot understand what they read" (p. 2). Clearly, we need to help many middle-grade students become more proficient readers. And this can happen, if educators make good instructional decisions, such as those we present below, that are rooted in sound theory and backed by well-designed research.

The Cognitive–Constructivist View of Reading

The cognitive–constructivist view of reading emphasizes that reading is a process in which the reader actively searches for meaning in what she reads. This search for meaning depends very heavily on the reader's having an existing store of knowledge, or *schemata*, that she draws on in that search for meaning. In fact, the active contribution of the reader is significant enough to justify the assertion that she actually constructs much of the meaning she arrives at in reading.

The Cognitive Orientation

The earliest influence behind this view comes from cognitive psychology, which attempts to provide a window on the brain, focusing on how the mind processes information. For the past 35 years, the cognitive orientation has been the dominant force in educational psychology. Two characteristics of this orientation are particularly important to our discussion here. First, the cognitive approach views learners as active searchers for meaning rather than passive responders to external stimuli; much of the meaning an individual derives from a situation is thought to be constructed by the individual. Second, it places great importance on the development of knowledge as a crucial part of an individual's intellectual development, and views knowledge as central to intellectual activity. What a student already knows has a great deal to do with what she can learn and how much time and effort that learning will take.

Within these two broad dimensions of the cognitive orientation, four theoretical constructs are especially important to understanding and fostering students' learning and thus are particularly relevant to effective teaching: schema theory, the interactive model, automaticity, and metacognition.

Schema Theory. One of the central theories of cognitive psychology and one of the most important concepts influencing current thinking about reading is that of *schemata* (the plural of schema). Schemata are units of knowledge that individuals internalize. As Rumelhart (1980) has pointed out, they constitute our knowledge about "objects, situations, events, sequences of events, actions, and sequences of actions" (34). We have schemata for objects, such as cars; for situations, such as being in a restaurant; for events, such as weddings; and for sequences of actions, such as driving to and from work. Schemata constitute our knowledge about the world. We make sense out of what we read by attempting to fit the information we glean from a text to an existing schema. If, for example, we read about a waiter serving a meal, we immediately evoke our restaurant schema, and evoking that schema provides us with a wealth of information beyond that in the text. We know that customers can order a variety of foods from a menu, that the waiter will bring their food, and that they will need to pay for it when they are finished. Among the types of schemata that influence our understanding as we read are general knowledge of the world and its conventions, specific knowledge about various subjects, and linguistic knowledge—which includes some understanding of different patterns of textual organization. Importantly, having appropriate schemata for texts we read is crucial to understanding. As Adams and Bruce (1982) put it, "Without prior knowledge, a complex object such as a text is not just difficult to interpret; strictly speaking, it is meaningless" (23).

The Interactive Model of Reading. The interactive model of reading, another concept advanced by Rumelhart (1977), presents a number of concepts closely related to the concept of schema theory. Interactive models can be best understood when contrasted to text-based and reader-based models. Text-based models assume that the text is of utmost importance and that the reader processes text by first recognizing lower-level units and then repeatedly synthesizing lower-level units into more and more complex units. In this view, the reader might first perceive letters, then synthesize several letters to form words, then synthesize several words to form a phrase, and so on. The point is that in this view the processing operates in a single direction, from the text to the reader.

Reader-based models are the antithesis of text-based models. Reader-based models assume that the reader is of utmost importance and that the fluent reader processes text by first hypothesizing about the content of text and then selectively sampling the text to confirm or disconfirm the hypothesis. In this view, the reading process begins with the highest-level unit possible (meaning in the mind of the reader) and deals with lower-level units (for example, words) to a limited extent. Again, the processing operates in a single direction, in this view, from the reader to the text.

Interactive models differ from these one-directional models by assuming that readers arrive at meaning by simultaneously using information from several knowledge sources. These knowledge sources include letter-level knowledge, word-level knowledge, syntactic knowledge, and various types of world knowledge or schemata. Information moves simultaneously in two directions; the reader's background knowledge and the information that she gleans from the text interact to produce meaning.

Recognizing that reading is an interactive process serves as a caution against overemphasizing the role of readers' schemata in text comprehension. As we noted, readers' schemata are vital to their understanding texts; however, that does not mean texts are unimportant (Stanovich, 1994). For example, you would not understand much from a description of a baseball game unless you knew something about baseball. However, a *Sports Illustrated* article about the Oakland A's will convey a very different meaning than a *Boy's Life* story about a Little League team. Although no text is ever fully explicit, neither are texts vacuous. Texts constrain meaning; for example, no competent reader who knew anything about sports would interpret the Little League story as being about basketball. Good readers learn to rely appropriately on the text and on prior knowledge, and to adjust their relative reliance on the two, as appropriate for a particular text and a particular situation.

Automaticity. LaBerge and Samuels first explained the importance of automaticity to proficient reading in 1974, and since that time the importance of this straightforward concept has been universally recognized. An automatic activity is one that can be performed instantaneously and without conscious attention. Reading demands that a number of processes—for example, recognizing letters, recognizing words, assigning meaning to words, linking words to form propositions, and linking propositions to form larger units of meaning—be performed at the same time. If these processes are not automated, they demand attention. The mind's attentional capacity is limited. In reading, some processes—dealing with the meanings of sentences and longer units—demand attention. Other processes must be automated so that they do not demand attention. Otherwise, the brain's limited attentional capacity will be overburdened, and the reader will not be able to read with understanding.

In particular, two closely related processes must be automatic. One of these is recognizing words. Readers must automatically recognize the vast majority of words they encounter as they read. They cannot afford a mental process such as, "Oh. Let's see. Yes, this word is *intervention.*" The other process that must be automatic is assigning meaning to words. Readers must develop rapid access to word meanings. Thus, in addition to recognizing a word automatically, they must automatically (instantly and without conscious attention) assign meanings to the majority of words they encounter as they read. They cannot afford to go through a mental process such as, "*Intervention.* Now, what does that mean? Oh, yes. It means to interfere with something."

Metacognition. As applied to reading, metacognition refers to a person's knowledge about his or her understanding of a text and about what to do when comprehension breaks down. As Garner (1987) has noted, accomplished readers have metacognitive knowledge about themselves, the reading tasks they face, and the strategies they can employ in completing these tasks. For example, on beginning this section, a reader might realize that she has no prior knowledge about metacognition (self-knowledge), notice that the section is brief (task knowledge), and decide that the strategy of reading the section through several times would be fruitful (strategy knowledge).

In this example, the reader exhibited metacognitive knowledge prior to beginning reading. However, readers can also make use of metacognitive knowledge as they are reading or after they have completed a text. In fact, active awareness of one's comprehension while reading and the ability to use effective fix-up strategies when comprehension breaks down are essential to becoming an effective reader, and lack of such metacognitive skills is viewed as a particularly debilitating characteristic of poor readers. Whimby (1975) has given a particularly apt characterization of a metacognitive reader.

> A good reader proceeds smoothly and quickly as long as his understanding of the material is complete. But as soon as he senses that he has missed an idea, that the track has been lost, he brings smooth progress to a grinding halt. Advancing more slowly, he seeks clarification in the subsequent material, examining it for the light it can throw on the earlier trouble spot. If still dissatisfied with his grasp, he returns to the point where the difficulty began and rereads the section more carefully. He probes and analyzes phrases and sentences for their exact meaning; he tries to visualize abstruse descriptions; and through a series of approximations, deductions, and corrections, he translates scientific and technical terms into concrete examples. (91)

Teaching students to be metacognitive is one of the most important and challenging tasks you face, and it is a task we address in detail in Chapters 4 and 5. Good readers, then, bring their schemata, or units of knowledge about the world, to each act of reading, applying that knowledge to the texts they are reading. They read with automaticity, freeing their minds to focus on meaning. This focus on meaning allows them to be metacognitive about their reading, and notice if and when they stop understanding the text. Noticing difficulties allows them to employ various strategies to get them back on the road to meaning. In this view of reading, the reader is actively engaged in constructing knowledge from text. This active construction is an integral part of another theoretical orientation that has shaped our view of teaching and learning, social constructivism.

Pause and Reflect 1.1

Think about the last physical activity that you have tried to master—skiing, rollerblading, tennis, horseback riding. What was it like to perform the activity as you were trying to learn it? Were you able to think about how much you were enjoying what you were doing, or were you too focused on doing each part of the activity correctly? Did you have a coach who helped you notice when you were doing something wrong? Did you learn to notice your mistakes and correct them as you were performing the activity? Until you were able to perform the activity without thinking about each individual step, you had not achieved automaticity. Until you learned how to notice mistakes and self-correct, you had not developed sufficient metacognition about the activity. Once you had achieved automaticity and metacognitive awareness of your performance, you were able to have fun. So it is with reading. ■

The Social–Constructivist Orientation

The social–constructivist orientation has become increasingly influential in education over the past decade (Fosnot, 1996). This orientation is different from, but complementary to, the cognitive psychological orientation to reading. Here, we discuss three aspects of constructivist thinking and its relevance to teaching. First, we discuss the general concept of constructivism; next, we deal specifically with social constructivism; and, finally, we consider the importance the social–constructivist orientation gives to the contexts in which students learn.

Constructivism.   We introduced the notion of constructivism in discussing cognitive psychology when we pointed out that much of the meaning an individual derives from a situation is thought to be constructed by the individual himself or herself. For those who take a strong constructivist position, our knowledge of the world—whether it is knowledge gained from a text or knowledge from any other source—is not the result of phenomena in the real world. It is the result of our interpretation of those phenomena. The meaning we attain is, in fact, constructed by ourselves. Inherent tendencies in the ways we think, categorize, and process information shape the meanings we construct.

Social Constructivism.   Social constructivism begins with acceptance of the basic constructivist position, but then goes beyond this to take the position that it is the social world within which we live—our interactions with our friends, acquaintances, and the larger community—that shapes our understanding of reality. As Gergen (1985) has explained, we understand the world in terms of social considerations, considerations that are themselves the result of interchanges among people. Therefore, the process of understanding is not a direct outcome of viewing the real world; rather, it is influenced greatly by the social world in which we live. Social constructivism is a relativistic notion because our social and cultural backgrounds vary. Whether we are interpreting a text or some other phenomena, we do not all see the same thing. Given the importance of our socio-cultural contexts, it is vital that teachers try to know about their students' lives both in and out of school. This becomes increasingly important as our students become more diverse, children whose experiences are less and less like those of their teachers. One way to learn about students' home lives is described in Teaching Idea 1.2.

Social–constructivist thinking has influenced educational practice. It is one of the factors motivating the interest in and endorsement of small-group work, particularly cooperative learning. If much of what a child learns or understands comes from her social interactions with others, then schools need to provide students with many opportunities for productive social interactions. All students benefit from this, and research indicates that cooperative group work can be an especially effective way to work with English-language learners (Gersten & Baker, 2000; Jimenez, 2000). We certainly agree with this position, and we point out opportunities for cooperative work throughout the book.

Social–constructivist thinking is also consonant with transactional theory. According to reader-response, or transactional theory (Galda and Guice, 1997), making meaning from literary texts is very much influenced by both the personal and

Teaching Idea 1.2
Discovering Who Students Are Outside of School

Ask your students to write about their lives in any or all of the following ways:

- Have them keep a diary for one week in which they record what they do before and after school.
- Ask them to write a letter to you in which they introduce themselves and their families and friends.
- Give them disposable cameras and have them photograph people and places that are important to them and then create a collage with captions.

- Using the same photographs, have them write descriptions of the photographs and why that person or place is important to their lives.
- Have students create a symbol for themselves and describe why it is a good symbol.
- Ask students to write brief character sketches of three people who are important to them.

the social contexts that surround every reader. We discuss transactional theory below.

The Significance of Context.   Social–constructivist thinking has also led educators to a realization of the importance of the contexts of students' learning. Think of contexts in terms of the texts students read, the immediate context of instruction, and the larger context of the place of reading in their school world and their world outside of school.

Reading educators have come to believe that the majority of the texts that students read should be authentic and complete. *Authentic* texts are those written by authors for the primary purpose of engaging or informing children and adolescents. These are contrasted with *contrived* texts, those written or modified by educators for the purpose of teaching some sort of reading skills. Worksheets can be viewed as contrived texts, or texts out of context. They are also usually partial texts. Complete texts—texts that constitute whole, understandable, and enjoyable units of discourse—are much more effective than partial or excerpted texts. Even when a particular chapter from a novel can be understood when it stands alone, it is still only a piece of a larger text, whereas as a short story is meant to stand alone, as a complete text. Although the occasional use of contrived or partial texts might be an efficient way to teach a particular skill or strategy, the basic reading fare in any classroom should be authentic, complete texts.

Instructional context is also important to consider, as there are problems inherent in using artificial materials, such as contrived texts, in artificial settings. Thus, asking students to complete worksheets that require them to circle prefixes and suffixes, or teaching them how to identify the main idea by working with paragraphs specifically written to teach main ideas, is problematic. While it is some-

Middle-grade students enjoy reading and talking together.

times efficient and effective to pull material and teach strategies and skills out of context, it is vital that students work with the newly learned material or skill in an authentic context, with authentic texts, as soon as possible. Until students can use what you are teaching in contexts that are meaningful and functional, the skills and material that you teach are, in a very real sense, meaningless. Unless students can transfer the knowledge of what you are teaching to new situations and experiences, your teaching has not helped them develop the schemata necessary to further learning.

The broader context in which children read—the literate environment in the classroom and the literate environment in their worlds—is the final context to consider. These contexts have a great influence on students' motivation and engagement in the work of literacy, as we discuss in Chapter 2. Simply put, if students can't see a meaningful reason to engage in the task of becoming fully literate, they won't. Creating a supportive and vibrant literate environment in the classroom, and helping students understand the uses and power of literacy in their own lives, is an important part of teaching.

Transactional Theory: Response to Literature

Just as the cognitive–constructivist view has transformed the teaching of reading, transactional theory, also known as reader-response theory, has transformed the teaching of literature by bringing to the foreground the essential work of the reader in the creation of meaning. Literature is open to the interpretation of its readers, but reading is shaped by the text being read. Transactional theory describes reading as a transactional, temporal, social, cultural, and transformational activity.

When middle-grade students are engaged with books they learn about themselves and the world around them.

Reading as Transactional

The idea of reading as a transaction between reader and text was first proposed by Louise Rosenblatt in 1938. In her view, active readers bring themselves with them when they read. They bring experience, expectations, knowledge, preferences, attitudes, values, and beliefs to the act of reading, along with varying degrees of reading proficiency, but the text itself, the words on the page, guides and shapes the meaning that readers create (Rosenblatt, 1976, 1978). The old metaphor of a careful reader mining a text to discover an author's meaning (which the teacher knows) has given way to a new vision of readers actively creating meaning with the text, filtering the words on the page through all that they know and feel to create a meaning that is at once unique to an individual and shared and shaped by the text itself and the cultural context in which readers are situated. The author is also a part of the picture, as shown in Figure 1.2.

In Figure 1.2, the intersection of readers, others (including the author), and text represents the shared meaning of any given text, where the intended meaning of the author, encoded in the text, and the constructed meaning of readers, created with the text, are congruent. As Purves (1993) argues, this constitutes the accepted meaning of any given text within a particular cultural, literary, and experiential context. The area where text and reader intersect represents the significance of the text to individual readers. Simplistically, this might play out as follows: We read a story about a mother and child going to visit the child's grandmother. We can agree on the basic story, but the significance of the story in our own lives depends on the connotations of the words in the text. Words such as mother, or grandmother, or child, will reverberate with our own significance, our own embellished meaning. This creation of individual significance and shared meaning is at the heart of transactional theory. Langer (1995) calls this process *envisionment*.

Figure 1.2 **A Model of Response to Literature**

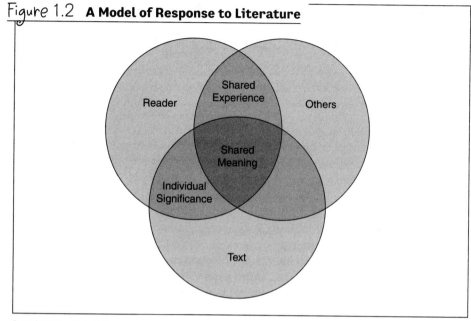

Based on Purves (1993)

Pause and Reflect 1.2

Recall the last time you sat and talked with another person about a book. It might have been during your book club's last meeting, a chat with a friend about a book that she recommended that you read, or a chance encounter with a stranger at your local bookstore. What were the similarities in your response to the book you discussed? What were the differences? What might be the reasons behind these similarities and differences? ■

Reading as Temporal

Reading is an event in time and across time. Langer (1995) describes the temporal dimension of reading in four parts: being out and stepping in to an envisionment, being in and moving through, being in and stepping out to think about what is known, and stepping out and objectifying the experience. As you begin to read you move from the real world into the world of the text, whether narrative, descriptive, or expository. As you move through the text you are creating meaning with the guidance of the text. At points you may step out of the envisionment that you have created and think about what you know, then step back into the text and continue. You may also step out of the text and look at it as an object, perhaps thinking in terms of structural or stylistic analysis, of logical argument, of effective presentation of information.

Teaching Idea 1.3
Helping Students Think about Approaches to Text

Find two brief passages of narrative fiction in the textbook that you use and write a set of directions for reading each passage. For passage 1, make your directions such that they focus students' attention on information that you wish them to retain (efferent reading). For passage 2, make your directions such that they focus students' attention on the experience that they create while reading (aesthetic reading). Have students read the passages and then discuss the difference in the reading experiences. Then do the same with two passages of expository nonfiction. Discuss with students how different types of text require different approaches.

How readers work with texts to create meaning differs according to the stance, or approach to text, that governs the evocation. Readers, Langer (1995) argues, read some texts in a manner that is *point driven*, in which they focus on an increasingly evident point—on the idea, information, or concept that is the subject of the text. Rosenblatt (1978) calls this *efferent* reading, in which readers seek to carry away knowledge for use in the real world. From a different stance, readers read for a *horizon of possibilities*, (Langer), or aesthetically (Rosenblatt). Reading from an aesthetic stance focuses on the experience of the text itself, the virtual experience that readers create for themselves with the guidance of the words on the page. Unlike efferent reading, aesthetic reading does not equip readers to immediately act in the real world, but it does allow them to contemplate life, and to build values.

Most reading varies along a continuum between aesthetic and efferent (Rosenblatt, 1978), even when a text signals that one or the other is a more appropriate stance. For example, those who love to cook might read a well-crafted cook book from both an aesthetic and an efferent stance. An aesthetic reading would include reading and thinking about enticing recipes, imagining what they might taste like, how they might look, and creating them virtually, or in the mind's eye. An efferent reading would note ingredients needed, time required, and would probably result in a grocery list and, eventually, a good dinner. Generally, a more efferent stance is most effective with nonfiction texts, especially those with an expository structure, while a more aesthetic stance is most effective with fiction and poetry. Good readers understand how to vary their stance according to the types of text they are reading. One way to introduce students to the idea of different stances is described in Teaching Idea 1.3.

Reading as Social and Cultural

Reading as a social and cultural process is an idea rooted in the social–constructivist tradition. Although reading is often thought of as something people do alone, we all read in the company of others, in a "community of readers" (Fish, 1980), even when reading to ourselves, alone in a room. While some readers belong to multiple reading communities—family, friends, and other groups—most students operate most of the time in the community of readers made up of their teachers and peers in the classroom. This community generates expectations that influence how students read, and how they respond to what they read. Students learn ways of taking meaning from text based on the directions for reading that are given, the assignments to be completed, and the responses of others in that community. What students talk about and how they talk about it are structured by the teacher and others who comprise the classroom community. When individual readers share their personal meanings with others, these meanings become part of a socio-culturally constructed interpretation of a text. Students test, alter, and enlarge their sense of meaning while talking about texts with others, or responding through writing, acting, singing, or drawing. As students share their personal meanings with each other, one person's responses to the text interweave with the responses of others. Additionally, other books that students have read influence the meanings that they create.

There is an even broader community at work in shaping how readers read as well as how writers write. Broad cultural expectations influence how people read, and the values, attitudes, and world views that readers bring to any text interact with the values, ideas, and world view of the author who has created that text. When what you read reflects your social and cultural understandings and beliefs, it is difficult to notice how that influences your reading, but when you read books that challenge your assumptions, these assumptions become evident. Even your understanding of the author's historical context is shaped by your own. (See Lewis, 2001, for an extended description of how the socio-cultural context affects how people read literature.)

Reading as Transformational

Not only do readers transform words into meaning, but when readers engage with texts, they have the opportunity to transform themselves as well. When engaged readers read, there is the potential to increase knowledge and to build values. Reading nonfiction texts transforms the knowledge readers hold as they take in new information and alter concepts. Reading fiction and poetry transforms readers through the creation of virtual experiences that add to readers' real-world experiences. This increased repertoire of lived-through experience offers readers more opportunities for understanding both literature and life. Because these virtual experiences don't require immediate action (Britton, 1970), readers are able to think about these experiences, to contemplate them in a manner that allows readers to construct their values as well as add to their well of experiences. The opportunity to help students shape the way they look at and interact with the world is perhaps the most exciting aspect of teaching literature. The books students read and and how they read them will make a difference.

Concluding Remarks

Middle-grade students are in a time of tremendous transition. They are moving from childhood to adulthood, and their physical, social, emotional, and intellectual attributes and capacities are changing, both over the period of adolescence and within any given moment. The demands that school places upon them change as well, as they increasingly must read to learn in a variety of domains. This challenge demands teaching that is based in sound theory and grounded in research. A cognitive–constructivist orientation to reading and a transactional perspective on literature are important theoretical orientations that are backed by extensive research. They form the basis for sound and effective literacy teaching.

When middle-grade students discover the possibilities that are inherent in reading, they discover meaningful purposes for engaging in the work of literacy—seeing that they are not alone as they read stories about others grappling with life issues similar to theirs, discovering new knowledge that unleashes their curiosity and drives them to find out more, and realizing that the world of books can take them places they haven't yet even imagined. Planning for and watching this happen is a wonderful experience.

▪ EXTENDING LEARNING

1. Select an aspect of cognitive–constructivist or transactional theory that interests you and gather a few research articles that explore this. Write a brief (three- to five-page) paper in which you explain the research, and why it matters to you as a teacher, to your peers. Then form small groups with various expertise and teach each other what you know.

2. Observe middle-grade students in your own or another teacher's reading, language arts, or content-area class. What do they look like? What do they say? What do you see them doing? How do they respond to the tasks the teacher sets? Describe this either orally or in writing to a peer and then discuss the following: What can you infer from what you see? Why might your inferences be incorrect?

3. Think about where you are teaching or will teach and identify community resources that can help you learn about your students' lives outside of school. Visit those community organizations and share what you discover with your peers.

Chapter 2

Motivation and Engagement

Although there is no single key to literacy, motivation is hugely important.

Steve is in his tenth year as an elementary teacher, and in those 10 years he has really learned how to make things work. As soon as you walk into Room 4-B, you realize that this is a teacher who cares about and respects kids and learning. The room itself invites discovery and learning. Desks are arranged so that Steve can use whole-group instruction when he wants to, but there are tables and a rug area available for small group work and discussion. The room also has a library center with an inviting collection of books, computers, a table for writing and doing research, a small tent for quiet reading and contemplation, and a couple of bean bag chairs that invite readers. Eye-catching bulletin boards highlight class projects and topics being studied. On the boards are lists of class activities, rules for procedures and behavior, class chore lists, progress reports on class and group projects—and lots of student work.

Of course, the classroom's physical environment is not the real draw. It's what goes on here. At the beginning of the day, as the students come into the room, Steve greets them by name. As the lessons begin, Steve's enthusiasm for teaching and learning are contagious. The students respond to his explanations of new concepts or assignments with animation and enthusiasm. Whether students are working in groups or alone—reading or writing—it is clear: they view the classroom as an interesting and rewarding place. They value their pursuit of learning. They are actively involved in learning, and, in fact, are learning.

The atmosphere Steve has created and the activities he provides make it obvious that Steve cares about his students and enjoys being their teacher. His classroom looks and feels like other highly motivating classrooms. It is filled with energy as he and his students work together to learn. Indeed, it reflects what Bogner, Raphael, and Pressley (2002) saw in the most engaged classrooms they observed:

> What was so striking about the most engaged classrooms was that the positive motivating instruction was so dense that it was nearly impossible for the observers to keep up with it. One second the teacher might be praising a child for working hard on a challenging writing assignment and the next second the teacher could be scaffolding another child's reading. (p. 161)

Good teaching and strong motivation and engagement, that's what Steve has accomplished. The two go hand in hand; you can't have one without the other, and that fact is reflected throughout this book. In this chapter, however, we concentrate specifically on motivation and engagement.

Motivation and engagement are essential to effective classrooms. As Bogner and her colleagues suggest, the best teachers saturate their classrooms with motivation. Yet as they and many others who have observed classrooms note, most teachers do not saturate their classrooms with motivation, and in some cases engage in a good deal of behavior that is unmotivating. Moreover, there is strong evidence that while the vast majority of children begin school with high expectations for success in reading and in school generally, by the upper elementary and middle grades many children are much less motivated and much less positive about school (McKenna, 2001; Pressley, Dolezal, Raphael, Mohan, Roehrig, & Bogner, 2003; Wigfield, 2000). We believe that middle-grade teachers can and must reverse this trend, and we are encouraged by the fact that there is a strong and consistent body of available information on how to do so. The remainder of the chapter presents that information.

In the next section, we discuss the concept of a literate environment, the most general concept we present here. In the section following that, we discuss the concepts of attribution theory and learned helplessness, two closely related concepts that account for the lack of motivation in many middle-grade students. In the section following that, the longest section of the chapter, we discuss specific approaches you can take to increase motivation. These include ensuring student success, providing appropriate challenges, grouping students to promote learning and positive attitudes, and using praise and other methods of directly motivating students. In the last section of the chapter, we present summaries of research-based suggestions for motivating students, partly to reinforce the ideas we present in the chapter and partly to make the point that there is a great deal of agreement about how to motivate and engage learners.

Creating a Literate Environment

The phrase *literate environment* describes the sort of classroom, school, and home environment in which literacy will be fostered and nurtured (Goodman, 1986). A literate environment includes demonstrations of literacy in action by competent others, time devoted to the practice of literacy, materials that support engagement in literacy, choice about literate activities, and a safe and supportive classroom climate.

Demonstration

One of the most important components of a literate environment is the modeling done by people that children respect and love. In the best possible literate environment, children's teachers, principals, parents, brothers and sisters, and friends read a lot and openly display the pleasure reading gives them, the fact that reading opens up a world of information and ideas to them, the value they place in reading, and the satisfaction they gain from reading. To be most effective, of course, this modeling should occur not just once but repeatedly—all the time, really. Also, this modeling should include repeated demonstrations such as your reading along with students during a sustained silent reading period, your looking up an answer to a question children have in a book, and your sharing a favorite poem with the class. It also includes many direct testimonials in which you say things such as "Wow! What a story," "I never realized that monarch butterflies were so incredible until I read this article," or "Sometimes I think the library is just about my favorite place."

Teachers who frequently demonstrate their enthusiasm and give direct testimonials such as these find that their enthusiasm is contagious and their students catch the reading bug from them and from one another. Fifth-grade teacher Mary Lou Flicker has her own testimonial to the power of modeling.

> I never realized the importance of modeling the kinds of behaviors I would like my students to emulate until one rainy day in March. Normally the kids eat outdoors on picnic tables, but during this unusual California downpour we were forced inside for lunch recess. After the kids finished eating, I told them they could play games together quietly, draw on the chalkboard, read, whatever.
>
> Instead of doing paperwork or watching the kids, I decided to read a book that a friend had recommended, Betty Bao Lord's *In the Year of the Boar and Jackie Robinson.* The book really grabbed my attention, and for a time I was fully absorbed in it, virtually forgetting the class. After I'd read a chapter or two, I sort of came out of my spell and looked around the room. To my amazement, there in the library corner, sat Ramon, one of my least-motivated readers, a kid who hardly ever read by choice, fully absorbed in the backup copy of *In the Year of the Boar and Jackie Robinson* from the class library. Later in the day, when I told Ramon I was so pleased to see him reading, he said, "Well, you looked like you was having such a great time reading that Jackie Robinson book that I just had to find out why!"

Several things about this experience were motivating to students. First was Ms. Flicker's modeling of engaged reading. Second was that she showed students how much she valued reading by spending class time on reading. Third was that she praised her student's good behavior.

Time

Demonstrating the value of reading goes beyond demonstrating your own engagement and includes scheduling class time for reading, whether independent or assigned. Regularly scheduled time for independent reading such as sustained silent reading tells students that teachers really care about reading. Time in class to read assigned texts also tells students that reading is important. Too often, reading is relegated to homework, or as a filler when there is time left after the real work of school is finished. But reading *is* the real work of the classroom! Time devoted to the pleasure of books and other texts tells students that you value books and want students to do so as well.

We know that reading independently improves reading fluency and reading achievement more generally (Allington, 1984; Knapp & Associates, 1995; Taylor, Frye, & Maruyama, 1990; Taylor, Pressley, & Pearson, 2002), but most students do not do enough of it. Most authorities estimate that middle-grade students spend only about 15 minutes per day doing silent reading in school. It's difficult to become good at something that you do for only 15 minutes a day.

Fifteen minutes a day of in-school reading could, of course, be augmented with independent reading at home; but again, studies demonstrate that children, unless they are already avid readers, simply do not make the time to read at home. Anderson, Wilson, and Fielding (1988) discovered that among the fifth-grade students they studied, 50 percent read only 4 minutes a day or less, 30 percent 2 minutes a day or less, and 10 percent not at all. They also found that independent reading time in school and time spent listening to books read aloud by the teacher were important factors in motivating students to read. All in all, we believe that students should do at least 30 minutes of in-school reading a day. This figure includes time spent reading in both language arts classes and in other content area classes.

Reading aloud to students is another way to demonstrate how much you value reading, and it also becomes an opportunity to teach students about the rewards that reading brings. What you choose to read aloud can serve to entice students to broaden the scope of their reading interests. It allows you to introduce new authors, new genres, and new ideas. It creates a communal experience that students can use to understand new texts that they read, new ideas that they consider. Reading aloud offers you the opportunity to talk about writing in a way that is concrete and engaging; students enjoy learning about how writing works when they are engaged with a text.

Reading aloud can also become a way to share engaging fiction and nonfiction with students who might not be able to read it on their own. Middle-grade students who are struggling readers are often given texts that they can read but do not enjoy because the book has been written for younger readers. One of the reasons to engage in the hard work of becoming a fluent, strategic reader is the joy that books can bring. All readers need to experience the power of a well-written story, poem, or piece of nonfiction so that they can remember the reward that reading can bring. Of course, reading aloud can be particularly beneficial for English-language learners, whose skills with oral English may be considerably stronger than their skills with written English. Think of engaging with a text through a teacher read-aloud as a carrot, a motivation to read. If you are fortunate enough to have class sets of texts, so that students can see the words as you read aloud, so much the better.

Time to demonstrate your engagement with texts, time for reading, and time to read aloud are all important components of a motivating classroom. Students also need time to talk about what they read with others. Although we often think of reading as an independent, solitary activity, those of us who are avid readers know the joy of talking about what we have read with others. Especially in the middle grades, the social nature of reading in the company of others can become a powerful motivating force, encouraging students to read, to read with understanding, and to share their ideas with others. Transactional theory, discussed in Chapter 1, highlights the interesting tension between individual response and collective understanding, or between significance and meaning. When students have the opportunity to talk with one another about what they read, they come to realize that there are many ways to respond to a text, and they also have the opportunity to enlarge their own repertoire of responses by listening to those of others. We discuss this more in Chapter 7. Time to talk about texts with others helps students understand the dynamic nature of engaged reading, even as it motivates them to engage in more reading.

Materials

Another important component of a literate environment is the physical setting in which children read. In the best possible literate environment, the classroom is filled with books, books that are readily accessible for students to read in school or take home. The walls are covered with colorful posters that advertise books and the treasures they offer and that showcase students' responses to what they have read. There are several inviting places to read—a carpeted corner where students can sit on the floor and read without interruption, bean bags or other comfortable chairs that entice young readers to immerse themselves in a book, places where students can gather in groups to read to each other or discuss their reading, and some tables for students to use to write about what they're reading. An attractive space encourages people to spend time in it, and time spent reading and responding is exactly what you want to encourage.

The texts that you select for your classroom library are another crucial component of a motivating literate environment. Certainly some books will be in your classroom because they fit within your curriculum in some way, as we discuss in Chapter 3. Integrating a curriculum through literature is one important way to help students make sense of what they are learning. When what they are learning in school is seamlessly integrated rather than piecemeal, students learn more. Reading well-written texts becomes a tool students can use to learn more about topics and ideas they are interested in, even as the texts they are reading can serve to unify the curriculum. And this kind of reading gives students a purpose to practice the craft of reading.

Teaching Idea 2.1
Assessing Students' Reading Attitudes and Interests

It's important that you get to know your students as readers early in the academic year. You can find out about their reading habits and preferences by having one-on-one book conferences with each of them, but a faster and more efficient way to get the information you need is to give them a brief written survey to fill out. You can easily create a survey that will give you the information you need with questions such as the following:

- Do you like to read? Why or why not?
- Are you reading anything for fun at this time? What is it? Why do you like it?

- Do you have any favorite authors or titles? Why are these favorites?
- Is there a certain kind of text that you prefer—books, magazines, fiction, nonfiction, etc?
- How do you choose what to read when you go to a library or a book store?
- What do you do if what you are reading is too hard or too easy for you?
- What makes a good reader?

Other important considerations reflect the diversity of your classroom—the range of abilities, interests, and cultural, linguistic, and social backgrounds of your students—as well as the diversity of the larger society outside your classroom.

Most of the texts in your classroom collection will be there because they meet the needs, abilities, and interests of your students. Assessing your students' attitudes toward reading and reading interests, as detailed in Teaching Idea 2.1, is an important step in selecting texts that will be engaging to them.

Finding out about your students as readers is vital to being an effective, motivating teacher. You can also find books that your students will probably like by looking at the annotated lists of *Adventuring with Books* (NCTE), *Best Books for Young Adults* (ALA), "Children's Choices" (every October in *The Reading Teacher*), "Notable Children's Trade Books in the Field of Social Studies" (in the May/June issue of *Social Education*), "Outstanding Science Trade Books for Children" (in the November issue of *Children and Science*), and the "Young Adult Choices" (every November in the *Journal of Adolescent and Adult Literacy*). Lists can also be found online at *www.reading.org*, *www.ala.org*, and *www.ncte.org*.

Another effective strategy for identifying books that your students might enjoy is to talk with your school or public librarian. Good librarians are trained to recognize books that many children will find engaging. They also have access to the American Library Association's resources and can give you lists of books that librarians have selected as those that will interest middle-grade readers. There are also resources such as the National Council of Teachers of English publication, *High Interest, Easy Reading*, which is updated regularly.

You will also want to build a collection that reflects the wide range of reading levels in your classroom. You will need material that supports your struggling readers as well as challenge them, and material that will support and challenge competent and avid readers as well.

The social, linguistic, and cultural background of your students and of the greater society is yet another important factor in selecting books. Readers shape their view of themselves and of the world partly through what they read. Reading about people who are similar to and different from ourselves is important for everyone. Recognizing yourself in a book is a powerful affirmation that you are part of the human endeavor—and the world of books. Recognizing the humanity of others who might seem different from ourselves is an important part of becoming a citizen of the world. Literature can act as both a mirror and a window for readers (Galda & Cullinan, 2002), reflecting their own lives and offering a chance to understand the lives of others. Perhaps the best books function to offer an experience that is similar to looking through a window at twilight. At first you can see through the window into another place but, as the light gradually fades, you end up seeing yourself (Galda, 1998; Galda & Cullinan, 2006). Thinking and talking about experiences like this can help students develop an understanding of themselves and others. And reading books from many cultures exposes students to many wonderful authors.

Since the early 1990s, the publishing industry has responded to the increasing diversity of North America by publishing a slowly growing number of excellent books that reflect this diversity. Unfortunately, the number of books by and about people of color published in any given year hovers around 3 or 4 percent—a far cry from the number of students of color who attend school. Books that reflect linguistic diversity—bilingual texts—or those that offer international perspectives, are even more scarce. Nevertheless, over the past 15 years a number of excellent books that enrich a classroom collection have been published.

Books that are excellent offer readers authentic glimpses of others' lives. When the portrayal of these lives is situated in a specific cultural context, it's extremely important that they be culturally authentic. Evaluating the cultural authenticity of books about people from a culture different from one's own is a challenge, but there are a number of resources that can help you find culturally diverse literature and that can help you learn how to think about issues surrounding cultural authenticity. Some of these resources are listed in Figure 2.1.

Another factor that needs to be considered when selecting literature for a classroom collection is the quality of that literature as writing. Well-written literature will produce good, avid readers. Poorly written literature is not likely to produce either. In Chapter 3, we discuss this matter in detail.

Choice

Scheduling ample time for reading and responding and finding materials that will engage readers are crucial components of a motivating literate environment. Add the element of choice to this mix, and it becomes even more powerful. Simply put, students need to have choices about what they read and what they do to respond to their reading. This does not mean that you never assign selections for students to read or tasks for students to complete after they have read. It does mean that you

Figure 2.1   **Resources for Finding and Evaluating Culturally Diverse Books for Middle-Grade Readers**

Some basic questions to ask yourself as you are selecting culturally diverse literature are these:

- Does the book qualify as good literature?
- Is the culture accurately portrayed, demonstrating diversity within as well as across cultures, if appropriate, and does it avoid stereotypes?
- Is the book a positive contribution to an understanding of the culture portrayed? (Galda & Cullinan, 2002, p. 279)

As you are learning to evaluate literature in terms of literary excellence and cultural authenticity (see Chapter 3), you may want to rely on published lists of books that have been carefully evaluated by experts in the field. Even expert teachers consult these references as an effective means of keeping up with new and excellent multicultural literature.

Publications

- Harris, V. (1997). *Using multiethnic literature in the K–8 classroom.* Norwood, MA: Christopher-Gordon.
- Helbig, A. K., & Perkins, A. R. (2000). *Many peoples, one land: A guide to new multicultural literature for children and young adults.* Westport, CT: Greenwood.
- International Board on Books for Young People. (quarterly). *Bookbird: A Journal of International Children's Literature.* Basil, Switzerland: Author.
- Miller-Lachmann, L. (1992). *Our family, our friends, our world.* New Providence, NJ: Bowker.
- National Council of Teachers of English. (multiple editions). *Kaleidoscope: A multicultural booklist for grades K–8.* Urbana, IL: NCTE.
- Stan, S. (2002). *The world through children's books.* Lanham, MD: Scarecrow.
- Tomlinson, C. M. (1998). *Children's books from other countries.* Lanham, MD: Scarecrow.

Lists and Awards

- Notable Books for a Global Society (February issues of *The Reading Teacher*), International Reading Association/www.reading.org
- Coretta Scott King Awards (American Library Association/www.ala.org)
- Pura Belpre Award (ALA)
- Mildred Batchelder Award (ALA)
- Publication lists from publishers such as Lee and Low, Jump at the Sun/Hyperion, Kane/Miller Book Press, Open Hand, Children's Book Press, Arte Publico, and North–South Books, all of whom focus on culturally diverse literature.

Also, review journals, such as those described in Chapter 3, that are excellent resources for finding quality literature that represents cultural diversity.

structure regular opportunities for students to choose their own reading materials and to choose their own response mode. Allowing students some choice often helps motivate them to spend time reading.

Independent reading is one such opportunity. Although students, especially those who are struggling readers and many English-language learners, need support and guidance in selecting books that they can and will want to read, students also ought to be able to choose their own books for independent reading. Some teachers insist that students choose only from the classroom or school library. We suggest that, if reading is the goal, students ought to be able to read all kinds of texts, including newspapers, comic books, and magazines. If we want students to spend time reading, we must allow them to choose what they read.

Choice is almost always a great motivator.

Sometimes teachers are able to offer students limited choice even in the texts they read as a whole class or small group. Offering students a small range of titles, all of which will allow you to meet your curricular goals, helps students feel a part of the instructional environment. So, too, does choice about what to do with the texts they have read. By offering students various options for responding to their reading, you increase the likelihood that they will enjoy the task.

Time, materials, and choice all foster engagement with books. Teaching Idea 2.2 offers a suggestion for helping students develop an interest in poetry that is based on these motivating elements, including time for browsing through books, something that often looks unproductive but has been found to be important in this particular instance.

Classroom Climate

A final and equally important component of a literate environment is the atmosphere in which children read. In the best possible literate environment, everything that happens in the classroom sends the message that reading—learning from what you read, having personal responses to what you read, talking about what you read, and writing about what you read—is fantastic! In such a classroom, students are given plenty of time to read, they are given ample opportunities to share the information they learn and their responses to what they have read with each other, they are taught to listen to and respect the ideas of others, and they learn that others will listen to and respect their ideas. A literate atmosphere is a thoughtful atmosphere in which values and ideas are respected—values and ideas in texts, one's own values and ideas, and other people's values and ideas.

Teaching Idea 2.2
Poetry Browsing to Create Interest

Teacher lore has it that it is difficult to get middle-grade students engaged in poetry. For whatever the reasons, unless it is humorous verse by authors such as Shel Silverstein and Jack Prelutsky, middle-grade readers tend to avoid poetry. But this doesn't always have to be the case. McClure, Harrison, and Reed (1990) found that, given time and choice, middle-grade students came to really enjoy poetry, even selecting books of poetry for independent reading. After assembling a collection of poetry that might interest middle-grade readers, McClure and colleagues added it to the classroom library, displaying the poetry collection so that students were tempted to look at the books. Then they gave students time to browse, to dip in and out of books, finding poems they enjoyed and wanted to read to their buddies, and then moving on. Over time, this freedom to simply enjoy and sample a lot of poetry without any task being assigned broke down the students' initial negative attitudes. Hansen (2004) found that fifth-grade students developed a wider repertoire of poetry types and poetic elements that they enjoyed once they had been exposed to a wide variety of poems and had discovered how poets manipulate language to create the effects they desire.

This kind of climate is developed when teachers help students learn how to discuss and share what they read in a positive and supportive manner. One way students learn to do this is through your modeling how to be positive and supportive as you scaffold students' reading experiences. Direct instruction on ways to conduct themselves in the classroom also helps set the right tone, and we discuss this more in Chapter 7. Trust, respect, and responsibility are important ideas in a safe and supportive classroom, and talking about these concepts and how the successful operation of the class rests on them is crucial, especially at the beginning of the year.

Pause and Reflect 2.1

Describing Your Own Literacy Experience in the Middle Grades

Think about your experience as a reader in grades 5 through 8. Did you read for pleasure or only for school? What kinds of books did you read? Were you ever given time to read in class? How did you feel about that? Did you ever talk with others about the books you were reading? What kinds of assignments did you have to complete when you finished reading a book? How did those assignments affect your attitude toward reading? ■

The Importance of Positive Attributions

Providing ample time, engaging materials, appropriate choices, and a supportive classroom climate will help you create a classroom that encourages the development of motivated, engaged readers. However, it is also important that you understand some of the internal factors that relate to motivation, to how students' perceptions influence their performance.

Educators and psychologists have been studying motivation for many years. One of their most persistent findings is that a major influence on motivation is the way people view their own successes and failures, what has come to be called *attributions*. A closely related finding is that the result of repeatedly failing is *learned helplessness*. In this section, we discuss each of these important concepts.

Attribution Theory

Attribution theory helps to explain and underscore the importance of success. Attribution theory deals with students' perceptions of the causes of their successes and failures in learning. As Wittrock (1986) explains, in thinking about why they succeed or fail in reading tasks, students can attribute their performance to ability, effort, luck, the difficulty of the reading task, or a variety of other causes. All too often, children who have repeatedly failed in reading attribute their failure to factors that are beyond their control—to an unchangeable factor such as their innate ability, or to a factor that they can do nothing about, such as luck. Once this happens, children are likely to lose their motivation to learn to read and to doubt their ability to learn. From the children's perspective, there is no reason to try because there is nothing they can do about it. Moreover, as long as they do not try, they cannot fail; you cannot lose a race if you do not enter it.

We will say more about what teachers can do to assist students in developing more positive attributions in the section of this chapter on Concrete Approaches to Motivating Students. In the meantime, Murphy and Alexander (2002) provide a very important general observation on how we can do so:

> Although there are a number of reasons for students' lack of motivation, teachers should recognize that students are often unmotivated about tasks or subjects in which they believe they will not succeed. To overcome such beliefs, teachers can structure incremental activities that allow students to build their abilities, and these small successes will enable students to believe in their ability to achieve. (pp. 17–18)

Learned Helplessness

As Johnston and Winograd (1985) have pointed out, one long-term outcome of children's repeatedly attributing failure in reading to forces that are beyond their control is their falling into a passive failure syndrome. Children who exhibit passive failure in reading are apt to be nervous, withdrawn, and discouraged when they are faced with reading tasks. They are unlikely to be actively engaged in reading, to have goals and plans when they read, to monitor themselves when they are reading to see if the reading makes sense, or to check themselves after reading to see if they have accomplished their reading goal.

Obviously, we need to avoid this debilitating cycle of negative attributions and passive failure. Seventh-grade teacher, Jerry Guntar, suggests four approaches.

> By the time they get to seventh grade, many students have experienced a good deal of failure and feel like they can't do anything about it. The first, and almost certainly the most powerful, way I have found to help students understand that they are in control of their learning is to show them that they can succeed: Make students' reading experiences

Figure 2.2 **Techniques for Engaging All Learners**

- Take the time to recognize students' strengths and build on them.
- Take the time to find out about the students' worlds and use familiar metaphors and experiences from that world.
- Create an atmosphere of family and caring in your classroom.
- Honor and respect students' home cultures.
- Help students to feel connected to community, to something beyond themselves.
- Validate students' home language by providing them with texts in that language, utilizing volunteers who speak that language, and encouraging the use of the home language during group activities.
- Take the time to learn words in students' home language and use them.

successful ones. Make them so frequently successful for students that they will be compelled to realize that it is they themselves and not some outside force that is responsible for their success.

Second, I tell students that their efforts make a difference, and when they are successful in a reading task, I talk to them about the activities they engaged in to make them successful. If, for example, after reading an informational piece about dinosaurs, students successfully answer several questions that they generated before reading, we discuss how generating those questions beforehand helped them focus their attention so that they could answer the questions as they read.

Third, I avoid competitive situations in which students compare how well they read a selection to how well others read it and instead focus students' attention on what they personally gained from the selection.

Finally, I try to provide a number of reading activities in which the goal is simply to enjoy reading, have fun, and experience something interesting and exciting rather than only offering reading activities that are followed by answering questions or some other sort of external accountability.

Unfortunately, negative attributions are all too frequent among poor children and children who are English-language learners. Lisa Delpit's (1995) suggestions for working with poor urban children and Robert Jimenez's (2000) suggestions for working with Latino students relate directly to motivating and engaging students who are often marginalized in mainstream classrooms. We summarize some of their suggestions in Figure 2.2.

Pause and Reflect 2.2

Ensuring Students' Success

Consider Jerry Gunther's emphasis on the importance of success and think about a middle-grade student you know (or perhaps a student you remember from your own middle-grade years) who is often unsuccessful with reading. Now think of a reading assignment you could give this student that would virtually ensure his success. Consider the reading selection you would use, what purpose you would ask the student to achieve as he reads, and what you would do to help him achieve this purpose. We will say more about ensuring students' success in the next section of this chapter, and suggest a number of specific approaches to doing so throughout this book, but for now rely on your experience and intuition. ■

Concrete Approaches to Motivating Students

Like Jerry Guntar, we believe that there are many teaching techniques that can break the cycle of learned helplessness and help students become motivated and engaged readers. The most powerful include ensuring student success, providing appropriate challenges, effective grouping, and promoting academic values and goals.

Ensuring Student Success

A dominant thought motivating not just this chapter but the whole of this book is the overwhelming importance of success. Research has repeatedly verified that, if students are going to learn effectively, they need to succeed at the vast majority of tasks they undertake (Brophy, 1986; National Research Council, 2004; Pressley et al., 2003). This of course applies to the reading students do just as it does to their other schoolwork. Moreover, if students are to become not only proficient readers but also avid readers—children and later adults who voluntarily seek out reading as a road to information, enjoyment, and personal fulfillment—then successful reading experiences are even more important.

A successful reading experience includes at least three features. First, and most importantly, a successful reading experience is one in which the reader understands what he reads. Of course, understanding may take more than one reading, it may require your assistance or that of other students, and it will often require the reader to actively manipulate the ideas in the text. Second, a successful reading experience is one that the reader finds enjoyable, entertaining, informative, or thought provoking. Of course, not every reading experience will yield all of these benefits, but every experience should yield at least one of them. Third, a successful reading experience is one that prepares the student to complete whatever task follows the reading. Finally, note that all students—English-language learners and less-skilled readers as well as accomplished readers—need to meet with success.

To a great extent, children's success in reading is directly under your control. You can select and encourage students to select tasks, materials, and supporting activities that all but guarantee success. For example, suppose you have a group of sixth-grade students who read at about 150 words a minute and a 10-minute period in which they will be reading. Giving students a selection slightly shorter than 1,500 words will ensure that they at least have time to complete it, while giving them a selection much longer than 1,500 words will leave them frustrated and ensure failure. As another example, suppose you have a group of seventh-grade students who will be reading a science chapter on the ecology of fresh water lakes but who have virtually no concept of ecology, who have never even thought about the relationships among organisms and their environment. Preteaching the concept of ecology will greatly increase the likelihood that students will understand the chapter and not simply flounder in a sea of new ideas.

Further, by including a wide selection of adolescent literature in your students' reading diet you can easily offer them opportunities to experience texts that they are able to read successfully during independent reading, small book discussion groups, or even background reading for content they are studying in science or social studies. There is a wide range of difficulty levels in books for children and

Teaching Idea 2.3
Creating a Book Review File

Middle-grade students are deeply involved in their social lives, so building on their desire for social connections can help you interest them in a wide variety of books. Although only a few students might read a book because you, the teacher, told them it was good, most students will read a book that a peer has recommended. Susan, a seventh/eighth grade English teacher, developed a quick and effective book review system. When a student finished reading a book, he went to the file (a small box that held 5×8 index cards) and looked it up by the author's name. If someone else had read it, there was a card on file; if not, the student created a card with the author's last name, first name, and book title. Then, whether on a new card or adding to the comments of others on an existing card, the student wrote a one- or two-sentence opinion of the book. This file became a favorite aid when students were looking for new books for independent reading, and often sparked impromptu conversations between students who had all read the same book. It was also an opportunity for students to learn the difference between writing an opinion with a supporting reason and writing a brief summary. Summaries weren't allowed in the file.

adolescents, a much greater range than is found in textbooks, which are, after all, geared for a particular grade level. Stocking every classroom library with books—fiction and nonfiction—that span the reading levels of your students allows all students to select texts with which they can be successful. As students come to know the books in the classroom and their own abilities and interests, they can begin to make appropriate selections. Being free to browse, to read a bit before deciding whether or not they will stick with a book, or to talk with others who have read that book, helps students learn which books they can and want to read. This is also a perfect opportunity for students to be able to share their evaluation of books with others, as Teaching Idea 2.3 describes. Sometimes, students challenge themselves to read a book that might be beyond their comfort level because classmates' talk about the book has piqued their interest.

Providing Appropriate Challenges

Having stressed the importance of success, at this point we want to qualify our argument by stressing the parallel importance of providing appropriate challenges for students. Saying students should succeed at the reading tasks you ask them to complete and that you should do everything possible to ensure success does not mean giving them only texts they are completely comfortable with. Unless readers undertake some challenging tasks, unless they are willing to take some risks and make some attempts they are not certain of and get feedback on their efforts, there is little room for learning to take place. In order to develop as readers, children need to be given some challenges. As Csikszentmihalyi (1990) learned from three decades of research on what makes people's lives happier and more meaningful, facing significant challenges and meeting those challenges is one of the most self-fulfilling and rewarding experiences people can have. However, when you present students with challenges, you need to be certain that they clearly understand the goals toward which they are working, to give them challenges appropriate for their skills, and to provide them with whatever support they need to meet these challenges. This is, of course, true for all students, but it is particularly true for those students who have often found school difficult. In the following classroom scenario, which is based on an article by Sampson, Sampson, and Linek, (1994/1995), you will see how fifth-grade teacher Gail Tollison creates a successful reading experience that includes providing appropriate challenges and supports for her students.

> Five students sit at the same table reading about lightning bugs in their science texts. Sarah is reading merely to finish the assignment, daydreaming about what she will do that evening. Carlos, on the other hand, reads with enthusiasm—he had caught lightning bugs the night before, released them in his room, and fallen asleep to their steady blinks. Paul reads with the fascination of a new discovery. He has recently moved from Alaska, where there are no lightning bugs. Marinda discovers something she didn't know about lightning bugs and quickly moves from being a passive reader to an actively involved one. Josh reads as he always does, word by word, with no real interest in the content. Around the room, other groups of five students also sit at tables reading the same text.
>
> When they finish reading, Mrs. Tollison tells the class they will be exploring the topic of lightning bugs. They will be working in groups of five using an approach called Circle of Questions. After establishing the groups, she gives the groups 3 minutes to brainstorm the questions they have about lightning bugs.
>
> After 3 minutes, Mrs. Tollison calls time, draws a circle on the board, and invites each group to share their questions. She writes the questions around the circle as the students share them.
>
> Mrs. Tollison next encourages students to review and examine their questions to see what categories of questions they can find. Using colored chalk, she circles items that belong in specific categories, for example, questions about what makes lightning bugs flash circled in blue, questions about physical attributes circled in red, or questions about reproduction circled in green. Each group then chooses a category in which to become experts.
>
> In their groups, students reread the text, searching for answers to the questions in their category. A recorder for each group writes down the answers and where they are found in the text. When all of the groups have finished researching their questions, the class meets as a whole, and the reporter from each group shares the information the group discovered with the class. Mrs. Tollison writes the answers and their sources by the appropriate questions on the Circle of Questions chart (Figure 2.3).
>
> While Mrs. Tollison records the answers, students discuss whether the text adequately addressed their initial questions or if additional research will be needed to flesh out their knowledge.

Figure 2.3 **Circle of Questions**

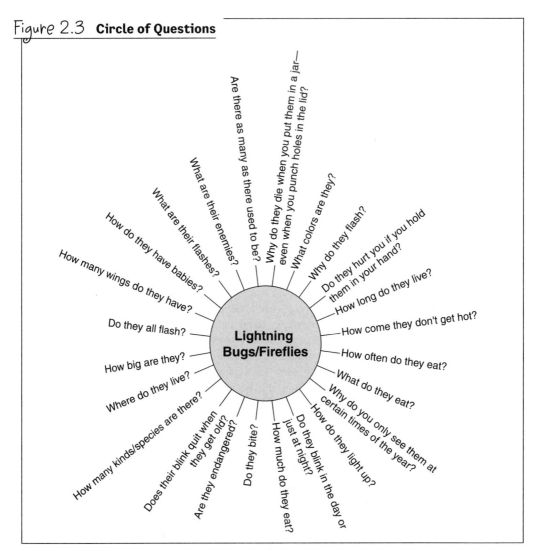

Are there as many as there used to be?

Why do they die when you put them in a jar—even when you punch holes in the lid?

What are their enemies?

What colors are they?

What are their flashes?

Why do they flash?

How do they have babies?

Do they hurt you if you hold them in your hand?

How many wings do they have?

How long do they live?

Do they all flash?

How come they don't get hot?

How big are they?

How often do they eat?

Where do they live?

What do they eat?

How many kinds/species are there?

Why do you only see them at certain times of the year?

Does their blink quit when they get old?

How do they light up?

Are they endangered?

Do they blink in the day or just at night?

Do they bite?

How much do they eat?

Lightning Bugs/Fireflies

From Sampson, M. B., Sampson, M. B., & Linek, W. (1994/1995). Circle of questions. *The Reading Teacher, 48,* 364–365.

Can you see how this activity appropriately challenged the readers that were introduced at the beginning of the scenario? Perhaps word-by-word reader Josh began to change his view toward reading that day. As his classmates generated questions they had about the text, he saw that all readers, not just him, don't understand everything they read. Carlos gained self-esteem because his knowledge of fireflies enabled him to answer many of the group's questions. Paul discovered that an excellent way to clarify the ideas in a text is through group interaction with that text. Sarah, appointed recorder for the group, became an active, interested member of the team. Miranda came to realize that not all questions are answered by a particular text, and sometimes more questions are raised. The entire class was challenged

Groups of middle graders will often be diverse in many ways.

to do what real readers do—actively construct their own questions about a topic and find the answers.

Another way for students to be both challenged and supported comes in reading discussion groups. Talking with others about what they have read, what questions they have, and how they reacted to the story, poem, or information they've just processed is a natural part of discussion groups. Successful discussion groups quickly become places where students can say, "I didn't get it when . . ." and their peers can help them. We discuss this more extensively in Chapter 7.

Grouping Students to Promote Learning and Positive Attitudes

One of the most important decisions you make in your classroom is that of how to group students. Students can be grouped in a variety of ways for a variety of purposes, yet in all too many cases grouping has not been used effectively and has had a negative effect on many students, specifically those students placed in the low-ability groups. In this section, we discuss some of the reasons for grouping, some of the problems grouping has produced, various types of groups, and some guidelines for grouping.

Advantages and Disadvantages of Grouping. A typical class of 25 to 30 students brings with it 25 to 30 different sets of interests, abilities, attention spans, personalities, and reading skills; and it is very difficult to attend to each of these when working with the class as a whole. When teaching the entire class as a single group, teachers tend to teach to an imaginary mean; that is, they gear their instruction to what they perceive to be the middle range of interest, attention span, personality, ability, and so on. Such instruction does not meet the needs of those who are not in this range. Furthermore, in large-group situations, it is tempting for the teacher to do most of the talking, asking only an occasional question and, even then, allowing only one or two students to respond. Thus, most students play a passive role.

Dividing students into smaller groups is often helpful for a number of reasons. First, it is generally easier to keep smaller groups of students on task than it is to keep larger groups on task. Smaller groups tend to facilitate direct instructional engagement for more children and for a longer period of time. Second, smaller groups allow you to provide instruction designed to meet the needs of specific students, thus maximizing each student's learning. Finally, smaller groups allow more students to be actively involved in instructional activities. In a group of five, for example, it is possible for each student to respond to a question before you either run out of time or test the patience of the other students.

Given these advantages, it is not surprising that students have often been grouped for reading instruction. Unfortunately, however, grouping has typically been based exclusively on reading ability. During much of the past century, students in the United States were grouped homogeneously for reading instruction, with the typical classroom having one high-, one middle-, and one low-ability group (Anderson, Hiebert, Scott, & Wilkinson, 1985). More recently, teachers and researchers have found that ability grouping results in a number of disadvantages, particularly for students in low-ability groups. As compared to students in other groups, students in low-ability groups are often given less time to read, spend more time on worksheets and less time being actively instructed, and are asked fewer higher-order questions. Additionally, students in the low-ability groups often suffer affective consequences of grouping, including lowered self-esteem, lowered motivation to succeed, and negative attitudes toward reading (Allington, 1983; 1994). Finally, there is much concern about the permanence of group membership; students who are placed in a low-ability group in kindergarten and first grade are all too likely to stay in the low-ability group throughout the elementary school years (Juel, 1990).

Effective Grouping Options. The finding that membership in the low-ability group is often all too permanent has led teachers to develop a variety of grouping options, many of which deliberately include heterogeneous groups of students. Using a variety of groups gives children opportunities to learn how to interact with and learn from others who are in some ways different from them. Using a variety of groups also allows you to create appropriate groups for the various goals you have for students. Some of the many useful types of groups include Proficiency Groups (short-term groups of students who share a common strength or a common instructional need), Deliberately Heterogeneous Groups (groups specifically set up to counteract the potentially negative effect of proficiency groups), Linguistically Diverse Groups (groups that deliberately include native-English speakers and English-language learners), Formal Cooperative Groups (heterogeneous groups of students specifically taught how to work together as a team), Interest Groups (short-term groups of students sharing a common interest), Book Clubs, Literature Groups or Literature Circles (a particular sort of interest group in which students read the same selection and meet to discuss it), and Project Groups (groups designed to work together on a particular project such as making a video or preparing a dramatic presentation).

When deciding how to group students, there are many factors to consider. Here are some of the most important ones:

- your general instructional objectives
- your specific objectives for individual children
- the material your students will be reading
- your students' individual strengths
- students' abilities to work with others in the group
- the number and types of groups you can successfully manage
- the absolute injunction that no student be repeatedly assigned to the low-ability group

Having presented a variety of options for grouping, we obviously believe that students will profit from participating in many types of groups. Still, becoming adept at grouping students is a challenge. We suggest that you meet that challenge by first becoming comfortable with two or three types of grouping and then gradually adding other grouping alternatives as your classroom management and grouping skills become stronger.

Additionally, we do not mean to suggest that there is no place for whole-class instruction. Whole-class instruction does have a place. Whole-class instruction is useful when you wish to reach all students at once. Spending 5 or 10 minutes with the entire class before students begin working individually or in small groups allows you to touch base with all students, answer their questions, and hear their concerns. However, because lengthy whole-class instruction seldom continues to command students' attention and often invites off-task behavior, whole-class instruction should generally be kept brief and focused.

Book Club (McMahon, Raphael, Goatley, & Pardo 1997) is one good example of a combination of whole class, individual, and small group work. A typical session might begin with 5 to 10 minutes of a teacher read-aloud or a brief lesson about reading strategies, literary elements, or even book club procedures. This is followed by 10 to 15 minutes of students reading, then 5 to 10 minutes of writing in response logs, then 10 to 15 minutes of discussion in small groups. The culminating activity brings the whole class together again for 5 to 10 minutes while the teacher encourages groups to share what they have discussed. This basic structure allows students to take advantage of the opportunity to work in varied grouping structures. In the remainder of this book, we present examples of many kinds of groups working together effectively. We discuss Book Club in more detail in Chapter 10.

Promoting Academic Values and Goals

Ultimately, motivation and engagement are intrapersonal values, and it is the student himself who must become motivated and engaged—with school and schooling. The fact is that a good deal of schoolwork is just that, *work*, and we need to find ways to help students truly value that work. One approach to doing so is to reinforce students when they demonstrate that they are valuing and "doing" school; for example, complementing a student who has been turning in his homework daily. Another approach is to provide students with role models who express a commitment to education. Teachers are certainly one role model and an important one. But in some ways, other students are even more important role models. One of the many reasons that it is important for lower-performing students to be grouped with higher-performing students is that the higher-performing students can serve as academic role models. Still another approach is for teachers, administrators, and counselors to encourage all students to take advantage of educational opportunities that they currently have or that will be available to them in the future. Discussing with a middle-school student the many possibilities he will find in high school is well worthwhile.

Still another approach to promoting academic values and goals is to offer students choices, something we discussed earlier in the chapter. In fact, a large body of research and practice indicate that "students are more likely to want to do schoolwork when they have some choice in the courses they take, in the material they study, and in the strategies they use to complete tasks" (National Research Council, 2004, p. 48). One choice that is particularly important in many of today's classrooms is that of language. At appropriate times, English-language learners ought to be allowed to use their native language in reading, writing, responding, and taking tests. Situations that provide no choices can leave students with a sense of powerlessness, and a sense of powerlessness is more likely to lead to alienation than to engagement. Saying that students should have choices does not, however, mean that they should have no structure and no limits. Middle-school students value structure, but it needs to be structure that affords them some opportunities to make choices.

Our final suggestion for promoting academic values and goals is to make learning experiences enjoyable. We have already said that a good deal of schoolwork is indeed work, and there is no getting around that. But nothing says that work cannot be made as enjoyable as possible. If, for example, students are learning how to make inferences, teachers can find texts that require inferences that students will enjoy reading. For example, jokes often require inferences and are wonderful practice. Stories also often require inferences about, for example, a character's motivation for what he is doing. Speculating about why a compelling character is behaving in a particular way is much more interesting than filling out a worksheet designed to test students' ability to make inferences.

Perhaps students are working on their critical thinking skills and learning how to distinguish between fact and opinion, or differentiate fact, theory, and belief. They can spend time doing rather boring worksheets, or they can read interesting expository texts about things they are interested in and then discuss those texts in terms of fact, opinion, belief, and theory. Excellent nonfiction for adolescents that begs to be analyzed in this way includes the many books on space by authors such as Patricia Lauber and Seymour Simon, books that explore dinosaurs and their extinction, books about evolution, and many biographies, especially those about figures from the more distant past. Books such as Diane Stanley and Peter Vennema's *Bard of Avon: The Story of William Shakespeare* directly address these issues, allowing students to see how good authors differentiate fact and opinion, and thus how they, as readers, can do so as well.

Finally, we have one suggestion about a widely used practice that very frequently does not promote academic values and goals. That practice is putting too much emphasis on extrinsic rewards. If the primary reason a student reads is to get points, a free pizza, or some free time on Friday afternoon, then he is not likely to do much reading when points, pizza, and free time are not in the offing. We are not suggesting you can't use some extrinsic rewards, but we are saying not to use too many of them.

Pause and Reflect 2.3

Promoting Academic Values

Suppose that it is the first week of school and you are talking to your sixth graders about the upcoming year and the goals you have for the class. Suppose too, that one of your goals is to convince students that although school work can be challenging, it is worth doing well and that doing their school work well will give them a sense of accomplishment and pride. Jot down what you might say to them. Then, consider what you could do in class over the next several weeks that would drive home your point that schoolwork can be both challenging and rewarding. ■

Fostering Higher-Order Thinking and Deep Understanding

As you may have noticed, Chapter 7 of this book has the same title as this section: Fostering Higher-Order Thinking and Deep Understanding. Our major purpose for devoting an entire chapter to these topics is that we believe that they are absolutely crucial to success both in school and outside of school. Lower-order thinking and shallow understanding are not the cognitive tools students need to succeed, thrive, and contribute in the 21st century. Equally importantly, and very fortunately, emphasizing higher-order thinking and deep understanding in your classroom also motivates and engages students (Knapp & Associates, 1995; Taylor, Pearson, Peterson, & Rodriguez, 2003). Completing a worksheet that requires a young reader to answer a set of rote questions on the events in Jerry Spinelli's *Loser* simply is not as engaging as trying to figure what it is about Zinkhof that repeatedly gets him in unfortunate situations. Similarly, learning a little bit about a lot of topics is usually not as interesting as studying a few topics in depth. In fact, almost any topic becomes interesting once you begin to understand it deeply. Several years ago, adult author Mark Kurlansky wrote a book, *Cod*, that dealt with "the fish that changed the world." In researching that book, he became interested in salt, used of course in preserving cod, and wrote another book, *Salt: A World History*. Both books are fascinating. Even topics like cod and salt—as you learn more and more about them, and of course as you discover the impact they had on civilization—become interesting. That does not mean you should ask middle-grade students to develop a deep understanding of cod or salt, but it does suggest that some pretty mundane topics can become interesting when people develop a deep understanding of them.

Ensuring Active Participation, Using Cooperative Activities, and Including Variety

Regardless of whether students are involved in higher-order thinking and deep understanding, they are going to be more motivated and they are going to learn more if they're engaged in active learning rather than more passive activities. This is true for middle-school students and for college students; and if you are using this book as part of a college class, we hope you are engaged in active learning activities as part of that class. Such activities as constructing models, role playing, doing experiments, creating examples, and comparing and contrasting actively involve and interest students. Students in one study (Boaler, 2002), for example, noted that "you learn more by doing something on your own" (p. 38), "you feel more proud of the projects when you done them yourself" (p. 38), and "because you had to work out for yourself what was going on, you had to use your own ideas" (p. 68).

Cooperative learning is one form of active learning that has become very widely used, and this is fortunate. Importantly, the advantages of cooperative learning occurred in a variety of domains. Students in cooperative groups showed superior performance in academic achievement, displayed more self-esteem, accommodated better to mainstreamed students, showed more positive attitudes toward school, and generally displayed better overall psychological health. Students in cooperative groups displayed better interpersonal relationships, and these improved interpersonal relationships held regardless of differences in ability, sex, ethnicity, or social class (Johnson & Johnson, 1989). Moreover, cooperative learning has been shown to be successful in teaching students how to resolve conflicts (Johnson & Johnson, 2002). Finally, cooperative learning can create a classroom in which students share the responsibility for each other's learning rather than compete with each other. This is a very positive situation, particularly for students who often do not do well in school and may become alienated in classrooms where they are too often on their own (Cohen, 1994).

A number of authors (Aronson & Patnoe, 1997; Cohen, 1994; Johnson, Johnson, & Holubec, 1994; Slavin, 1987) have described approaches to cooperative learning, and using more than one approach can provide variety and accomplish somewhat different purposes. Moreover, as the title of this section suggests, variety itself tends to be motivating and engaging for students. No one likes to do the same thing in the same way all the time, and sometimes adding variety just to add variety makes good sense. For example, if you typically have independent reading on Fridays, sometimes it might be good to put it on another day for no reason other than varying the schedule. Of course, too much variation is not the goal, particularly for many middle-grade students.

Making Connections to Students' Cultures and Lives Outside of School

It is not at all surprising that students are more engaged and motivated to learn if they feel that what they are learning is related to their out-of-school lives. Although not every topic in the curriculum is going to be connected to students' home lives and cultures, some of it certainly should be. One of the easiest ways to do this is to carefully select the reading material for your classroom so that it reflects the issues, concerns, and cultures of your students, as we discussed earlier in this chapter. At the same time, however, we must admit that assuring cultural matches is easier said than done.

Kristen, a teacher who works with Somali immigrants, discovered the there is very little available literature that accurately reflects the lives of her students, so she decided to ask students and their families to create books for their classroom library. She asked students to get family members to tell them stories—stories about life in Somalia, stories about their journey to the United States, stories about the things that happened to them when they arrived. She then asked students to tell and write stories about their own lives. And she gave her students cameras to take photographs of people and places in their home and neighborhood. Next, she typed up their texts and they arranged the photos or drew pictures to illustrate their words, then put their books together, complete with title page, dedication page, and publication information. The result was a number of books, bound at a local copy center, with content that was culturally specific to her students. Kristen didn't stop there, of course; she found trade books and magazine articles that related to her students' lives in other ways, and added these to her growing library.

Her students invested in the classroom library by writing some of the books, and were motivated and eager to read their own, those of their peers, and the trade books and magazine articles that Kristen gathered. Her effort to find literature that was culturally relevant to her students became a wonderful opportunity for writing and a strong motivator for reading for these students.

While a culturally diverse library is important no matter who you teach, it's also important to think about the universals that engage middle-grade students. Reading about topics like family, friends, relationships with the opposite sex, growing up, struggling for independence, and becoming self-reliant can draw your students into the world of reading and help them realize that reading, even the reading they do in school, often relates to their lives outside of school.

Class projects can also help students connect home and school. Rather than researching and writing about a topic that has little connection to their community, students can choose to pursue a topic that is relevant to their lives. For example, a group of middle-grade students in the Pacific northwest spent a school year researching and writing about how pollution had destroyed the salmon stream that ran by their school. They read, discussed, and wrote while they also cleaned up the stream. The result was a cleaner stream, heightened community awareness of issues of pollution, and a book, *Come Back, Salmon!* that chronicled their project. Eventually, the salmon even came back.

Your students all come from families and communities that have, as Moll (1992) describes it, "funds of knowledge." It's up to you to tap into that knowledge and bring it into your classroom. Connecting school and home is an important part of helping students value what they are learning in school.

Praising Students, Rewarding Them, and Helping Them Set Goals

Praise can be a very effective motivator, and it is certainly a widely used tool. One study, for example, showed that beginning teachers used praise and punishment as their motivational approach more than 75 percent of the time (Newby, 1991). Nevertheless, praise is not without its potential drawbacks. Most importantly, it must be honest, and students must perceive it as honest. According to Guthrie and Wigfield (2000), effective praise is given only in response to students' efforts and achievements, specifies just what students have accomplished to earn the praise, and helps students better appreciate their work. Guthrie and Wigfield also note that effective praise makes it clear to students that they should attribute their success to effort and fosters their understanding of the strategies that they used to accomplish the task for which they are being praised.

Rewards other than praise—points, stars, books, pizzas—can sometimes be effective in the short run. However, one of the most consistent and strongest cautions in the literature on motivation is that extrinsic rewards can undermine motivation in the long run (Guthrie & Wigfield, 2000; National Research Council, 2004; Stipek, 2002). When students become accustomed to getting extrinsic rewards for reading, they may begin reading solely or largely to get the intrinsic reward and actually discontinue reading when the extrinsic rewards are no longer available. Our goal should always be to demonstrate to students that reading is worthwhile for its own sake—for the learning, enjoyment, and satisfaction that it brings. Our greatest tools in accomplishing this goal are giving students good books and other material to read and scaffolding their efforts so that they can successfully do the reading.

Goal setting is another important component of motivation. Students who set goals to learn certain content or processes, such as understanding a difficult concept or being able to self-check as they read, are more motivated to learn than students who do not. Teachers who help their students set appropriate learning goals are helping to foster students' long-term engagement and learning (Ames, 1992; Maehr & Midgley, 1996).

Concluding Remarks

Creating motivating and engaging classrooms is essential for all grade levels, but it is particularly essential for middle-school students, who need a great deal of support and encouragement. Creating motivating and engaging classrooms means creating a literate environment—a place, a space, and an atmosphere where reading and learning thrive. In motivating and engaging classrooms, students learn to attribute their successes and failures to factors under their control. And in motivating and engaging classrooms, teachers employ myriad approaches to motivating students—including but not limited to ensuring student success, fostering higher-order thinking, and making connections to students' cultures and lives outside of school.

We close the chapter with three sets of recommendations for motivating students. The first is a set that Pressley and his colleagues (2003) gleaned from the work of Brophy (1986, 1987), recommendations made nearly 20 years ago. The second is a set that one of us (Graves, 2004) gleaned from the work of Pressley and his colleagues (Bogner et al., 2002; Dolezal et al., 2003; Pressley et al., 2003). The third is a set made by the National Research Council (2004) based on research in urban schools. As you read them, we hope that you will notice two points. First, the three sets of recommendations overlap a good deal with each other. Second, the recommendations overlap a good deal with the recommendations we make in this chapter. Our point is this: We know how to motivate and engage students. Our task now is to put this knowledge into action.

Motivational Strategies Gleaned from Brophy

- Model interest in learning. . . . Communicate to students that there is good reason to be enthusiastic about what goes on in school. The message should be that what is presented in school deserves intense attention, with the teacher doing all that is possible to focus students' attention on important academic matters.
- What is being taught, in fact, should be worth learning!
- Keep anxiety down in the classroom. Learning should be emphasized rather than testing.
- Induce curiosity and suspense, for example, by having students make predictions about what they are about to learn.
- Make abstract material more concrete and understandable.
- Let students know the learning objectives so that it is very clear what is to be learned.
- Provide informative feedback, especially praise when students deserve it.
- Give assignments that provide feedback (to your students and to yourself).
- Adapt academic tasks to students' interests and provide novel content as much as possible. [Do not cover material students already know just because it is the mandated curriculum.]
- Give students choices between alternative tasks—for example, selecting one of several books to read.
- Allow students as much autonomy as is possible in doing tasks. Thus, to the extent students can do it on their own, let them do it.
- Design tasks to contain an engaging activity [for example, role playing], product [for example, a class-composed book], or game [for example, riddles]. (Pressley et al., 2003, pp. 27–28)

Motivational Strategies Gleaned from Pressley and His Colleagues

- Demonstrate your deep concern for students.
- Do everything possible to ensure students' success.
- Scaffold students' learning.
- Present appropriate challenges.
- Support risk-taking and help students realize that failures will sometimes occur.
- Encourage students to attribute their successes to their efforts and to realize that additional effort can help avoid failures.
- Encourage cooperative learning and discourage competition.
- Favor depth of coverage over breadth of coverage.
- Communicate to students that many academic tasks require and deserve intense attention and effort.
- Make tasks moderately challenging. (Graves, 2004, p. 448)

Motivational Strategies Listed by the National Research Council

- a challenging but individualized curriculum that is focused on understanding
- knowledgeable, skilled, and caring teachers
- a school culture that is centered on learning
- a school community that engenders a sense of support and belonging, with opportunities to interact with academically engaged peers
- strong ties linking the school and students' families and communities
- an organizational structure that services and addresses students' nonacademic needs
- opportunities to learn the values of schoolwork for future educational and career opportunities (National Research Council, 2004, p. 14)

In the remainder of this book and in our day-to-day teaching in our own classrooms, we keep these recommendations at the center of our thinking. We encourage you to do the same. With motivation and engagement, great things are possible: Students can learn deeply, they can remember important information, and they can use what they learn in school in their lives beyond the classroom. They can do all of this while enjoying the activities in your classroom, enjoying school, and becoming committed lifelong readers.

■ ▬▬▬▬▬▬▬▬▬▬ EXTENDING LEARNING

1. Spend some time observing a middle-grade classroom other than your own. Take notes on what you see. What opportunities for engaging in literacy activities are present? How welcoming is the physical setting? What materials are available? Then watch how the teacher and students interact in the classroom.

Is the atmosphere safe and supportive? Are students enthusiastic and engaged? Finally, create a list of things to do and things to avoid doing in order to best motivate students.

2. The list that you created in the previous activity represents your judgment based on your observation. Other sources of information deserve to be considered. One source is the teacher you observed. Talk to the teacher and get his or her perceptions on what motivates students and which specific things he or she does to motivate them. The other source is, of course, students. Talk to a half-dozen or so students and get their perceptions of what is and is not motivating in their classrooms. Once you have the teacher's and some students' perspectives, compare them to your list and revise or fine-tune your list as seems appropriate.

3. Find resources such as *Adventuring with Books* (NCTE), "Children's Choices" (*The Reading Teacher*), "Notable Children's Trade Books in the Field of Social Studies" (*Social Education*), "Outstanding Science Trade Books for Children" (*Children and Science*), "Young Adult Choices" (*Journal of Adolescent and Adult Literacy*), and *Best Books for Young Adults* (ALA), and look for books that you think will engage middle-grade readers. Then find some of the books and read one or two of them yourself. Were you engaged? What are the common qualities of the books that engaged you? Do you think the qualities you value are the same as those that middle-grade students value? If you're uncertain about the answer here, you might talk to some middle-grade students about their reading preferences.

■ ▒▒▒▒▒▒▒▒▒▒ **BOOKS FOR MIDDLE-GRADE STUDENTS**

Kurlansky, M. (2002). *Salt: A world history.* New York: Walker and Company.

Kurlansky, M. (1997). *Cod. A biography of the fish that changed the world.* New York: Walker and Company.

Lauber, P. (1990). *Seeing Earth from Space.* NY: Scholastic.

Lauber, P. (1996). *You're Aboard Spaceship Earth.* NY: HarperCollins.

Lord, B. B. (1984). *In the year of the boar and Jackie Robinson.* New York: Harper & Row.

Prelutsky, J. (1984). *The New Kid on the Block.* Illus. James Stevenson. New York: Greenwillow.

Prelutsky, J. (1990). *Something Big Has Been Here.* Illus. James Stevenson. New York: Greenwillow.

Prelutsky, J. (1996). *A Pizza the Size of the Sun.* Illus. James Stevenson. New York: Greenwillow.

Silverstein, S. (1974). *Where the Sidewalk Ends.* New York: HarperCollins.

Silverstein, S. (1981). *A Light in the Attic.* New York: HarperCollins.

Silverstein, S. (1996). *Falling Up.* New York: HarperCollins.

Simon, S. (1985). *Jupiter.* New York: Morrow.

Simon, S. (1985). *Saturn.* New York: Morrow.

Simon, S. (1987). *Mars.* New York: Morrow.

Simon, S. (1987). *Uranus.* New York: Morrow.

Simon, S. (1992). *Our Solar System.* NY: Morrow.

Simon, S. (1992). *Venus.* New York: Morrow.

Simon, S. (1998). *Destination Jupiter.* New York: Morrow.

Spinelli, J. (2002). *Loser.* New York: Joanna Colter Books.

Stanley, D., & Vennema, P. (1992). *Bard of Avon. The story of William Shakespeare.* New York: Morrow/Avon.

3

Literature for Adolescents

Adolescent literature is as varied in content and scope as its adolescent readers.

A group of students, middle-school age, sit on the floor of the local book store, surrounded by piles of books, talking. Some of the books are those old childhood favorites—*Charlotte's Web* and *Tuck Everlasting*—that they just can't give up, even though they read them when they were 9 and 10. There are books that are marketed for adults in those piles, things that these middle-grade readers find intriguing. *The Handmaid's Tale* and *The Perfect Storm* are being passed around and examined. Most of the books in the piles, however, would be classified as adolescent literature. Books by authors such as Laurie Halse Anderson, Richard Peck, Chris Crutcher, Will Hobbs, Jacqueline Woodson, Angela Johnson, Avi, and Walter Dean Myers are handed around and looked at. As they hold the books, students talk to each other, saying things like "Oh, that's such a good book," or "I loved *Monster*. I wonder if *Fallen Angels* is good, too." Over time they sort through the books and decide what they are going to take with them. Not surprisingly, the book selections represent a wide range of genre, authors, topics, and audience. Both *Charlotte's Web* and *The Handmaid's Tale* are in the final selection.

These students are young adolescents, and they have selected a very wide range of books. So, what is adolescent literature? On one hand, adolescent literature is any book that adolescents choose to read, whether it was written and marketed for an audience of children, adolescents, or adults. Using this definition, both *Charlotte's Web* and *The Handmaid's Tale*, marketed for children and adults, respectively, could be considered adolescent literature.

In this chapter we first define adolescent literature, and then discuss how to evaluate quality of language, illustrations, and other literary considerations. Next, we consider elements of narrative fiction as well as several genres, or types, of narrative fiction. We go on to a discussion of both nonfiction texts and poetry for adolescent readers. Finally, we present resources for finding good books and discuss how to make wise selections and deal with censorship.

Defining Adolescent Literature

The term adolescent literature is generally applied to those books written for a target audience between the ages of 12 and 18. Some make a further distinction between adolescent literature and young adult literature, with some young adult audiences extending from 16 into the early 20s. Here we consider adolescent literature as books written specifically for an audience between fifth and twelfth grade, and we focus on those books and authors who write for middle-grade readers, knowing that both reading ability and maturity vary widely in these students.

Aside from the intended audience, adolescent literature is usually indicated through the content of the literature as well. Themes and concepts that are explored in these books are usually ideas that are important to adolescents, with themes of maturation, love, belonging, friendship, social justice, and family quite common. Issues that are included in adolescent literature include sex, rape, teen pregnancy, sexual identity, drugs and alcohol, bullying and violence. Further, the characters in adolescent narrative fiction are usually adolescents themselves, rather than younger children or adults. Nonfiction for adolescents includes an immense range of topics in many areas—history, sociology, science, art, music, technology. Finally, books for adolescents are generally more complex than those for younger children, in both structure and content.

Often, when we hear the word literature, we think immediately of poetry and narrative fiction, but adolescent literature encompasses various types of nonfiction as well. A basic distinction in adolescent literature is that between fiction and nonfiction. Fiction is, by definition, not actual. While it may be plausible, or seem real, fiction is, in fact, *made up* by the author. On the other hand, nonfiction is actual, a presentation of actual events, persons, discoveries, facts, and concepts, artfully arranged by the author.

Another useful distinction is between poetry, narrative, and expository prose. Poetry is marked by condensed language and a reliance on form and sound. Narrative fiction creates a *secondary world* (Tolkien, 1964) of story into which readers can enter as they read, a world that includes characters working to solve a problem. Narratives also are marked by a temporal dimension—they occur over time. Although a story might not be presented sequentially, it occurs sequentially. Expository nonfiction does not seek to tell a story but, rather, to present ideas and facts in order to build concepts and theories. Adolescents need to have opportunities to read both fiction and nonfiction, to read narrative, poetic, and expository prose. Above all, they need to have many opportunities to read well-written texts, regardless of type. As we discuss in Chapter 2, reading adolescent literature is a motivating experience for most middle-grade readers because this literature speaks to their interests and experiences, questions and concerns. Average readers, gifted students, those who struggle with reading, and English-language learners all benefit when they have the opportunity to be engaged with well-written books.

Pause and Reflect 3.1

Think about the books you are currently or have just finished reading. What is it about each book that you like? What interests you? What engages you? What makes the book good, and in what way? ■

Selecting Books for Adolescents

There are general criteria for excellence that apply across any text. Excellence in language and, if appropriate, illustration are always important. Look for books that have interesting language used in interesting ways and illustrations that are outstanding visual images.

Language

- Books should contain interesting words used in interesting ways, rich language that stimulates readers' curiosity.
- Even prose should contain rhythm, figurative language, and imagery.
- Dialogue should sound natural.
- Essential vocabulary should be defined in context.
- Descriptions should be fresh and vivid.
- Language should reveal the writer's enthusiasm and passion.

Illustration

- Images should be outstanding examples of visual art—whether oil, watercolor, pen and ink, or photograph; cartoon or representational; folk or surrealistic.

- Image and text should work together to tell a story or illuminate a concept or an idea.
- Images should reflect and extend the words on the page, providing essential information to the reader in both story and informational texts.
- Images should enhance the mood of a story or poem, the ideas in nonfiction texts.

Other Literary Considerations

Narrative

- The plot should be logical and consistent and be understandable by the audience.
- Characters (protagonists) should be full-dimensioned and dynamic; they should engage readers.
- The story should evidence unity of character and action.
- The setting should be vivid and detailed, easily pictured by readers.
- Themes should unify and create a multilayered story; they should be understandable by, and important to, readers.

Expository/Descriptive

- The sequence and development of ideas should be logical, leading to concepts.
- There should be differentiation between fact and opinion, theory and belief.
- The interrelationships between facts, and between facts and theories, should be clear.
- Facts should be current, complete, and accurate and there should be audience-appropriate scope.

Within the broad distinctions among narrative fiction, poetry, and nonfiction, there are particular dimensions that are important to consider when deciding on the quality of a particular text. Each genre also has its own special characteristics and thus its own special criteria for excellence. Add to this the need to consider the illustrations when evaluating picture books or graphic novels.

Understanding Narrative Fiction

Writers of narrative fiction have many techniques at their disposal as they create their unique secondary worlds. Narrative fiction is created through the manipulation of literary elements such as setting, characterization, plot, and theme, and is realized through the unique style of the author.

Setting

Stories occur at a particular time and in a particular place, and that constitutes the setting of a story. Sometimes settings are relatively vague, sometimes referred to as *backdrop* settings, but even sketchy settings are important. The setting might be as vague as "small-town America," or "large urban high school," or "summer at the swimming pool," but where the story takes place still influences both characters and action. *Integral* settings, on the other hand, are quite detailed and clearly function to further the action or define a character. A setting can act as an antagonist, or enemy, as in adventure stories in which the characters are in conflict with nature. Setting also can illuminate character, as it does in biography, or set mood and foreshadow events, as an historical setting might do. Setting can even function as a symbol, such as the American West, symbolizing freedom and adventure. Whether backdrop or integral, setting creates the context in which characters play out the action. For example, in Lois Lowry's *The Giver*, the story is deeply rooted in the futuristic dystopian setting that Lowry creates. Without this setting, the problems that the protagonist confronts wouldn't arise and he wouldn't be able to make the decisions that change his life.

Characterization

Characterization is the way in which authors create believable, memorable personalities that are so vivid that readers feel that they recognize them as real, if not actual. Good authors create protagonists, or main characters, that are *round* because they have multiple character traits, and *dynamic* because they mature and change over time. Authors do this by showing a reader how a character looks, thinks, feels, and acts through actual description by a narrator, through the thoughts, words, and actions of the character, or through the thoughts, words, and reactions of other characters. Just as we get to know other people through how they look, what they say and do, and how others feel about and act toward them, so, too, do we get to know fictional characters.

In addition to round, dynamic main characters, writers also create other characters that support a story. These characters might be multidimensional as well, and might change across the course of the story, or they might be flat characters with only one or two dimensions, or archetypal characters—the strict teacher, the supportive mother, the challenging coach—that populate the background of the story. These characters further the action of the story but do not dominate it. Sometimes they act as foils, standing in sharp contrast to the main character.

Believable, developed characters propel the action of a story, and the action of a story changes those characters. This is called "unity of character and action," and exploring this unity is something that many authors for adolescents seek to do. For example, Cassie in Mildred Taylor's *Roll of Thunder, Hear My Cry* both shapes and is shaped by the social climate of Depression-era rural Mississippi. As she discovers the extent of the influence that racism has on her life, she suffers; but she and her family also fight back when they can, and their attitude and actions make a difference in their world.

Plot

The plot is the action of the story, the sequence of events in which characters play out a role in some kind of conflict. Basic problem-types in adolescent narrative fiction include conflict within a character—self versus self—as well as between one character and another—self versus other. Many works of adolescent fiction include a conflict between self and society, as adolescents struggle to gain independence and to define for themselves the societal rules that they will follow. Finally, conflict between self and nature is also found in adolescent fiction, most often realized in what are popularly called adventure stories, such as Gary Paulsen's popular novel, *Hatchet*. In many books these types of conflicts are combined to form a multi-layered plot. Jean Craighead George depicts a young girl's struggle within her self, with her father, with society, and with the Arctic, as she seeks to define her place in the world in *Julie of the Wolves*.

There are varied plot structures in adolescent fiction, ranging from the chronological plot that is characteristic of fiction for younger readers, to a progressive chronological plot with sub-plots embedded, to plots that contain one or more flashbacks as characters recall past events, to parallel plots—in which two series of events occur together. Many plots contain subtle foreshadowing that contributes to the overall believability of the story. The quest tale, in which a protagonist leaves home or safety and ventures out into the world, only to return home a changed person, is popular in adolescent fiction. As the quest tale is often an apt metaphor for an adolescent's life, its popularity is not surprising. Karen Hesse's protagonist in *Out of the Dust* leaves home in order to discover that home is where she wants and needs to be. It is only through her leaving that she can recognize this.

Whatever the structure, plots need to be logically developed, contain a believable conflict that adolescent readers care about, and have the quality of verisimilitude, even if fantasy. One easy rule-of-thumb to use when evaluating plot is to ask whether the events that occur are coincidental or logical. Two coincidences is one too many. Unlike younger readers, however, adolescents often tolerate ambiguity, and the closed, happy-ever-after ending that marks most fiction for younger readers is not always found in fiction for adolescents. These readers can see the shades of gray or moral ambiguity that adults live with and understand that life is rarely, if ever, perfect. They can also understand that "what comes next" is often unpredictable. Jacqueline Woodson's *Miracle's Boys* ends on a hopeful note, but it is not at all certain that the boys will be able to sustain their family, given the pressures they face.

Theme

Moral ambiguity and the imperfections of life are two of the many issues that are explored by writers for adolescents. A theme is not the moral of the story, although many readers try their best to find a moral even when one is not apparent. Rather, theme is the big idea or thread of ideas that tie a story together. Most stories for adolescents have multiple themes, with the dominance of one over the other depending, in large part, on the way the book is read. Sometimes a theme is explicit, actually stated by a character or the narrator as in, "You have to trust yourself before you can trust others," from a story that explores themes of trust and self-worth. Often, themes are implicit, not directly stated in the text but inferred from the overall experience of the text. Themes, or the exploration of big ideas, provide the impetus for wonderful conversations about books and life.

Julia Alvarez probes issues of political oppression, freedom, and maturation in *Before We Were Free*, a novel set in the Dominican Republic during the Trujillo dictatorship. We watch a young girl becoming an adolescent as her extended family is shattered by political events, and we view these events through her eyes. By ex-

Teaching Idea 3.1
Exploring Narrative Fiction through Short Stories

Short stories contain all of the elements of narrative fiction in a condensed form and are perfect for helping students learn how these elements work together to create a memorable story. There are a number of collections of contemporary realistic fiction short stories, fantasy short stories, and science fiction short stories, most of which are organized thematically. Find one that you think students will engage with and create some discussion topics and writing prompts that will push them to explore how these stories work—each differently—to explore similar themes. Some books to get you started are:

Appelt, Kathi. (2000). *Kissing Tennessee and other stories from the Stardust Dance.* San Diego: Harcourt. Eight stories from eight different narrators revolving around the eighth-grade graduation dance.

Anderson, Rachel. (1989). *The bus people.* New York: Henry Holt. Six passengers on the bus for mentally handicapped students tell their stories, bracketed by two brief stories about the bus route and driver.

Armstrong, Jennifer. (2002). *Shattered: Stories of children and war.* New York: Knopf. Twelve authors tell stories of how war can affect children, both across history and across the world.

Carlson, Lori. (1994). *American eyes: New Asian-American short stories for young adults.* New York: Henry Holt. Ten authors explore the rough edges of the meeting between an Asian culture and Asian-American culture.

Cart, Michael. (2003). *Necessary noise: Stories about our families as they really are.* New York: HarperCollins. Ten contemporary authors probe what it is to be a family in the United States in the twenty-first century.

Ehrlich, Amy. (2001). *When I was your age: Original stories about growing up.* Cambridge, MA: Candlewick. In ten stories, contemporary authors for adolescents recount their own growing pains.

Fleischman, Paul. (1997). *Seedfolks.* New York: HarperCollins. Thirteen people—old and young, Vietnamese, Haitian, Hispanic, hopeful, and despairing—come together around a neighborhood garden.

Howe, James. (2003). *13: Thirteen stories that capture the agony and ecstasy of being thirteen.* New York: Atheneum. Much like being thirteen, these stories fluctuate between tragedy and comedy, always leaving hope.

Mazer, Anne. (1993). *America street: A multicultural anthology of stories.* New York: Persea Books. Fourteen stories by top U.S. writers about growing up in our diverse society.

ploring true events through the point of view of a fictional adolescent girl, Alvarez enables adolescent readers to think about these themes in a new way.

Themes in adolescent fiction range from the romantic and comic—love, success, maturation—to the tragic and ironic—alienation, despair, futility, hopelessness. The impact of a theme often has to do with the point of view in the narrative, or who is telling the story. An interesting exercise involves exploring short stories that are thematically similar, as Teaching Idea 3.1 suggests.

Point of View

Point of view concerns the voice through which a story is told. Many stories for adolescents are told from a *first-person* point of view, in which one of the characters recounts the story to the reader. This point of view is marked by the use of the pronouns

I and we. First-person narratives are very compelling, pulling readers into the heads of (usually) the protagonist. Adopting this point of view restricts the writer to telling the reader only that which the character can see, know, feel, think, and experience. First-person point of view is difficult to maintain, but offers a potentially powerful experience to readers. One reason many readers are so gripped by Laurie Halse Anderson's *Speak* is that it is told through the first-person narration of a young rape victim. The first-person narration in Francisco Jiminez's books *The Circuit* and *Breaking Through* pulls diverse types of adolescent readers into the life of a young Mexican boy who struggles to balance work, family, and school in his life as a migrant worker.

Writers who want a little more distance between their readers and the character who is telling the story often choose a *third-person limited* point of view. This point of view, marked by the pronouns he, she, and they, is usually limited to what a specific character could logically know, but is more detached. The reader isn't in the head of a character, but is hearing the story from that character's perspective.

Even more detached is the *omniscient* point of view in which the narrator is all-knowing and can reveal the thoughts and inner feelings of several characters, and move about in time and space to report events from an evenhanded position. Rather than seeing the story events through the protagonist's eyes, the reader sees the protagonist and the story world through the omniscient narrator's eyes. Finally, some authors use a *dramatic* point of view in which they reveal what can be seen and heard, but do not reveal inner feelings.

Although most books for adolescents are written from one of these perspectives, some authors employ more than one point of view, exploring central conflicts from the perspectives of several characters, often alternating by chapters. Using multiple narrators enables authors to provide various perspectives on the themes, characters, and events in a story. This is an increasing trend in adolescent literature. Books that do this include Ellen Wittlinger's *What's In a Name?*, Kathi Appelt's *Kissing Tennessee*, Paul Fleischman's *Bull Run*, E. L. Konigsberg's *The View From Saturday*, Virginia Euwer Wollf's *Bat 6*, Avi's *Nothing But the Truth*, and Paul Zindel's classic, *The Pigman*. These writers adeptly use multiple points of view to explore the variability in how we experience life.

Style

It can be argued that "style is all"—you won't have vivid settings, characters you care about, an engaging plot, or interesting exploration of themes without also having good style. Yet style is more than the mark of just a good story. It is the mark of a well-told, memorable story. Style encompasses the words an author selects, how these words are used, and the structures that they create. Stylistic devices such as figurative language (metaphor, similie, and personification) and imagery give writers the power to make their ideas come alive. The use of symbols adds depth and dimension to the ideas in a text, as they represent both literal and the figurative meanings. Allusions add a layer of meaning that nimble readers can enjoy, linking the story to the larger world of literature. The plot device of foreshadowing rewards alert readers with ample information for prediction and helps to create a sense of the inevitability of the outcome. Suspense increases the drama, and authors use the technique of

Adolescent literature spans many genres, including types of fiction.

cliff-hanger chapter endings to increase the suspense. Flashbacks, another plot device, allow authors to link past and current events and feelings to help develop cause and effect.

Natural dialogue, the use of dialect, and variations in vocabulary and syntax make characters' voices leap from a page. Mildred Taylor is particularly good at using dialect and dialogue to develop her characters. In *Roll of Thunder, Hear My Cry,* Taylor delineates her characters through their voices so well that it is possible to know who is speaking just by the vocabulary and syntax they are using. The voice of the protagonist in Laurie Halse Anderson's *Speak* is clearly that of a sarcastic, wounded, and frightened young adolescent girl.

Interesting narrative structures allow writers to tell stories in many different ways, and good writers select the structure that allows them to present their ideas most compellingly. Writers such as Karen Hesse, Jacqueline Woodson, Ron Koertge, and Virginia Euwer Wolf use poetry to create multilayered novels. Sharon Creech uses multiple narrators and journal entries to depict both an ocean journey and a coming of age story in *The Wanderer.* Art Spiegelman uses text and image to tell his story of *Maus: A Survivor's Tale*. Often, readers recognize an author's distinctive style, but sometimes authors take chances, creating new ways of enhancing the themes they are exploring. Walter Dean Myers did so in *Monster* when he alternated between the journal entries of his protagonist, Steve, and a movie script that allows Steve to distance himself from his own trial for murder. By including the journal entries, Myers gives us a picture of a young man who is frightened, hurting, and struggling with questions of guilt and innocence. The script allows readers to see the trial as

Figure 3.1 Genres and Subgenres in Adolescent Literature

	Fiction	Nonfiction
Narrative	Picture Storybooks/Graphic Novels	Authentic Biography
	Folklore	Narrative Nonfiction
	Fantasy*	
	Science Fiction*	
	Contemporary Realistic*	
	Fiction*	
	Historical Fiction*	
	Biographical Fiction	
	Memoir	
Exposition		Expository Nonfiction
Poetry		

*May also include mystery, adventure, romance, or drama

something almost unreal, yet so commonplace that the outcome is almost a foregone conclusion. The visual imagery that the script highlights helps Myers push the reader to consider how much we depend on what we see, rather than on what we know.

With so many books to select from, it is important to select the very best you can find. Works of narrative fiction that contain vivid settings, memorable characters, intriguing plots, resonant themes, and that are written with an engaging style enrich our lives and those of our students, both within and outside of the classroom. Fortunately, there are many books in several genres that meet these criteria.

Genres in Narrative Fiction

Within the broad distinctions of narrative and nonnarrative and of poetry, fiction and nonfiction, several genres and subgenres make up the body of work that we call adolescent literature. In this section we consider the genres that are narrative fiction: picture books/graphic novels, folklore, fantasy, science fiction, contemporary realistic fiction, historical fiction, and memoir. Entwined within these major genre categories are several subgenres. Adventure stories, sports stories, animal stories, romances, mysteries, and humorous stories can be found in many genres, but represent a particular type of story, whether because of the conflict in the plot (as in adventure stories or mysteries), the topics (as in sports stories, animal stories, or romance), or the mood, as in humorous stories (Galda and Cullinan, 2006). Figure 3.1 lists the major genres and subgenres.

Picture Books/Graphic Novels. Unlike the other genres, this genre is defined by its format rather than its content. The content of picture books and graphic novels spans the other genres, but the format always contains the essential dimension of visual representation. In picture books and graphic novels, the meaning is conveyed as much or more by the visual as by the verbal; visual and verbal work together to create the whole.

Although most literature that adolescents read is not written in a picture book format, some picture books are completely appropriate for adolescent audiences. Further, there is an increasing interest in graphic novels, that unique blend of picture and text, among adolescent readers. In either case, the reciprocal relationship between image and text is crucial for building meaning. Whether looking at the multiple story lines in David Macaulay's *Why the Chicken Crossed the Road* or enjoying the clever rendition of Avi's *City of Light, City of Dark,* Neil Gaiman's *The Wolves in the Walls* or Art Spiegelman's *Maus: A Survivor's Tale* books, adolescent readers learn to balance their verbal literacy with their visual literacy, and become increasingly skilled in both.

Books that combine the verbal and visual to attain meaning cannot be judged on words alone but are, rather, evaluated in terms of how the verbal and visual are entwined: how illustrations reflect and extend the mood, setting, characterization, plot, theme, concept, or idea presented in the words and, in turn, how the words reflect and extend the illustrations.

Folklore. One type of narrative fiction in adolescent literature is folklore, stories that originated in the oral tradition and have been handed down orally through the generations before they were recorded in print. Folklore includes many types of stories—myths, folk tales, fairy tales, tall tales, legends and hero tales, and folk songs. Until recently, the range of folklore that was available for young readers in U.S. schools was primarily confined to the Western European tradition. Fortunately, folk stories are now available in a wide range of single and collected works from around the world. Myths and hero tales are still probably most often studied in the middle grades, although with the increasing availability of folklore from around the world, middle-grade students might also be studying the cultural variations of classic folk and fairy tales such as *Cinderella* or *Little Red Riding Hood.* Folklore appears in anthologies that center on a particular theme across many cultures, anthologies that reflect a particular culture, or in individual editions. All three formats are useful in middle-grade classrooms.

Mythology and Pourquoi Stories.   Myths are stories developed by people who sought to explain both natural phenomena and human behavior. They center on the creation of, or reasons for, phenomena and, sometimes, the behavior of the gods who were believed to be responsible for these phenomena. Not long ago the study of mythology in the middle grades rarely went beyond Greek and Roman myths. Today, there are numerous examples of creation myths and *pourquoi* (why) stories from around the world. Collections such as Virginia Hamilton's *In the Beginning: Creation Stories from Around the World,* and hundreds of individual titles allow students the pleasure of enjoying these imaginative tales, the opportunity to experience the universality of the human urge to make sense of the world, and the experience of thinking about the same phenomenon from varied cultural perspectives.

Hero Tales. Hero tales, or epics and legends, present the larger-than-life exploits of a hero. Epics focus on the courageous deeds of humans in their struggles with other humans and with the gods. Two famous epics, *The Odyssey* and *The Iliad,* are often studied in the middle grades. These stories are also available in editions written specifically for the adolescent audience, such as Adele Geras's *Troy*, a retelling of the story of *The Iliad*. Legendary heroes, based in reality but exaggerated so that they have crossed into legends, are often popular with middle-grade readers. Nancy Springer's series of books about King Arthur, including *I Am Mordred*, offer different perspectives on the well-known legend, as does Kevin Crossley-Holland's trilogy, *The Seeing Stone, At the Crossing Places*, and *King of the Middle March*.

In the 1980s, a renewed interest in the folklore of the many cultures that make up North America resulted in several excellent collections of North American folklore that are appropriate for middle-school readers. Middle-school readers enjoy the cleverness, interesting language, and some of the history behind the African American oral tradition in Virginia Hamilton's *The People Could Fly: American Black Folk Tales* and *Her Stories: African American Folktales, Fairy Tales, and True Tales*; Julius Lester's *The Tales of Uncle Remus: The Adventures of Brer Rabbit, Further Tales of Uncle Remus: The Misadventures of Brer Rabbit, Brer Fox, Brer Wolf, the Doodang, and Other Creatures*, and *The Last Tales of Uncle Remus*; and James Haskins' *The Headless Haunt and Other African-American Ghost Stories*. Joseph Bruchac's *Flying with the Eagle, Racing the Great Bear*, and John Bierhorst's collections such as *The Deetkatoo: Native American Stories About Little People* present powerful tales from varied Native American traditions. Paul Goble's picture books featuring tales from the Plains Indians, such as *Buffalo Woman, The Girl Who Loved Wild Horses*, and *Star Boy* incorporate Plains Indians visual symbols in the illustrations that illuminate the gripping stories. Laurence Yep retells stories told by Chinese immigrants to America during the building of the railroads in *The Rainbow People* and *Tongues of Jade*. Paul Robert Walker's *Big Men, Big Country: A Collection of American Tall Tales* is designed to bring these favorite stories to an adolescent audience.

Whatever the origin or form of folklore, qualities that distinguish excellent folklore include:

- language that reflects the oral origins through rich, natural rhythms and vivid imagery
- language that begs to be read aloud
- language and illustrations (if applicable) that reflect the cultural heritage of the tale

Fantasy. Fantasy, another type of narrative fiction, has its roots in folklore. Fantasy is about people, places, or events that could not happen in the real world. Animals talk, small creatures act as people do, time slips, and the forces of good and evil battle using magic. While clearly unrealistic, well-crafted fantasy creates a sense of plausibility through carefully developed characters, a logical plot, and often vivid settings, as authors explore universal truths around ideas about morality, destiny, and other philosophical dilemmas. Perhaps more than any other genre, fantasy requires the "willing suspension of disbelief."

There are many types of fantasy, including animal fantasy, miniature worlds, quest tales, and literary lore. Fantasy stories are often developed through the use of devices such as time slips and magic. Many adolescent readers enjoy fantasy, while many others reject it, especially if they have not had a recent good experience with the genre. Many teachers, too, tend to shy away from fantasy (and science fiction), which results in many students never giving the genre a chance and thus missing some wonderful books. Fantasy writers, in fact, would argue that fantasy is one of the most powerful genres, in that it confronts essential human dilemmas in a manner that realistic fiction cannot do, thus presenting truth in a way that realistic fiction cannot.

To thoroughly explore, for example, the devastation of war in a realistic contemporary or historical novel for middle-grade readers might be inappropriate, or at least painful. Fantasy, however, can grapple with the horrors of war through, for example, the lives of rabbits Fiver and Hazel in Richard Adams' *Watership Down* in a way that allows young readers to think about this disturbing reality. Fantasy, as Newbery Award–winning Susan Cooper (1981) argues, both asks more of and gives more to a reader.

Animal Fantasy. This type of fantasy is both a popular and a relatively easy way into the fantasy genre for young adolescent readers. Fifth- and sixth-grade boys, in particular, are often captivated by animal fantasies such as Brian Jacques's *Redwall* series in which animals battle one another as the forces of good and evil clash in the world of Redwall.

Quest Tales. Stories in which the hero leaves home, encounters challenges and succeeds, and returns home a changed person are also popular with adolescent readers. Some, such as *The Golden Compass, The Subtle Knife,* and *The Amber Spyglass,* all part of Philip Pullman's His Dark Materials series, offer quest tales in a grand scope. Pullman infuses his novels with the classic story of loss and redemption told in both the Bible and Milton's *Paradise Lost.* Franny Billingsley's *The Folk Keeper* is a quest tale that weaves Celtic folk lore, coming of age, and self-discovery into a gripping romance.

Literary Lore. These tales, stories based on a folk story but extended and extrapolated well beyond the original tale, are often popular with adolescent readers, especially those who recognize the kernel of the story as a familiar childhood tale. Novels such as Gail Carson Levine's *Ella Enchanted,* Donna Jo Napoli's *Crazy Jack,* and Robin McKinley's *Beauty* offer adolescent readers beautifully told stories to enjoy and ponder.

The line between fantasy and realistic fiction has begun to blur as authors increasingly experiment with literary devices such as magical realism. In *Skellig,* David Almond creates a story that blurs that line. Adolescent readers enjoy debating whether or not the character Skellig was real or imaginary, what he symbolized, and why the young protagonist needed to encounter him. Qualities that distinguish excellent fantasy include:

- a detailed fantasy world that is believable within an interesting story
- imaginative events that are logically consistent within the story world
- multidimensional characters with consistent and logical behavior
- meaningful themes that provoke readers to think about life

Science Fiction. Science fiction is similar to fantasy but is built upon a scientific possibility, a hypothetical structure that allows authors to explore what life might be like if we take science to its logical conclusion. "If we do this, then what might life be like" is the basic question of science fiction, and these stories, while not realistic now, present possible future realities. As science and society change, so do the premises of science fiction. It is no longer science fiction to write of lunar exploration. With the collapse of the Soviet Union and the lessening of nuclear tensions, many science fiction writers turned away from hypothesizing about the aftermath of a nuclear Armageddon and began exploring other, contemporary issues such as the effects of overpopulation through the miracles of modern medicine, or the effects of ecological imperialism run wild. Mind control, a classic science fiction theme, continues to be explored by authors today.

Lois Lowry's novel *The Giver*, first in a trio that includes *Gathering Blue* and *Messenger*, explores what life would be like if society were able to control many of the emotions that are part of being human. Thus there is no desire, no love, no pain, no anger, no emotion of any kind in the Community. There is also no history. Everything is perfectly arranged, with dinner delivered and dishes removed, jobs handpicked by the Elders, one of whom is the Receiver, who holds all of the memories, horrible and wonderful, in his own mind. Adolescents who read this book find it quite compelling, as it calls into question many of the easy answers that people rely on to manage their lives. The open-ended conclusion allows multiple interpretations until the next books in the series are read.

Mind control through medical procedures, cloning, and drug cartels are all explored in Nancy Farmer's *The House of the Scorpion*. Against this backdrop Farmer creates a very likeable and realistic character who learns some very hard truths and has to make some difficult decisions as he matures. In this novel the setting is so carefully detailed that it seems completely real, and the questions Farmer raises about what it means to be human spark interesting discussions.

Qualities that distinguish excellent science fiction are similar to those for fantasy, and include:

- an interesting story based on a scientific possibility, with well-developed characters, an engaging and believable plot, and a meaningful theme that provokes readers to think about life
- internal consistency in plot and character

Contemporary Realistic Fiction. Contemporary realistic fiction explores current reality, life as it is lived now. These stories are possible, and very plausible, even though they are invented by an author. Characters, events, and settings all could possibly be real, even though the stories are fictional. Contemporary realistic fiction includes survival stories, like Gary Paulsen's *Hatchet* and the other books in that series, in which characters are pitted against their environment. Many mysteries are contemporary realistic fiction, in which characters seek to solve a problem. In E. L. Konigsburg's *Silent to the Bone*, the protagonist solves the mystery of who abused his best friend's baby sister, while his friend is in such a state of shock that he quits speaking. There are many authors whose contemporary realistic fiction novels would fall into the subgenre of sports stories. In books such as those written by Chris Crutcher or Rich Wallace, the protagonists are usually very involved in sports and their involvement plays a big role in the plot, which most often reflects a theme of maturation, both physical and social.

Themes that permeate contemporary realistic fiction include various relationships—friends, enemies, lovers, parents, siblings, grandparents; the painful process of growing up and gaining independence; and the life choices adolescents make about sex, drugs, alcohol, and violence. Honor, courage, perseverance, morality, and loyalty are issues that adolescents think about, and contemporary realistic fiction helps them consider possibilities. Laurie Halse Anderson puts readers in the mind of a young girl who is the victim of rape and subsequent shunning by her peers in the powerful novel, *Speak*. Paul Fleischman's *Whirligig* allows readers to share in a young man's remorse and repentance after his accidental killing of a young girl. Jacqueline Woodson explores a teenager's feelings about homosexuality and race in her books *From the Notebooks of Melanin Sun* and *The House You Pass on the Way*. An Na allows readers to feel the pain of being an immigrant and the anguish of living with an abusive father in *A Step From Heaven*. And Walter Dean Myers brings readers into the courtroom as a Harlem teenager is on trial for murder in *Monster*. There is probably a piece of contemporary realistic fiction that explores just about any issue that is important to young adolescents. Qualities that distinguish excellent contemporary realistic fiction include:

- a setting that is vivid and realistic and supports the events of the story
- characters who are multidimensional and dynamic, credible and free of stereotypes
- believable problems solved in realistic ways
- integral themes that are important to adolescents
- natural dialogue that is appropriate to the characters

Historical Fiction. Historical fiction is in many ways like contemporary realistic fiction but set in the past. These plausible stories of life in the past are based on real events and real people, but are fictional depictions of life in a particular time and place. Some historical fiction novels are thoroughly grounded in a particular place and event that is a documented part of history. Laurie Halse Anderson's *Fever, 1793* is set in Philadelphia during the yellow fever epidemic. Although the protagonist is a fictional young woman, how she lives, thinks, dresses, and acts all reflect the carefully detailed time and place. Other characters in Anderson's novel, such as Robert Peale, are actual historical figures. Mildred Taylor's Logan family saga, of which *Roll of Thunder, Hear My Cry* is one part, is set in rural Mississippi during the Depression. The values, racial attitudes, and ways of life are all historically accurate, the setting is detailed and vivid, and the characters are all fictional, although based on her family's stories.

Today we enjoy a plethora of outstanding historical fiction novels set in times ranging from prehistory to the Vietnam era. These books allow students to engage with a good story, and also help them come to understand that history was lived by people, often people much like themselves, and that history impacts life, as it so clearly does in these novels. In outstanding historical fiction, the larger, historical dilemma is reflected in the problems of the characters. For example, Walter Dean

Myers' *Fallen Angels,* a novel set during the Vietnam Conflict, reflects the national political and social divide that characterized that era and extends this into the lives of the characters, collectively and individually. Further, historical fiction presents history from a variety of perspectives and in a variety of voices. In adolescent literature, the Civil War era is seen from the point of view of Yankees as well as Confederates, blacks who are slaves, blacks who are free, white slave holders, white abolitionists, pro-war and anti-war activists. No history textbook has the breadth of perspectives that historical fiction presents. Qualities that distinguish outstanding historical fiction include:

- historical accuracy in events, attitudes, and issues
- a vivid, integral, and accurate historical setting
- authentic language patterns that are still understandable by modern readers
- multidimensional and dynamic characters whose feelings, behavior, and values reflect the historical period
- an integral theme that reflects larger historical concerns in the particulars of the story
- a plot that is accurate in terms of historical events and opportunities

Memoir. Biography, autobiography, and memoir all tell the story of the life or a portion of the life of a real person. Although biographies can be mostly fictional, the good ones are authentic, grounded in facts, and fall into the nonfiction category. On the other hand, memoirs are based on real events in the life of the author, but are interpretive accounts in which events are selected, arranged, and constructed to bring out a particular theme or personality trait.

Memoirs are an increasingly popular genre and young readers are gravitating to them. Authors of memoirs do not attempt to cover the full scope of their lives but rather select and present particular incidents that help readers understand the emotional reality of their lives. Francisco Jiminez does this beautifully in *The Circuit* and *Breaking Through,* episodic stories about his childhood and adolescence as a migrant worker. Chris Crutcher, author of many books for adolescents, has departed from the usual chronological plot and written an unusual memoir that is structured around memorable themes in his own life and his writing, *King of the Mild Frontier.* Like all good memoirs, these books are marked by:

- multidimensional, fully human characters
- engaging writing
- rich social details
- textured presentation of time and place
- insight into how their early lives shaped the authors' later life and work

Understanding Nonfiction

Nonfiction—whether narrative, descriptive, or expository—is rooted in fact; it is a disciplined exploration of someone's life, of a concept, or of ideas. Nonfiction writers, just like fiction and poetry writers, have an obligation to present their material in the most appropriate and appealing manner possible. Nonfiction is focused on conveying information, facts, and concepts rather than telling a story. Although most

Teaching Idea 3.2
Critical Reading with Nonfiction

Nonfiction offers a perfect opportunity for students to learn to recognize how authors distinguish between fact and opinion, how assumptions influence the presentation of facts, and how to determine the accuracy of a particular selection. Note with your students how authors are careful to use words such as know, determined, and understand, as opposed to words such as think, hypothesized, and predict. By listing verbs that indicate fact and those that indicate opinion or supposition—as well as qualifiers that help to distinguish between the two, you push students to notice those qualifiers, or the lack thereof, in the nonfiction that they read, making them more critical consumers of nonfiction material, including their textbooks. By examining, with your students, exposition for the underlying assumptions that color the interpretation of facts, and noticing how the arrangement of facts can determine how they are understood, you enable your young readers to see the power in the language of exposition. By comparing author qualifications, source lists, and processes, you also help your students understand the difference between superficial and deep knowledge of a subject. Finally, teaching students to recognize the structures they find in nonfiction, and how to use common features such as a table of contents or index, also helps students learn to read and understand how to navigate the many textbooks they encounter.

works of nonfiction are expository or descriptive, some, such as biography, do adopt a narrative framework. In biography, however, narrative is not the focus; it is an expressive technique used to convey information rather than to create a fictional story world. Indeed, in authentic biography the world is not fictional.

The information that is conveyed in nonfiction is more variable than most adults imagine. There is a great deal of nonfiction published each year, and almost every conceivable topic can be found in nonfiction. From famous people to space travel, cultural variation to the history of the chair; nonfiction explores the world, past and present. Nonfiction that connects with every aspect of the school curriculum is readily available. Books such as Delia Ray's *A Nation Torn: The Story of How the Civil War Began* enliven the study of history. Others, such as Roy Gallant's *The Day the Sky Split Apart: Investigating a Cosmic Mystery* add interest to the science curriculum. And still others, including Jan Greenberg and Sandra Jordan's *The Painter's Eye: Learning to Look at Contemporary American Art*, or Melvin Burger's *The Science of Music*, enhance the arts curriculum.

Somewhere at the beginning of the middle-grade years, many students begin to become increasingly interested in reading nonfiction, and this interest grows during adolescence, regardless of reading ability (Carter & Abrahamson, 1990). This interest is closely tied to content—students are interested in books on a topic that intrigues them. Sometimes students feel that reading nonfiction is easier than reading fiction. It certainly is easier to learn when new ideas and information are presented in a meaningful, vivid manner, and outstanding nonfiction does just that. A rich array of excellent nonfiction generates interest in and excitement about new ideas. Students who are allowed to pursue their interests through the reading of nonfiction soon learn to think critically about the books they are reading, as described in Teaching Idea 3.2.

No single textbook can have the depth or breadth of information available in an array of nonfiction texts. Further, a grade-level textbook is written at one reading level, thus it is often too challenging for some students and not challenging enough for others. Nonfiction adolescent literature contains books about any subject at a wide variety of reading levels. Nonfiction books also are especially useful in providing appropriate instructional experience for English-language learners (Bernhardt & Kamil, 1998).

Students who read nonfiction have more practice at getting information from expository text than do students who never read nonfiction, and this practice serves them well as they are building their comprehension skill. They also have the benefit of many models of well-written nonfiction texts on which to build as they write their own nonfiction texts. Thus, familiarity with nonfiction helps adolescent readers develop as critical readers and writers of nonfiction texts. No matter what the topic, quality nonfiction is noted for its style, organization, and accuracy.

Style

Style is important in nonfiction just as it is in fiction and poetry. Writers of nonfiction, like writers of fiction, select words with care, choosing those that best convey their ideas. Well-written nonfiction is often filled with metaphors that allow readers to understand complex concepts, and with vivid language and engaging rhetorical devices that stimulate a reader's curiosity. Many compelling nonfiction authors directly address the reader, asking "you" to engage with them in an exploration of an interesting idea. This engaging style also reflects the writers' enthusiasm for a subject. Nonfiction writers are also careful to arrange their works to help readers see the interrelationships between facts and how those facts are, in turn, related to theory. *The Life and Death of Adolf Hitler*, by James Cross Giblin, is written in such a compelling fashion that, even though a reader might already know a lot about the subject, the urge to keep reading is strong. Giblin manages to end each chapter with a cliff-hanger that provokes readers to want to read more.

Organization

The manner in which a work of nonfiction is organized is extremely important. Effective writers create a logical sequence and development of ideas, explore the interrelationships among facts, and lead a reader to conceptual understandings. The careful organization of ideas results in a unified text. Jim Murphy's *Blizzard! The Storm That Changed America* combines individual narratives of those who experienced the story, with information about the broader political, social, and technological context in a manner that allows readers to both experience and learn about this defining nineteenth-century event. In addition, organizational features such as a table of contents, glossary, indices, bibliography, and appendices allow readers to find information easily and to go beyond the book as they explore the topic.

Accuracy

Because nonfiction is not fiction, accuracy is extremely important. Good nonfiction writers deal with facts that are current and complete, presenting varied points of view on the topic, if they exist, and distinguishing between fact, theory, belief, and opinion. Further, successful writers adjust the scope of the book to suit the intended audience. They also cite their own qualifications, sources, and processes. Books by notable nonfiction writers such as Seymour Simon, Jim Haskins, Milton Meltzer, Patricia and Frederick McKissack, and others exemplify the qualities that distinguish exemplary nonfiction.

Expository and Narrative Nonfiction

Most of the nonfiction written for adolescents is either narrative nonfiction, in which information is presented within a narrative frame, or expository nonfiction, in which facts and ideas are presented in an orderly, logical fashion. The best nonfiction texts present facts that are accurate, complete, and within the scope of their audience, in a vivid, engaging, passionate manner. The authors arrange these facts in a way that pushes the reader to go beyond the facts themselves, developing concepts and understanding the material in light of other relevant knowledge. Almost always, the facts that are presented are only the beginning, as the focus on overarching themes becomes the driving force behind the writing.

Expository Nonfiction

Jennifer Armstrong's *Shipwreck at the Bottom of the World* is an interesting text to explore with students, especially when comparing it with books on the same subject that are marketed for adults. Armstrong does a remarkable job of recreating the hardships that Ernest Shackleton and his men had to endure after they were stranded in the South Pole ice, the social structures that were operating at the time, and the larger political climate, all the while exploring the qualities of leadership that enabled Shackleton to save all of his men. A combination of narrative and expository structures, liberal use of original photographs, diary excerpts, and citation of resources give credibility to the information that Armstrong provides.

Phillip Hoose's *The Race to Save the Lord God Bird* is much more than a chronicle of the gradual extinction of the ivory-billed woodpecker. As he documents the history of the bird, he also explores the meaning of extinction. This theme is made explicit in the first line of the introduction to the book: "To become extinct is the greatest tragedy in nature." He also describes the origins of the science we now call ecology, the field techniques that biologists used as they studied this rare bird, and the first major conservation movement that was sparked by the work on the ivory-billed woodpecker. Maps, glossary, thorough source notes, and an index add to the utility of this magnificent, timely book.

Excellence in expository nonfiction is marked by:

- current, complete facts; distinction between fact and theory
- logical development and sequence of information
- attractive, reader-friendly format and design
- illustrations that extend and explain the information presented
- an overarching theme or themes that tie the information to larger concepts

Authentic Biography

Authentic biographies are grounded in the historical record. They can be chronological, recounting the important events in the subject's life in sequential order, or episodic, highlighting only a certain period or periods in the subject's life. Many biographies focus on a single subject, but an increasing number of collective biographies are structured around a theme or unifying principal. Books such as Judith St. George's *In the Line of Fire: Presidents' Lives at Stake* and Joyce Hansen's *Women of Hope: African Americans Who Made a Difference* are collective biographies that adolescent readers enjoy.

Biographies are about all sorts of people. Walter Dean Myers presents the story of Sarah Forbes Bonetta, a young woman who was the protégé—and prisoner—of Queen Victoria, in *At Her Majesty's Request: An African Princess in Victorian England.* Alison Leslie Gold's *A Special Fate: Chiune Sugihara, Hero of the Holocaust* tells the story of the Japanese consul in Lithuania who defied his government and issued thousands of transit visas to Jews in Eastern Europe. James Cross Giblin chronicles the life of one of history's villains in *The Life and Death of Adolf Hitler* and Russell Freedman presents *Martha Graham: A Dancer's Life.* A rapidly increasing number of biographies are available to feed any adolescent's curiosity about notable people.

Any good biography explores the interaction between an individual and the world he or she lives in, exploring the unity of character, action, and context. Qualities that distinguish excellent biographies for adolescents include:

- accuracy or truthfulness of information
- richly rendered social details that illuminate setting, plot, and characterization
- a multidimensional, fully human character as the subject
- engaging writing
- illustrations that help readers visualize time and place as well as illuminate the character of the subject.

Understanding Poetry

Poetry is difficult to define. It is generally marked by the precise use of condensed language, and relies on imagery, figurative language, devices of sound, and form to call attention to something in a fresh and insightful manner. There are many types of poetry available to adolescent readers and many contemporary poets who write for them. Poems range in form from narrative to concrete, lyric to haiku, and the range of poetic devices used in poetry for adolescent readers mirrors the range available in poetry for adults. The difference is that poems for adolescents capture the adolescent experience—from elation to anguish, confidence to fear, childhood to adulthood. Often, adolescents have lost (or never developed) the habit of reading and enjoying poetry, but they can learn to love it if they are allowed to browse through the many wonderful collections of poetry for adolescents that are available today. Paul Janeczko's collections, such as *Looking for Your Name: A Collection of Contemporary Poems,* are all aimed at adolescent readers, and those readers respond to them enthusiastically. Collections such as *19 Varieties of Gazelle* and *This Same Sky* by Naomi Shihab Nye offer adolescents poetic glimpses of life in various cultural contexts. Extended narrative poems or collections of poems that support a narrative structure, such as

Teaching Idea 3.3
Poetry Out Loud: Exploring Sound and Meaning through Choral Reading

Put some of your favorite poems on overheads and explore with your class some of the many options for reading them out loud. You might want to begin with poems that are already arranged to be read chorally, such as those in Paul Fleischman's *Joyful Noise, I Am Phoenix,* and *Big Talk.* Another good way to begin is to use lyrics from songs that are popular with your students. The point is to get your students to experiment with how sound enhances meaning. After you've broken the ice over several days, put other poems on the overhead, poems that you and your students will have to talk about before perform-ing them. Demonstrate and discuss *tempo* (fast/slow), *stress* (emphasis), *tone* (serious/comic), and *volume* (loud/soft), and experiment by read-ing a poem in different ways. Then introduce the notion of grouping voices (unison, choruses, single voices paired with other single or choral voices, cumulative voices) and experiment with them. Divide the class into small groups, pass out copies of different poems (one for each group), and ask students to plan and perform. If you do this over time, students will begin to automati-cally think of how sound works to enhance mean-ing in the poetry they read and write.

Lindsay Lee Johnson's *Soul Moon Soup,* Karen Hesse's *Out of the Dust,* or Jacqueline Woodson's *Locomotion* offer adolescent readers the opportunity to engage with lyri-cal, poetic language while reading narrative fiction.

Figurative Language and Imagery

Poets use figurative language and imagery to help readers see with a poet's vision. This allows them to create meaning beyond the literal use of the words, to engage readers' imaginations and point them toward seeing the world in new ways. Effec-tive similes, metaphors, personification, and imagery are appropriate to and un-derstandable by the adolescent reader, and integral to the meaning of the poem, not simply tacked on as embellishment. Poet Eve Merriam compares morning to a clean sheet of paper in her poem, *Metaphor,* and any one who has ever gone to bed hop-ing that tomorrow will be better relates to that idea.

Sound

Sound is an important tool for creating meaning, and poets have a whole range of poetic devices that relate to sound from which to select. Rhyme, rhythm, alliera-tion, assonance, and onomatopoeia are all elements that can be manipulated by a poet to enhance the meaning of, and the reader's aesthetic experience with, poetry. The poetic elements call attention to particular words, phrases, and sounds and help the reader know how to read a poem. Elements of sound add depth to a poem; they should reflect and extend the ideas that the poet is exploring. Paul Fleischman is a master of this in *Joyful Noise* and *I Am Phoenix,* both collections of poems for two voices that rely on sound to create meaning. These collections are an excellent way to introduce students to choral reading, an effective technique for exploring the sound–meaning relationship in poetry, as suggested in Teaching Idea 3.3.

Form

Form is another tool the poet uses to create meaning. Adopting particular poetic forms, such as *mask* or *apostrophic* poetry, gives poets the license to assume new voices and new roles as they take on the mask of, or address, a particular object. *Free-verse* writers make careful use of line breaks and white space to enhance their meaning, and *concrete* or *shape* poetry also allows writers to use visual as well as verbal cues to enhance meaning. Whatever the form, and there are many, the form itself should enhance the ideas the poet is exploring. Barbara Juster Esbensen melds form and meaning in *Echoes for the Eye: Poems to Celebrate Patterns in Nature*.

There are wonderful collections of poetry available for adolescent readers, collections that will entice them and help them enjoy their experience with poetry. Naomi Shihab Nye, Liz Rosenberg, Paul Janeczko, Cynthia Rylant, and others have given us a splendid array of choices. Quality poetry for adolescents consists of:

- beautiful language that calls attention to something in a new, fresh way
- language that stirs emotions in its readers
- the artful use of a wide array of poetic tools to convey meaning

Building a Classroom Collection

Being able to distinguish between mediocre and excellent adolescent literature is an important skill, but only the beginning of being able to build a useful classroom collection. Teachers must also know how to find out about good books, both old and new, and be able to select among them to build a collection that meets the needs of their students. A useful classroom collection contains books that relate to the curriculum—reading, writing, literature study, science, social studies, and other cross-curricular connections. As we discuss in Chapter 2, it needs to contain books that reflect students' interests and abilities and will stretch those very interests and abilities. The classroom library also should reflect the cultural diversity of our world. Further, a good classroom collection contains books that you will want to teach and to spend time with, as well as books that are on the shelf for students' independent reading choices. The books in your classroom need to offer students the opportunity to see themselves and others, to think about life, and to learn about their world.

How can you use literature to enhance your curriculum? If the curriculum is thematically-organized, select books that allow students to explore those themes. Science and social studies teachers and language arts teachers who team with them will select many books that support the science or social studies curriculum. A writing curriculum is enhanced by books that exemplify the types of writing that students will do. Teachers who use literature to structure or support the reading curriculum make sure they have books that allow them to teach and students to practice the reading strategies they are working with. Literature study is strengthened by selections that help students learn appropriate literary concepts.

Classrooms that promote reading offer opportunities for students to find good books.

Pause and Reflect 3.2

Think about what you are or will be teaching and jot down some of the ways that you can use adolescent literature to strengthen or shape what you do. Then think about some of the books that you have read and where they might fit your needs. What kind of reading do you need to do to get ready for next year? ■

Finding Good Books

Talking with other teachers about books that they like and find useful is certainly one way to find out about books, but, pleasant as it may be, this strategy takes you only so far. Fortunately, journals that regularly review books and websites about the many awards and prizes in the field of literature can aid you in your continuing search for good books for your classroom.

Journals/Books. One of the most useful journals you will find is the *Journal of Adolescent and Adult Literacy*. This journal is published eight times a year by the International Reading Association (www.reading.org). Focused on the teaching of reading to adolescents and adults, this journal includes interesting, timely articles on teaching, reviews of professional and classroom materials, and reviews of books for adolescents. Another journal of interest is the *English Journal*, published by the National Council of Teachers of English (www.ncte.org). This journal focuses on teaching English to adolescents.

There are many fine journals that explore children's and adolescent literature, and a great one to begin with is *The Horn Book Magazine* (magazine@hbook.com). This journal features articles about literature, authors, and illustrators, and contains excellent, substantial reviews of new literature. It is published six times a year.

There are also several books that can help you find the best of the books published each year. Many of these are listed in Chapter 2 as resources for finding high-quality, culturally diverse literature. The National Council of Teachers of English periodically updates a useful publication titled *Your Reading: A Booklist for Junior High and Middle School Students*. Yet another excellent resource is *Best Books for Children: Preschool through the Middle Grades*.

Awards and Prizes. The John Newbery Medal has been awarded annually since 1922 to the author of the most distinguished contribution to literature for children published in the United States in the preceding year. Many of these books, both medal winners and honor books, are books that are enjoyed by young adolescent readers. The award is administered by the Association for Library Services for Children (ALSC), a division of the American Library Association (ALA). The Michael L. Printz Award honors the author of an outstanding young adult book published in the preceding year. It is administered by the Young Adult Library Services Association (YALSA), a division of the ALA. This award was created especially for adolescent literature. The blurring of the boundaries between what is considered adolescent literature and what is considered children's literature, which is defined in the Newbery criteria as through age 14, was apparent in 2003 when Nancy Farmer's *The House of the Scorpion* won both a Newbery honor and a Printz honor.

The Coretta Scott King Award is administered by the Social Responsibilities Round Table and the ALA and given annually to an outstanding African-American author and illustrator whose work commemorates and fosters the work and dream of Dr. Martin Luther King, Jr. The Pura Belpre Award is presented biennially to a Latino/Latina writer and illustrator whose work best portrays the Latino cultural experience in an outstanding work of literature for children and youth. It is cosponsored by the ALSC and ALA, and the National Association to Promote Library Services to the Spanish Speaking.

The Robert F. Sibert Award is administered by the ALA and seeks to recognize outstanding informational books. Information about these and other awards is available at the website for the American Library Associaton, www.ala.org.

The Boston Globe–Horn Book Awards are sponsored by *The Boston Globe* newspaper and *The Horn Book Magazine* and, since 1976, honor a work of fiction, poetry, nonfiction, or illustration. Information about this award can be found at www.hbook.com.

The National Council of Teachers of English sponsors the Orbis Pictus Award. This award honors the author of an outstanding nonfiction book. Information can be found at www.ncte.org. The International Reading Association also sponsors awards for literature, including the IRA Children's Book Award, presented for a book published in the preceding year by an author who shows unusual promise. Information about this award can be found at www.reading.org.

Selection versus Censorship

Teaching with adolescent literature is invigorating. It is also a challenge for many reasons, one of which is the threat of censorship. With so many excellent books written on an unprecedented wide range of topics and themes, it is almost inevitable that someone will attempt to censor the books that middle-grade students are reading. Carefully considering the books that one's own child reads is acceptable, no matter what our personal stance on books, raising children, or censorship might be. Parents do have the right to monitor their child's reading, and can insist that a teacher offer their child an alternative to any book that they, the parents, find inappropriate. This parental right goes beyond its boundaries, however, when parents or anyone seek to censor the reading of others. Suppressing the reading material of others is censorship. Carefully choosing reading material that is appropriate for particular readers and particular purposes is selection. Censorship and selection are quite different.

The National Council of Teachers of English enumerates five differences between censorship and selection.

1. Censorship excludes specific materials; selection includes specific material.
2. Censorship is negative; selection is affirmative.
3. Censorship seeks to control the reading of others; selection seeks to advise or suggest the reading of others.
4. Censorship tries to indoctrinate and limit access to information and ideas; selection tries to educate and increase access to information and ideas.
5. Censorship focuses on specific, isolated parts of a work, while selection considers the interrelationship among parts and the work as a whole. (National Council of Teachers of English, 1983, p. 18)

The National Council of Teachers of English (www.ncte.org), the International Reading Association (www.reading.org), the American Library Association (www.ala.org), and the National Coalition Against Censorship (www.ncac.org) have helped libraries and school districts establish policies that protect students and teachers against attempts at censorship. The web sites of these organizations contain useful information and detailed procedures to follow in the case of a censorship attempt. Most school districts have established procedures to follow in the event of censorship. Find out what these are and be prepared to follow them. NCTE published *Guidelines for Selection of Materials in English Language Arts Programs*, in which they set out general principles for selection. Their Anti-Censorship Center (www.ncte.org/about/issues/censorship) offers information about what to do when a book is challenged, a link to a site for reporting a censorship incident, and a list of other sites that contain new reports of censorship. It also provides a link to written rationales for the most commonly challenged books and a link to the NCTE Guideline, The Students' Right to Read, which includes a form for would-be censors to fill out. The ALA's Office for Intellectual Freedom publishes a list of frequently challenged books, and their *Hit List for Young Adults* provides resources for withstanding challenges to frequently challenged books.

One of the best defenses against censorship is wise selection. This includes careful attention to the quality of the book being selected as well as thorough consideration of the academic value of the book. Know why you have selected the books that you teach and that line the shelves of your classroom library. And as you select these books, keep in mind the standards that your school and community hold. With so many wonderful books to choose from, selecting excellent texts that support learning and are not offensive to the majority of the larger community is not such a difficult task.

Concluding Remarks

Literature for adolescents encompasses a vast array of books, spanning many different genres, a range of reading levels, and more reading interests than you might be able to imagine. The best of this literature is carefully crafted poetry and prose, both fiction and nonfiction, narrative and expository, that has been written with an adolescent audience in mind. These books speak to the hopes, dreams, fears, worries, and passions of adolescents in a manner that engages readers. Indeed, these books can be so powerful in the lives of adolescents, it is vital that we select carefully—only offering the best that we have.

Excellent books have the potential to change the lives of middle-grade readers. They can change attitudes toward reading, helping students become better readers because they are willing to do the hard work of reading when the book is good. Wanting to find out what happens, gather knowledge, and experience ideas is a powerful motivating force for learning to read well. Excellent books help students move beyond a functional literacy—with which they can perform adequately in the literate world—to a more passionate literacy. Literature for adolescents brings the content of all curricular areas alive, offering readers a breadth and depth that textbooks cannot. These books can help all students become avid readers. Perhaps Anna Quindlen says it best at the end of her tribute to books, *How Reading Changed My Life* (1998):

> Perhaps it is true that at base we readers are dissatisfied people, yearning to be elsewhere, to live vicariously through words in a way we cannot live directly through life. Perhaps we are the world's great nomads, if only in our minds. . . . Books are the plane, and the train, and the road. They are the destination, and the journey. They are home. (p. 70)

■▬▬▬▬ EXTENDING LEARNING

1. Using the sources presented in this chapter, select five books that are narrative fiction, two books of poetry, and four nonfiction books, both expository and narrative. Read these books, responding to them in a journal. Consider what you think the books are about, what you liked about them, what you didn't like (if anything), and what you noticed about the author's craft. If you teach science, social studies, or another curricular area, find at least two pieces of narrative fiction and two books of poetry, as well as six to seven pieces of nonfiction in your area of expertise.

2. Begin and keep a Teacher's Notebook about the books you read, hear about, and read about, noting why you have entered the title on your list. When you can, begin to read these books, noting your evaluation of each one and why you think middle-grade readers might enjoy it, and how you might use it for instruction.

3. Get to know a particular author of books for adolescents by reading that author's works, noting aspects of craft. Find biographical information from published memoirs, brief articles about writing by the author, or interviews. *Something About the Author* is an excellent beginning source.

■ BOOKS FOR MIDDLE-GRADE READERS

Adams, R. (1974). *Watership down.* New York: Macmillan.

Alvarez, J. (2002). *Before we were free.* New York: Knopf.

Anderson, L. H. (1999). *Speak.* New York: Farrar Straus Giroux.

Anderson, L. H. (2000). *Fever—1793.* New York: Simon & Schuster.

Apelt, K. (2000). *Kissing Tennessee and other stories from the Stardust Dance.* San Diego, CA: Harcourt.

Atwood, M. (1998). *The handmaid's tale.* New York: Doubleday.

Avi. (1991). *Nothing but the truth: A documentary novel.* New York: Scholastic.

Avi. (1995). *City of light, city of dark: A comic book novel.* New York: Scholastic.

Babbitt, N. (1975). *Tuck everlasting.* New York: Farrar.

Bierhorst, J. (1998). *The Deetkatoo: Native American stories about little people.* New York: Morrows.

Billingsley, F. (1999). *The folk keeper.* New York: Simon & Schuster.

Bruchac, J. (1993). *Flying with the eagle, racing the great bear.* Mahwah, NJ: BridgeWater Books.

Burger, M. (1989). *The science of music.* New York: HarperCollins.

Creech, S. (2000). *The wanderer.* New York: HarperCollins.

Crossley-Holland, K. (2001). *The seeing stone.* New York: Arthur A. Levine.

Crossley-Holland, K. (2002). *At the crossing-places.* New York: Arthur A. Levine.

Crossley-Holland, K. (2004). *King of the middle march.* New York: Arthur A. Levine.

Crutcher, C. (2003). *King of the mild frontier.* New York: HarperCollins.

Esbensen, B. J. (1996). *Echoes for the eye: Poems to celebrate patterns in nature.* New York: HarperCollins.

Farmer, N. (2002). *House of the scorpion.* New York: Athaneum.

Fleischman, P. (1985). *I am Phoenix: Poems for two voices.* New York: Harper & Row.

Fleischman, P. (1988). *Joyful noise: Poems for two voices.* New York: Harper & Row.

Fleischman, P. (1998). *Whirligig.* New York: H. Holt.

Freedman, R. (1998). *Martha Graham: A dancer's life.* New York: Clarion.

Gaiman, N. (2003). *The wolves in the walls* (D. McKean, Illus.). New York: HarperCollins.

Gallant, R. (1995). *The day the sky split apart: Investigating a cosmic mystery.* New York: Athaneum.

George, J. C. (1972). *Julie of the wolves.* New York: HarperCollins.

Geras, A. (2001). *Troy.* San Diego, CA: Harcourt.

Giblin, J. C. (2002). *The life and death of Adolf Hitler.* New York: Clarion.

Goble, P. (1982). *The girl who loved wild horses.* New York: Macmillan.

Goble, P. (1982). *Star boy.* New York: Bradbury.

Goble, P. (1984). *Buffalo woman.* New York: Bradbury.

Gold, L. (2000). *A Special fate: Chiune Sugihara, hero of the holocaust.* New York: Scholastic.

Greenberg, J., & Jordan, S. (1991). *The painter's eye: Learning to look at contemporary American art*. New York: Delacorte.

Hamilton, V. (1985). *The people could fly: American Black folk tales*. New York: Knopf.

Hamilton, V. (1988). *In the beginning: Creation stories from around the world*. San Diego, CA: Harcourt.

Hamilton, V. (1995). *Her stories: African American folktales, fairy tales, and true tales*. New York: Scholastic.

Hansen, J. (1998). *Women of hope: African Americans who made a difference*. New York: Scholastic.

Haskins, J. (1994). *The headless haunt and other African-American ghost stories*. New York: Harper-Collins.

Hesse, K. (1997). *Out of the dust*. New York: Scholastic.

Hoose, P. (2004). *The race to save the lord god bird*. New York: Farrar, Straus and Giroux.

Jacques, B. (1986). *Redwall*. New York: Philomel.

Janeczko, P. (1993). *Looking for your name: A collection of contemporary poems*. New York: Scholastic.

Jiminez, F. (1999). *The circuit: Stories from the life of a migrant child*. Boston: Houghton Mifflin.

Jiminez, F. (2001). *Breaking through*. Boston: Houghton Mifflin.

Johnson, L. L. (2002). *Soul moon soup*. Ashville, NC: Front Street.

Junger, S. (1997). *The perfect storm: A true story of men against the sea*. New York: Little Brown and Company.

Koertge, R. (2003). *Shakespeare bats cleanup*. New York: Candlewick.

Konigsburg, E. L. (1996). *The view from Saturday*. New York: Atheneum.

Konigsburg, E. L. (2000). *Silent to the bone* (J. Pinkney, illus.). New York: Simon & Schuster.

Lester, J. (1987). *The tales of Uncle Remus: The adventures of Brer Rabbit*. New York: Dial.

Lester, J. (1990). *Further tales of Uncle Remus: The misadventures of Brer Rabbit, Brer Fox, Brer Wolf, the Doodang, and other creatures*. New York: Dial.

Lester, J. (1994). *The last tales of Uncle Remus*. New York: Dial.

Levine, G. C. (1998). *Ella enchanted*. New York: HarperCollins.

Lowry, L. (1993). *The giver*. Boston: Houghton Mifflin.

Lowry, L. (2000). *Gathering blue*. Boston: Houghton Mifflin.

Lowry, L. (2004). *Messenger*. Boston: Houghton Mifflin.

Macaulay, D. (1987). *Why the chicken crossed the road*. Boston: Houghton Mifflin.

McKinley, R. (1978). *Beauty*. New York: HarperCollins.

Merriam, E. (1964). Metaphor. In *It doesn't always have to rhyme*. New York: Athaneum.

Myers, W. D. (1988). *Fallen angels*. New York: Scholastic.

Myers, W. D. (1999). *At Her Majesty's request: An African princess in Victorian England*. New York: Scholastic.

Myers, W. D. (2000). *Monster* (C. Ngers, illus.). New York: HarperCollins.

Murphy, J. (2000). *Blizzard! The storm that changed America*. New York: Scholastic.

Na, A. (2001). *A step from heaven*. Asheville, NC: Front Street.

Napoli, D. J. (1999). *Crazy Jack*. New York: Delacorte.

Nye, N. S. (1992). *This same sky: A collection of poems from around the world*. New York: Simon & Schuster.

Nye, N. S. (2002). *19 Varieties of gazelle: Poems of the Middle East*. New York: HarperCollins.

Paulsen, G. (2000). *Hatchet*. New York: Simon & Schuster.

Pullman, P. (1996). *The golden compass*. New York: Knopf.

Pullman, P. (1997). *The subtle knife*. New York: Knopf.

Pullman, P. (2000). *The amber spyglass*. New York: Knopf.

Ray, D. (1990). *A nation torn: The story of how the Civil War began*. New York: Dutton.

Spiegelman, A. (1986). *Maus: A survivor's tale: My father bleeds history.* New York: Pantheon.

St. George, J. (1999). *In the line of fire: Presidents' lives at stake.* New York: Holiday.

Taylor, M. E. (1976). *Roll of thunder, hear my cry.* New York: Dial.

Walker, P. R. (1993). *Big men, big country: A collection of American tall tales.* San Diego, CA: Harcourt.

White, E. B. (1952). *Charlotte's web* (G. Williams, Illus.). New York: HarperCollins.

Whittlinger, E. (2000). *What's in a name.* New York: Simon & Schuster.

Wolff, V. E. (1998). *Bat 6.* New York: Scholastic.

Woodson, J. (1995). *From the notebooks of Melanin Sun.* New York: Scholastic.

Woodson, J. (2000). *Miracle's boys.* New York; Putnam.

Woodson, J. (2003). *The house you pass on the way.* New York: Putnam.

Woodson, J. (2003). *Locomotion.* New York; Putnam.

Yep, L. (1989). *The rainbow people* (D. Wiesner, illus.). New York: HarperCollins.

Yep, L. (1991). *Tongues of jade.* New York: HarperCollins.

Zindel, P. (1968). *The pigman.* New York: Bantam Doubleday Dell.

4

Scaffolding Students' Comprehension, Learning, and Engagement with Text

Scaffolding can make every reading experience a successful one.

Imagine you get a call from a rich uncle saying he wants you to take a trip to Bolivia to investigate his landholdings there. The plane leaves in an hour. He will pay for everything. All you need to do is answer a few questions and write up a short report when you return. Your passport and inoculations are current and, being the adventurous person you are, you decide to go. But the trip is a disaster—no one is there to greet you, you brought the wrong clothes, you can't understand the language, the culture is confusing, and, what's worse, you can't even locate the landholdings. When you return, you scribble a note to your uncle. "The trip was a disaster. I was a failure. You may give me an 'F' as nephew."

What went wrong? For one thing, you weren't prepared to go to Bolivia. No one figured out what you needed to know and provided you with the infor- mation you needed for a successful trip. No one was there to show you around once you got there. In fact, no one did anything to help you in the challenging situation you faced. Consequently, and not surprisingly, when you returned all that you could recall of your trip was your failure.

Reading a story or expository text is something like taking a trip. Sometimes the territory may be quite familiar, other times very new. Whatever the case, one of our tasks as teachers is to help ensure our students a successful, meaningful journey. We can do this by sufficiently preparing students before reading, guiding them where necessary during reading, and providing them with meaningful experiences after reading. In this chapter, we refer to such assistance as *scaffolding*, and describe in detail what we call a Scaffolded Reading Experience (Graves & Graves, 2003), a flexible instructional framework designed to assist students in understanding, learning from, and enjoying each and every reading experience.

Scaffolding is one of the most widely discussed and widely endorsed instructional concepts (for example, Anderson & Armbruster, 1990; Applebee & Langer, 1983; Cazden, 1992; Clark & Graves, 2005; Pearson, 1996; Pressley, 2002; Routman, 2000; RAND Reading Study Group, 2002). Although different authors define scaffolding slightly differently, three closely related features are essential attributes of effective scaffolding. First, there is the scaffold itself, the temporary and supportive structure that helps a student or group of students accomplish a task they could not accomplish—or could not accomplish as well—without the scaffold. Second, the scaffold must place the learner in what Vygotsky (1978) has termed the *zone of proximal development*. As explained by Vygotsky, at any particular point in time, children have a circumscribed zone of development, a range within which they can learn. At one end of this range are learning tasks they can complete independently; at the other end are learning tasks they cannot complete, even with assistance. Between these two extremes is the zone most productive for learning, the range of tasks that children can achieve *if* they are assisted by someone more knowledgeable or more competent. Third, over time, the teacher must gradually dismantle the scaffold and transfer the responsibility for completing tasks to students. As Pearson and Gallagher (1983) have explained, effective instruction often follows a progression in which teachers gradually do less of the work and students gradually assume increased responsibility for their learning. It is through this process of gradually assuming more and more responsibility for their learning that students become competent, independent learners.

In this chapter, we discuss scaffolding and give a host of examples of how it can be used to foster middle-grade students' comprehension, learning, and engagement. We begin by discussing the roles that purpose, the selection, and the students play in planning reading activities. Next, we discuss the Scaffolded Reading Experience, the framework we use in supporting students' efforts. Following that, we describe and give examples of various kinds of prereading, during-reading, and postreading activities you might use to prepare and engage readers. Finally, we present a detailed example of a complete scaffolded reading experience.

The Purpose, the Selection, and the Students

Three elements come into play when considering the kinds and number of activities needed to foster successful reading experiences—the purpose for reading, the selection, and the students. These three factors will dictate what sorts of activities you design to foster a successful reading experience.

The Purpose

Let us first talk briefly about purpose. In the scenario we used at the beginning of the chapter, there was at least one explicit purpose for your journey to Bolivia—to find out about your uncle's landholdings there. Purpose is what motivates us, helps focus our attention, and gives us a goal, something tangible to work toward.

Without purpose, you have no way to measure your success. "Open your science books and read pages 16 to 20." "Why?" the student might ask. In this instance he might answer, "Because the teacher told me so. If I don't want to get into trouble, I'd better do it." This is not a very good purpose, in our estimation. "Read pages 16 and 17 to find out three interesting facts about Pluto" is a slightly more focused purpose, and you can measure students' success in achieving this purpose.

Purposes for reading are nearly as numerous and varied as the seashells along the beach. They might be singular or multiple, straightforward or complex. One reading purpose might be to simply enjoy a well-told tale, another to discover a story's theme or the differences and similarities between characters, another to learn something about the events that precipitated the cold war, and still another to find out how to make sourdough bread. Whatever the purpose for reading, you want to ensure your students' success in achieving it.

Purposes are determined by a number of factors. Among these are the students reading the selection, the selection itself, and what it is your students need to know, want to know, or will be empowered, enriched, or enlightened by knowing.

Purposes can be student generated or teacher generated. A student-generated purpose may begin with a student telling you, "I'm getting a guinea pig for my birthday, but I don't know what to feed it." You pull a book on guinea pigs from your library shelf. "I don't know what they eat either. Will you tell me when you find out?" By embracing student-generated purposes for reading, you will heighten interest in reading among all of your students, particularly those whose cultural experiences lead to purposes for reading that may be different from your own.

A teacher-generated purpose begins with a purpose in the mind of a teacher. Perhaps your social studies curriculum includes the study of Japan. You want your students to learn how to compare and contrast. Focusing your students' attention, as they read, on looking for similarities and differences between your state—which, of course, they are quite familiar with—and Japan will help you achieve your teacher-generated purpose.

The Selection

Of course, before you begin to create activities for a particular text, you will have read it and become acquainted with its topics and themes, its potentially difficult vocabulary and other potential stumbling blocks, and the opportunities it presents for instruction. The reading material itself will dictate how you want your students to approach it and what you want them to take away from it. A science chapter, for instance, will require a different kind of reading than a novel; thus, the activities you set up to prepare, guide, and enrich the reading experience will be quite different for each.

Say, for instance, a science chapter on electricity has a number of difficult concepts that your seventh graders will need to understand if they are to comprehend the thrust of the chapter. In this case, you will probably want to preteach these concepts before students begin reading on their own and encourage students to attend to these concepts while they are reading.

You may also decide to provide alternatives to independent reading for students in your classroom who read substantially below the seventh-grade level and would be unable to comprehend much of the chapter on their own. You might pair students for reading or have students work in groups where there is one reader who reads the text paragraph by paragraph, stopping after each paragraph for the group to discuss what was read and, as a group, write a one-sentence summary.

After all of your students have finished reading, in order to ensure depth of processing, you will want them to work with these concepts in yet another way, perhaps by having students make a chart listing the concepts and illustrating them. Providing opportunities for students to work with concepts in a variety of ways—through listening, writing, drawing, watching, and touching, to name a few—will be of particular benefit for students who may have missed some of the important concepts in their initial reading.

Suppose, as another example, that the class is reading Phyllis Naylor's *Shiloh*. This Newbery Medal Book will invite other, perhaps quite different, kinds of activities. As you are studying the novel, you realize what an outstanding job of characterization Naylor does, and decide that this is a good time to focus on this important literary device. Consequently, your prereading, during-reading, and postreading activities would focus on the elements of the novel that best illustrate characterization. Before students read the story, you give a mini-lesson on characterization, focusing on those devices that Naylor uses particularly well. As students read, you could have them look for her use of these devices. As a followup, you might let them revise a short segment of the novel, depicting one of the characters as quite different than he was in the book. This approach would lead students to a fuller understanding and appreciation of *Shiloh*, and to learning more about how authors create the vivid and interesting characters in their stories.

As explained by Louise Rosenblatt (1978) and as we have discussed in Chapters 1 and 3, the purposes for reading informational texts and literature are often quite different. In the first instance, we are usually reading to extract information we can do something with. In the second, our purpose is most often aesthetic; our primary purposes for reading literature are usually to enjoy, appreciate, and respond to it. In planning reading activities for students, we need to keep these differences in mind.

Different students will need different sorts of scaffolding.

Pause and Reflect 4.1

Considering Your Purposes in Reading Various Texts

People read some texts to gain information and some to enjoy and savor them. Think of a text you read solely to gain information. Now think of one you read solely for enjoyment. How did your reading of the two texts differ? Now consider something you read for both enjoyment and information. How did your reading of this dual-purpose text differ from your reading of the other two? What percentage of the time do you think you read solely for information, solely for enjoyment, and for both of these purposes? How do you think the percentage of time you give to reading for each of these purposes compares to the percentage of time typical middle-grade students spend reading for each of them? ■

The Students

When you are thinking about purposes and analyzing reading material, there is another factor that will be crucial in your planning—your students. Certainly, you want to do everything possible to guarantee their success. Therefore, whatever decision making you are involved in, your students' needs, concerns, and interests will be uppermost in your mind.

Say, for example, you are teaching a class of fifth graders who are average-to-poor readers living in a Midwestern city. Your social studies curriculum includes a unit on Australia, and one of the reading selections is an article on the Great Barrier Reef. Although your students may have heard of Australia and seen pictures of it in the media, you know they have not visited there; nor, for the most part, have they actually been to an ocean. To read this article successfully, these students will need prereading experiences that provide them with background information that helps fill the gaps in their repertoire of concepts about Australia, and about oceans, reefs, and other topics central to the article. Students from other countries might provide some of this information. If your class includes students from Cuba, Puerto Rico, or Haiti, for example, they could provide information on their experiences with the Atlantic Ocean. Both the Atlantic and Pacific oceans could then be discussed in preparation for the reading on Australia. Also, suppose the reading level of the article is about sixth grade; some of your students may need further assistance in understanding it. This may include preteaching potentially difficult vocabulary, then suggesting a reading strategy—such as recommending students to read the article quickly once to get its main thrust, then again slowly to pick up the details.

If, on the other hand, the students reading the selection on the Great Barrier Reef are skilled readers, the school is located in a West Coast beach town, and both interest and knowledge about the ocean are high, your prereading activities will be quite different. These may include having students discuss what they know about the topic before reading it, perhaps writing down what they know about Australia, reefs, and their experiences and knowledge of the ocean. After reading the article, the students might discuss what new information or ideas they discovered from the reading, what questions were brought to mind while they read, and where they might go to find the answers to those questions.

The Scaffolded Reading Experience

The activities you provide to foster students' comprehension, learning, and engagement with the texts they read can be divided into three categories—prereading, during-reading, and postreading. Although you will often want to provide students with something in each of these categories, such activities can range from something extremely brief to something quite complex. A straightforward short story or chapter book, such as the humorous novel, *Looking for Bobowicz: A Hoboken Chicken Story* by Daniel Pinkwater, might only require your saying, "This is a terrific . . . and funny . . . story. Read and enjoy!" then having students read the entire story silently and afterwards discuss whether or not they enjoyed the story, and if so, why. A challenging expository text, however, such as Marc Aronson's *John Winthrop, Oliver Cromwell, and the Land of Promise*—a nonfiction trade book that chronicles the parallel history between seventeenth-century Great Britain and colonial New England—might require several pre-, during-, and postreading activities. For prereading, you might provide activities that relate the reading to the students' lives and activate background knowledge. You might also preteach potentially troublesome vocabulary. As students are reading, you might have them write summaries of each section of the text. Postreading activities might include discussion, chart making, and demonstrations.

In the next three sections, we discuss some of the components of each of these three categories—prereading, during-reading and postreading. After that, we provide sample activities for each. Before we discuss these activities separately, there are several very important points to keep in mind. First, as noted in the previous section, the support you provide for students results from your considering the students, the selection, and the purpose or purposes of the reading. Second, as noted just above, what kinds of prereading, during-reading, and postreading

Figure 4.1   **Two Phases of a Scaffolded Reading Experience**

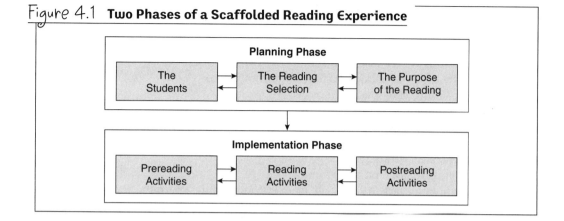

activities you engage students in and how much support you provide will vary dramatically from one situation to another. Third, prereading, during-reading, and postreading activities are interrelated; that is, each will affect and be affected by the others. The Scaffolded Reading Experience (SRE) framework, shown in Figure 4.1, depicts these relationships visually. As can be seen, you first plan the experience, taking into account the students, selection, and purpose; and then as a result of that planning, you implement a series of prereading, during-reading, and postreading activities appropriate to the situation. Fourth, we want to point out that the specific notion of scaffolding that underlies the SRE is slightly, but importantly, different from the notion of scaffolding more generally held. A scaffold is typically defined as a temporary supportive structure that enables a child to successfully complete a task he or she could not complete without the aid of the scaffold. In considering the scaffolding provided by SREs, we modify that definition by adding that, in addition to helping children complete tasks they could not complete without the aid of the scaffold, scaffolding can aid students by helping them better complete a task, complete a task with less stress or in less time, learn more fully than they would have without the aid of the scaffold, or enjoy and engage with the text more fully. Finally, we want to note that SREs can be designed for use with special students (Graves, Graves, & Braaten, 1996) and with English-language learners (Fitzgerald & Graves, 2004a; 2004b) as well as for all other students.

Prereading Activities

Obviously, prereading activities are those things you do with students prior to their reading a selection. No surprisingly, they are widely recommended for both native English speakers (for example, Cunningham, Hall, & Dufee, 1998; Fountas & Pinnell, 1996; Graves & Graves, 2003; Readence, Moore, & Rickelman, 2000; RAND Reading Study Group, 2002; Watts & Graves, 1997) and for English learners (for example, Aebersold & Field, 1997; Fitzgerald & Graves, 2004; Gibbons, 2002). Prereading activities serve multiple purposes. Possible prereading activities include:

- motivating
- relating the reading to students' lives
- activating or building background knowledge
- providing text-specific knowledge
- preteaching vocabulary
- preteaching concepts
- prequestioning, predicting, and direction setting
- suggesting strategies
- using students' native language
- involving English-language learner communities, parents, and siblings

We will now briefly consider the nature of each of these activities—what they are and why and when you might use them—and then give an example of each. Although we deal with each of these kinds of activities separately, as you read about them you will notice overlaps. For example, a motivating activity may also activate prior knowledge, introduce a new concept, and relate the reading to the students' lives. Similarly, a prereading activity targeted at teaching vocabulary may also activate prior knowledge. The final two activities listed are specifically designed for English-language learners, and can be used as prereading, during-reading, and postreading activities (Fitzgerald & Graves, 2004), so you will see them in all three lists.

Motivating

As you well know, most of the time we need to be motivated to do something—reading is no exception. Getting middle-school students to *want* to read is sometimes easy, sometimes not, but it is always essential. Think about yourself and the reading you are doing right now. What is motivating you to read this? In an ideal world, our motivation would be intrinsic, stemming from an internal need or desire that is fulfilled when we read. However, that is not always the case, particularly in school. We might hope that all students are intrinsically motivated to read what we feel is important and worthwhile for them to read, but the truth is that they sometimes are not. We need to motivate them to want to read, to light their fire, so to speak, so they feel that need and desire. Motivating activities, then, are any kinds of activities that help students delve into reading material willingly, even eagerly, knowing there is some sort of reward at the end—new knowledge, experiences, discoveries, excitement, laughter. It is there for them if they will but read.

Relating the Reading to Students' Lives

One of the principal ways of motivating students and a major step in making reading meaningful to students is to relate what they are about to read to their lives. Your goal is to draw students into the text by helping them recall aspects of their lives and the world they live in that are similar to those found in the selection. For example, before sixth-grade students read a biography on Martin Luther King, Jr., such as *The Life and Death of Martin Luther King, Jr.* by James Haskins, you might have students think about and discuss times in their lives when they felt that they were not treated as well as others, when they felt they were mistreated or treated unfairly. Having students think about these times and talk about them will help students understand better the concept of discrimination, a central theme in the biography. In addition, minority students may have stories that their parents have told them about being discriminated against in the United States, while students who have recently moved from other countries may have recent memories of discrimination. Helping students build bridges between their lives and the text will facilitate their understanding as well as their appreciation and enjoyment of what they read.

Activating or Building Background Knowledge

In Chapter 1, we explained that having appropriate background knowledge—*schemata*—is absolutely crucial to understanding text. By activating background knowledge we mean calling up from students' memories information they already have on a particular subject, information that will help them make connections between what they already know and what they glean from the text. We do this informally all the time. Before a party, your friend might say to you, "You remember my Uncle Pete, don't you? He's kind of short and tells jokes." You think for a minute and then say, "Sure. He's the one with the bald head and the belly laugh." At the party, when you hear a boisterous laugh and Uncle Pete calls to you from across the room, you can answer confidently, "Uncle Pete, hi!" Your background knowledge was sufficiently activated to make the connection.

For students, activating background knowledge before they read a story means providing activities that prompt them to bring to consciousness information they already know that will help them understand the upcoming text. The more students know about the topic of a text before reading it, the better they will understand it, learn from it, and appreciate it. Moreover, as reading authorities have repeatedly pointed out over the past several decades (for example, Anderson, 1984; Marzano, 2004), prior knowledge not only enables us to comprehend a text, it also helps us organize and remember what we have learned.

Given the vital importance of prior knowledge to comprehension and memory, it is critical to recognize that different students bring different stores of prior knowledge into the classroom and are thus differentially prepared to read some selections. Recognizing and accommodating to these differences in today's culturally and linguistically diverse classrooms is one of the major challenges any teacher faces. Yet it is a challenge that we must meet in order for all students to reach their potential as readers.

Sometimes, it is necessary to do more than activate background knowledge. Sometimes we need to build background knowledge because students lack the necessary background knowledge. If a biography about whaling presupposes knowledge about the New England coast and times in nineteenth-century New England and students do not have this knowledge, you may need to provide it for them before they begin the biography.

Providing Text-Specific Knowledge

Providing text-specific knowledge is called for when some aspect of the text itself is difficult enough that teaching students about it before they try to read it is needed. Suppose that your eighth graders are reading Jon Krakauer's gripping true-life adventure "A Bad Summer on K2" from *Eiger Dreams: Ventures Among Men and Mountains* (1990) and you think the descriptions of some of the technical mountain-climbing procedures are insufficient and may slow students down, even confuse them. It might be very helpful to teach about some of these procedures before students read the article, perhaps using drawings or photographs to provide students with concrete images to assist their understanding.

Preteaching Vocabulary

Because vocabulary is so important to comprehension and learning, we need to pay attention to the vocabulary in reading selections. Ideally, the selections students read should be composed primarily of words they know but include some words they do not know—words that will provide opportunities for expanding their vocabulary and the depth of their knowledge of individual words. Preteaching some of the most challenging and crucial words in an upcoming selection will foster both vocabulary development and comprehension. Like many sorts of instruction, preteaching vocabulary is important for all students but particularly important for English-language learners (Gordon, 2004).

In Chapter 8, we take a detailed look at a variety of word-learning tasks. Here we look briefly at one of those—teaching words that are new labels for known concepts. For example, before students read Jon Krakauer's "A Bad Summer on K2," you might preteach the words *bivouac, crampons,* and *rucksack* using the Context Plus Use of the Dictionary Procedure we describe in Chapter 8. With this procedure you give students each word in a context-rich sentence, have them look up the meanings in a dictionary, and then discuss each word and its meaning as a class. Using such a procedure, you can efficiently teach up to half a dozen or so words before students read a short story, article, or book chapter; and this is about as many words as you should typically deal with for a relatively short selection.

Preteaching Concepts

Preteaching concepts is both similar to and very different from preteaching words that do not represent new concepts. The above terms—*bivouac, crampons,* and *rucksack*—represent concepts that many eighth graders are familiar with and can be easily explained. A *bivouac* is a short stay at a camp site, *crampons* are metal spikes that fasten to your shoes to help you walk on ice or snow, and a *rucksack* is a backpack. Another term from "A Bad Summer on K2," *crevasse,* may represent a new concept for students, particularly if you want them to get a fairly good understanding of what a *crevasse* is. Teaching new concepts demands more work and more time than does teaching new labels for existing concepts. As we explain in Chapter 8, one useful procedure for teaching a new concept is to define it, note related concepts that it may be confused with, give examples of the concept (with *crevasse* we would probably show pictures), give non examples (again show pictures), and then let students identify examples and non examples. Again, teaching a new concept takes time and effort. Thus, while it may make good sense to preteach half a dozen or so new vocabulary words before students read a selection, it often appropriate to teach only one concept.

Prequestioning, Predicting, and Direction Setting

We group prequestioning, predicting, and direction setting activities together because they have a similar function—they focus students' attention on what to look for as they read. Prequestioning, predicting, and direction setting activities are important because without them students may not know what to attend to, and it is simply impossible for a reader to attend to everything in a reading selection.

Suppose your sixth-grade class has been studying nutrition and one student brings in a recipe from the Sunday paper for a stir-fry dish that is described as being healthy. Before students read the recipe, you might ask them to think about the question, "Is this a healthy recipe, or not?" as they read. In such an activity, you would ask them to be ready to defend their answers. Alternately, you might ask students to predict what the ingredients of a healthy stir-fry dish are likely to be, and then check on their predictions as they read. Or you could give students directions to identify the more and less healthy ingredients as they read the article. All three activities accomplish the job of focusing students' attention.

Of course, teachers are not the only ones to ask prequestions or set directions for reading. Student-generated questioning occurs when the students are asking their own questions about a selection and reading to discover the answers. For example, suppose that during the nutrition unit, students are asked to create a puppet play to teach the kindergarten and first-grade classes good eating habits. When they read material to prepare for their play, they will need to ask all sorts of questions in order to create an appropriate script: "What are good healthy foods that five- and six-year-olds will like?" "What are the unhealthy foods that children should avoid?" "Why are these foods unhealthy?" The answers to questions such as these will provide students with the raw material for their play.

Using Students' Native Language

When the going gets tough for English learners, when the gulf between students' proficiency in English and the task posed by the reading becomes wide and deep, one extremely helpful alternative is likely to be to use students' native language. Strategic use of native language is highly recommended by many professionals who work with English-language learners (Gersten & Baker, 2000; Kamil & Bernhardt, 2004). You might, for example, use Spanish to present a preview of a book like Seymour Simon's *Earthquakes* for some of your students. Or you might use Spanish to give your Spanish-speaking students directions for reading *Earthquakes*.

Involving English-Language Learner Communities, Parents, and Siblings

In all probability, there are other students in your class, students in other classes in your school, and people out in the community who speak both English and the languages spoken by your English learners. Getting the assistance of these children and adults in your classes has tremendous advantages (Kamil & Bernhardt, 2004). The most obvious advantage is that they can communicate effectively with your students who are not yet proficient in English. Another advantage is that, by helping your students, your resource people—if their English is not well developed—will improve their own English abilities. Still another advantage is the satisfaction, sense of belonging, and sense of pride that the resource people will get from assisting in your classroom. It is often difficult to convey to parents who are not proficient in English that they are welcome at school, that you really want to work with them to help their children succeed. By bringing parents into the school as resource people, you convey to them that they are not only welcome but needed! It is, to use a phrase that's trite but really does fit here, a Win–Win situation. As we noted earlier, both using the students' native language and engaging people resources are just as viable while students are reading a text or after they have read it as they are before the students read.

Suggesting Strategies

Suggesting strategies is a somewhat different kind of prereading activity than those discussed thus far in that the focus here is on suggesting ways in which students themselves might effectively approach the text to achieve their reading purposes. Moreover, when we say *suggesting* strategies, we do so because we believe that the strategies you suggest at this point in an SRE should already have been thoroughly taught and learned. We describe a very powerful approach to teaching comprehension and study strategies in depth in Chapter 5. Here we briefly consider suggesting them just before students read a text.

For example, before students read an expository selection you might suggest that they survey the selection's illustrations, graphs, headings, and subheadings, and then take notes as they read it. Another strategy you could suggest, one that can be used for any type of text, is that they read the title and the first few paragraphs, and then pose three questions that they think will be answered as they read. Of course, there are many other strategies you can suggest students use while reading, and some students will require a great deal of support in their use of strategies. As we just noted, we discuss a powerful procedure for teaching strategies in the next chapter.

Pause and Reflect 4.2

Situations in Which Preteaching Activities Are Likely To Be Needed

In what kinds of reading situations are prereading activities likely to be unnecessary? In what kinds of reading situations are prereading activities essential? ∎

Sample Prereading Activity: Prereading Questionnaire

By now, you are probably aware that the possibilities for prereading activities are almost limitless. But there is a common thread to all of them—each serves in one way or another to build a bridge from your students to the reading selection, the sort of bridge that was lacking for your hypothetical trip to Bolivia. So, when you think about prereading activities in general, think about building bridges, helping students cross from the known to the unknown. Think about what students need to know to understand, learn from, and appreciate a particular reading selection and how you can help launch them on a successful reading experience each and every time they read.

Teaching Idea 4.1 (p. 90) is a sample prereading activity. As you read through it, think about what it attempts to accomplish in preparing the reader to read with understanding and enjoyment. Does it motivate? Activate prior knowledge? Build text-specific knowledge? Relate reading to students' lives? Preteach vocabulary or concepts?

During-Reading Activities

Once you have built the bridge with prereading activities, students are ready to explore the world of the text that lies beyond it. During-reading activities include both things that students do themselves as they are reading and things that you do to assist them. Like prereading activities, during-reading activities are widely recommended for native English speakers (for example, Bean, Valerio, & Stevens, 1999; Beck, McKeown, Hamilton, & Kucan, 2001; Wood, Lapp, & Flood, 1992) and for English learners (for example, Aebersold & Field, 1997; Fitzgerald & Graves, 2004a, 2004b; Gibbons, 2002).

As we have stressed throughout this book, reading is a constructive, transactional process; that is, readers build meaning as they read, combining what they know with the author's words and coming up with meaning. One of our jobs as teachers is to make sure this meaning-building is taking place by fostering students' active involvement in thinking and reasoning about the text. You have already begun this process with prereading activities, but there are additional opportunities for supporting students' efforts as they read. Possible during-reading activities for an SRE include:

- silent reading
- you reading to students
- supported reading
- oral reading by students
- modifying the text
- using students' native language
- involving English-language learner communities, parents, and siblings

As we have noted, for English-language learners the final two activities are useful during-reading as well as prereading activities. A study guide in the students' native language, possibly prepared by a parent helper, is an example of a during-reading activity.

Teaching Idea 4.1
Sample Prereading Activity for Patricia MacLachlan's *Journey*

Students: Fourth-grade students of high reading ability in an ethnically diverse urban class that includes three English learners.

Selection: *Journey* by Patricia MacLachlan. When their mother goes off, leaving Cat and Journey with their grandparents, they feel as if their past has been erased until Grandfather finds a way to restore it for them by taking family photographs. This is a short novel, 83 pages, of high literary quality. Because it is a story that students may not select on their own, *Journey* is an ideal choice for in-depth reading in school.

Purpose: To engage students in the kind of thinking that will help them focus on the main themes in the story by connecting them with similar themes in their own lives.

Procedure: Before students begin reading *Journey,* create a display of cameras and photographs. Then, just prior to students' reading the novel, hold up the book and tell them that

Journey is a wonderful story written by Patricia MacLachlan. Explain that the story tells about a boy whose mother has left him and his sister to live with their grandparents and that two things are very important in the story—a camera and photographs. Ask students to describe the items you have displayed and to think about and discuss how and why photographs might be important in the story.

Next, explain that because of the significance of cameras and photographs in *Journey,* you want students to think about what parts these items play or have played in their own lives. Tell them that to help them focus their thinking, you have made up a questionnaire. Before distributing the questionnaires, read the questions on it aloud. Then, give a questionnaire like that shown in Figure 4.2, and ask them to complete it. Have one of your students help the English-language learners complete their questionnaires. After all of the students have finished their questionnaires and before they begin reading the story, give them an opportunity to share their ideas.

Figure 4.2 Questionnaire for *Journey*

Do you have a camera?   yes_____ no_____

If you do have a camera, what do you like to take pictures of? _____

_____

When do you use your camera most? _____

_____

Do you have family photographs at home?   yes _____ no _____

What do these photographs show? _____

_____

What do your *favorite* photographs show? _____

_____

Why do you like these photos the best? _____

_____

Which are your least favorite photographs? _____

_____

Why don't you like these photos? _____

_____

What do you think family photographs can tell us about ourselves? _____

_____

Why can we sometimes see things in photographs that we don't notice in real life?

_____

Silent Reading

Most of the time, adults read silently, and by the time students reach the middle grades, they should be doing most of their reading silently, too. To get good at something, you have to practice. To get *really* good at something, you have to practice a lot. Reading is no exception. To get really good at reading, you have to practice a lot. The more silent reading you can motivate students to do—both in class and out of class—the better they will become at this activity that will engage them throughout their lives. And of course the best possible situation is to create readers who desperately want to read a lot, who sneak in reading wherever possible.

Reading to Students

Reading to students should not be an activity reserved for primary-grade students. Hearing a story or piece of exposition read aloud is often a very enjoyable and rewarding experience for readers of all ages. As storyteller and author Bill Martin Jr. (1992) has said, "A blessed thing happened to me as a child. I had a teacher who read to me." It's fun to be read to. Some students of course, find listening easier than reading; this is certainly the case with many less-proficient readers and with some—but by no means all—English-language learners. For these students, reading aloud—or playing an audio tape for the same purpose—is sometimes very helpful. Also, reading the first chapter or the first few pages of a piece can help ease students into the material and also serve as an enticement to read the rest of the selection on their own. Reading to students can make difficult material accessible to students who find certain texts difficult, either because of their complex structure or difficult vocabulary. For example, seventh or eighth graders might not select David Almond's compelling novel *The Fire-Eaters* set in northern England in 1962 on their own. But reading the first several chapters aloud might entice them to read the entire text, and thus give them the joy of experiencing an exceptional piece of literature.

Pause and Reflect 4.3

Experiencing the Pleasure of Listening to Well-Read Literature

When have you last heard a talented reader read a good piece of literature? We suspect that for some of you it has been quite a long time. If so, go to your local library and check out an audio book you think you'll really enjoy. Listen to it and enjoy it, and then realize how you can bring this same experience to your students with your own oral reading. Of course, good oral reading takes practice. You may want to start by reading short selections, and by practicing them before you read them to the class. ■

Supported Reading

Supported Reading refers to any activity that you use to focus students' attention on particular aspects of a text as they read it. Supported reading often begins as a prereading activity—perhaps with your setting directions for reading—and is then carried out as students are actually reading. For example, to help students appreciate an author's craft and to give them examples of the sort of language they might like to sometimes include in their own writing, you might have them jot down examples of particularly colorful language as they read a novel written in free verse, such as *Soul Moon Soup* by Lindsay Lee Johnson. As another example, if you find that an expository piece on seashells is actually divided into half a dozen sections but contains no headings or subheadings, you might give students a semantic map that includes titles for the half dozen sections and ask them to complete the map as they are reading. Often, with supported reading activities, students' goal is to learn something from their reading rather than just read for enjoyment. Thus, supported reading activities are frequently used with expository material. However, it is also possible to guide students in understanding and responding to narratives, for example, to recognize the plot structure of a novel or to empathize with the protagonist of a short story.

Of course, one long-term goal is to motivate and empower students to learn from and respond to selections without your assistance. Thus, with less-challenging selections and as students become increasingly competent, your support can and should be less specific and less directive, and sometimes consist only of a prereading suggestion: "After reading the first chapter in Kathleen Krull's *Lives of the Presidents,* I have a suggestion for you. Try reading it with a partner and stopping after each section to take notes. This should help you understand and remember the material better." Or, if students are reading a narrative such as Elizabeth Levy's *My Life as a Fifth-Grade Comedian* you might say, "You'll find that Bobby is quite a character and that he changes a lot during the story. Using a journal to record the changes he undergoes and writing down how you feel about the changes may help you better appreciate what he's going through."

Oral Reading by Students

In some classrooms, oral reading by students is a relatively frequent activity, while in others it's a relatively infrequent one. As we previously mentioned, most of the reading students do once they leave elementary school is silent reading, and thus doing a lot of silent reading is important. Nonetheless, oral reading has its place. Certainly, poetry is often best and most effective when read orally, as are novels written in free verse such as Newbery winner *Out of the Dust* by Karen Hesse and *Soul Moon Soup* by Lindsay Lee Johnson. Also, poignant or particularly well-written passages of prose are often appropriate for oral reading. Martin Luther King Jr.'s "I Have a Dream" speech is the example that first comes to mind. Reading orally can also be helpful when the class or a group of students is studying a passage and trying to decide on alternate interpretations or on just what is and is not explicitly stated in the passage. Additionally, students often like to read their own writing orally. And, of course, having individual students read orally can provide you with very valuable diagnostic information. Thus, oral reading is something to include among the many alternatives you offer students.

Modifying the Text

Sometimes because of what is either required by the curriculum or what is available, students will be reading selections that present too much of a challenge due to their length or difficulty. In these cases, modifying the selections is appropriate. The most efficient way to modify a selection is to shorten it. Suppose the chapter on electricity in your sixth-grade science text is quite lengthy. After reading through it, you decide it is too much for your average- to low-ability readers to handle. In this case, you might have students read only selected portions of the chapter—the topics you feel are most important for them to understand. Assuming students can and will read the complete selection, will they get as much out of reading part of it? Of course not. But, assuming they cannot or will not read all of it, success in reading part of it is certainly preferable to failure in reading all of it.

Another way to make difficult material accessible to students is to tape record a selection for students to listen to as they read along silently with the text. You, or competent students, can make the recordings or you can check out or purchase commercial tapes and CDs. Recordings can make material accessible to less-able readers and provide a model for good oral reading. Additionally, in some cases it is possible to have a text or a summary of a text available in English-language learners' native languages.

Sample During-Reading Activity: Supported Reading

As was true with prereading activities, there are many different kinds of during-reading activities and many ways of varying individual activities. Once again, the three factors that will always determine the makeup of the reading experiences you provide for students are the selection, the students, and the purposes. Because the purposes for reading literature and reading expository materials are often different, during-reading activities for these two types of reading will also often be different. However, some activities can be modified to work for both literature and expository text.

Also, during-reading activities will overlap with both prereading and postreading activities. In other words, during-reading activities require both stage setting and followup. For example, if you want students to write journal entries as a during-reading activity, they need to know what to do, how to do it, and why they are doing it. The explanations and modeling used to prepare students to write takes place before they begin reading. Then, after students read the selection and write in their journals, postreading activities generally include a chance for them to share their entries with each other or with you.

Teaching Idea 4.2 is a sample during-reading activity for a nonfiction text that we want to assist students in understanding and responding to.

Postreading Activities

Postreading activities are those that students engage in after they read a selection. These kinds of activities grow out of prereading and during-reading activities and will involve students in various kinds of synthesizing, analyzing, evaluating,

Teaching Idea 4.2
Sample During-Reading Activity for Francisco Jimenez's *The Circuit*

Students: Sixth-grade students in a social studies class studying contemporary social issues. These are competent readers, but they live in an east coast suburb far removed from the setting and themes of the selection being read.

Selection: *The Circuit* by Francisco Jimenez. Francisco Jimenez, once a child migrant worker in California and an illegal immigrant in his childhood, is now a professor at Santa Clara University and the winner of several prestigious children's book awards for his memoir collections of his early life. *The Circuit* is a collection of 12 semi-autobiographical stories about migrant workers in the 1940s and 50s in California. The harsh reality of children's lives in this situation is heartrending, and Jimenez has a talent for befriending his reader and drawing out the reader's empathy. The stories are poignant and powerful, meant to stand alone or collectively to represent his childhood experiences.

Purposes: Jimenez has eloquently explained the purposes of his writing, and this during-reading activity is designed to achieve his purposes—"Through my writing I hope to give readers insight into the lives of migrant farm worker families and their children, whose back-breaking labor picking fruits and vegetables puts foods on our tables. Their courage, their hopes and dreams for a better life for their children, and their children's children, give meaning to the 'American dream.' Their story is the American story."

Procedure: This during-reading activity occurs after several substantial prereading activities. On the day before students begin the reading, the teacher has built background knowledge about the text and the author, related the reading to students' lives, and provided some text-specific information. And just prior to this during-reading activity, the teacher read the first story, "Under the Wire," aloud, and the class discussed it. For this activity, students work in pairs, reading each story silently and then pausing after reading each story to respond to one or two factual questions and one or two open-ended questions designed to foster reflection. Depending on the time available, students' skill and interest in the selections, and the teacher's goals, students can read and respond to several of the selections or to all of them. The questions for the first few stories following "Under the Wire" are shown below.

Story 1: "Soledad"
1. What mistakes did Panchito make? What were his parents most angry about?
2. How did Panchito feel? Can you remember a time when you were little when you tried to help but actually did something wrong?

Story 2: "Inside Out"
1. How do you feel about Panchito not being allowed to speak English?
2. Why do you think Panchito gave Curtis the drawing?

Story 3: "Miracle in Tent City"
1. How do you feel about the Jimenez's home?
2. What do you think might be wrong with Torito?

Story 4: "El Angel de Oro"
1. This story is dedicated to Miguel Antonio. Why do you think Francisco remembers this special friend so well? Do you remember any special friends from grade school? What do you remember? Why?
2. Why does Panchito put the fishing pole in the creek?

After reading and discussing the selections in pairs, which is likely to take a day or two, students meet for a large-group discussion of Jimenez's stories and the reflections he provokes.

applying, or simply savoring or sharing what they have read. Like prereading and during-reading activities, postreading activities are widely recommended for native English speakers (for example, Alvermann, 2000; Fountas & Pinnell, 1996; Graves & Graves, 2003; McKeown & Beck, 2003; RAND Reading Study Group, 2002; Schoenbach, Greenleaf, Cziko, & Hurwitz, 1999; Yopp & Yopp, 1992) and for English learners (for example, Aebersold & Field, 1997; Fitzgerald & Graves, 2004; Gibbons, 2002). Possible postreading activities for an SRE include:

- questioning
- discussion
- writing
- drama
- artistic, graphic, and nonverbal activities
- application and outreach activities
- building connections
- reteaching
- using students' native language
- involving English-language learner communities, parents, and siblings

What you hope to accomplish with postreading activities is for students to better understand the material and to realize and appreciate the greater implications of a narrative or an expository text, to take away from the experience not only new knowledge but a positive attitude regarding the beauty and power of written language. Note that the final two activities, which you have seen as prereading and during-reading activities, are also appropriate as postreading activities. For a postreading activity, it might be good to ask English-language learners to respond to the text using their native language.

Questioning

Asking students to answer questions about certain aspects of the text is often a natural outgrowth of what has taken place in the prereading and during-reading phases. For example, suppose as a prereading activity for Chapter 6 of Andrew Clements's engaging novel *Frindle,* you simply ask your fifth-grade students to predict what will happen in the chapter, and that as a during-reading activity they simply read the chapter silently. The first question to be asked during postreading might be, "What did happen in the chapter?" But of course such a question is only a starting point. Next, you want to encourage thinking beyond literal understanding, involving them in making inferences and perceiving relationships between and among ideas. Then, encourage students to examine how these ideas might apply to their own lives.

One way to ensure that you ask various types of questions is to deliberately consider three types of questions, which Pearson and Johnson (1978) have termed *text explicit, text implicit,* and *script implicit.* Assume that your fifth-grade students are reading a brief biography of S. Scott Momaday, the Pulitzer Prize–winning author in *Native American Biographies* (Globe, 1993). Text-explicit questions are directly answered in the reading selection. One text-explicit question you might ask after students read the Momaday biography is "When did he win the Pulitzer Prize?" The biography specifically states that he won the Pulitzer Prize in 1969. Text-implicit questions are answered in the reading selection, but they require that at least one inference be made. One text-implicit question you might ask about Momaday is "How did Momaday's winning the Pulitzer Prize influence his writing career?" The biography contains a good deal of information that answers this question, but it does not explicitly answer it. Script-implicit questions, as opposed to text-implicit questions, require the reader to use his prior knowledge in formulating answers. One script-implicit question you might ask after students have read the Momaday biography is, "How would you feel if, like Momaday, you often found yourself in situations in which your background and experiences were very different from those of others?" Obviously, this question is prompted by the Momaday biography, but much of the answer must come from the reader's schemata.

Another way to look at questions is in terms of who creates them. As we have noted, questions can be either teacher generated or student generated. The questions we posed for *Frindle* and the Momaday biography are examples of teacher-generated questions. Student-generated questions evolve from students' interests and their need or desire to know. After reading Milton Meltzer's *Crime in America*, which was published 1990, inquisitive eighth graders might well want to know how much the U.S. crime scene had changed since that time. Such inquisitiveness and probing to learn more is exactly what we want to encourage in students.

Discussion

Discussion gives students an opportunity to share their views and to listen to the opinions of others. It is a chance to extend students' thinking about the ideas, characters, events, or topics presented in the text and to promote connections between the text and students' lives.

Discussion must always take place in an atmosphere of trust. For students to take risks in expressing their thoughts, they need to feel secure in doing so. As we just noted, students should be encouraged and challenged to think about a text, not just to cite facts and figures, but to delve more deeply into meanings and implications. Discussion, which involves speaking and listening, is one way to accomplish this goal.

Of course, good discussions do not just happen. As a number of the authors in *Lively Discussions* (Gambrell & Almasi, 1996) explain at length, good discussion requires planning and effort on both your part and your students' part. To become proficient in discussion, students need explicit instruction, modeling, and many opportunities for practice. Students also need feedback from you and their peers on what has been learned in a discussion and on the process of the discussion itself. That is, you and your students need to talk about matters such as all students participating, students listening to each other and respecting each others' opinions, and the group's success in dealing with the topic.

Writing

As we noted in Chapter 1, this book does not deal in detail with writing instruction. We leave that to other books. But that does not mean that writing is not a terrific aid to reading. It is a fantastic tool to use in conjunction with reading. Writing is another way to help students become actively involved with the reading selection they have just read, whether for the purpose of better comprehending it or for possible applications of its themes. Writing requires that students really think about what they know. In prereading activities, you might have students write to engage their prior knowledge on a topic, as we suggested in the example on questioning. Postreading activities that involve writing will let them take the new information and ideas they have gleaned from the reading and synthesize or apply them in a new way.

Postreading writing activities should, as is the case with any of the other activities we have been talking about, relate to the initial purposes set for reading the material. If your purpose in having students read a chapter on electricity is for them to understand and remember what they read about electricity, then having them write a summary for each of the sections of the chapter is a useful writing activity. If your purpose is to have students respond personally to a text, you might ask them to write a paragraph telling how a certain poem made them feel. Or you might ask them to write their own poems based on an image or theme in the poem they read.

Reading selections can be the springboard for many kinds of creative writing activities. Say, for instance, before reading Laurence Yep's historical novella *Hiroshima*, you discuss with students how authors can create fiction within an historical context. After students have finished reading the book, you might suggest that they identify a recent historical event, perhaps a recent event at school, and write a brief sketch in which they are a character involved in the event.

Drama

Because most middle-grade students love to get into the act, dramatics of all kinds are often popular and they provide a wonderful way to involve students in the material they read. Plays, skits, storytelling, pantomimes, and readers' theater are all examples of dramatic activities in which students use their bodies and their voices as well as their minds. Postreading dramatic activities can serve as a welcome break from the quieter, more cerebral sitting-at-the-desk type activities.

Dramatizing an event or portraying a character in a story requires that students not only understand that event or character but make judgments on what to dramatize and how to portray various events and characters. In doing this the student must focus on what are the most important features about that event or character. After they read *Danger Marches to the Palace: Queen Lili'uokalani* by Margo Sorenson, you might have your sixth-grade students get into small groups and prepare skits that show some of the more important and exciting events in this biographical. Not only will planning such an activity help students better understand this particular piece of history, it will also give them the opportunity to learn from their classmates' skits. Also, students can write and perform their own plays.

Readers' Theater, in which students take the role of one of the characters in a story and read that part aloud, is yet another way to get students involved with a text. Good choices for Readers' Theater are stories that have several characters and a lot of action and dialogue.

Retelling stories is an excellent way for students to solidify their understanding of the structure of stories and to encourage literal, interpretive, and creative thinking. Retelling stories can be great fun, but we suggest that you do a good deal of modeling of storytelling before your students make their storytelling debuts. Students do their best retelling and gain the most in terms of understanding the structure of stories when they are very familiar with the story's sequence, characters, problem, and resolution before they attempt to retell it. Certainly, students may want to alter stories when they retell them, and storytelling offers some excellent opportunities for creativity, but students will profit from knowing what changes they are making and why they are making them.

Artistic and Nonverbal Activities

A myriad of activities are included in this category. Media productions such as videos, slide shows and photographic displays are examples of artistic postreading activities. For instance, after your fifth graders read the biography *Lincoln: A Photobiography* by Russell Freedman, they might create their own photo biographies of contemporary celebrities by clipping photos from magazines and newspapers, pasting them in a booklet, and writing simple texts to go with them. But photo biographies are certainly not the only way to respond to Freedman's text. Drawing, painting, cutting and pasting, working with clay or playdough, weaving, and making collages are other sorts of artistic activities that can be used to extend and enrich students' experience with this and other reading selections.

Another frequently used activity in this category involves some sort of graphic presentation—constructing charts, trees, maps, diagrams, schematics, and the like. For instance, after reading William Wu's "Black Powder," in which the Chinese American protagonist honors his father's death by performing a ceremony based on Chinese folk religion, seventh graders might create a chart in which they compare the elements of this ancient ceremony to a modern-day memorial service.

Other artistic and nonverbal activities involve bringing in artifacts or specimens or constructing models that are relevant to the reading selection. For example, after reading the informational book, *Insect Metamorphosis* by Ron and Nancy Goor, fourth graders might begin a class insect collection; and, after reading a chapter on the California missions, they might draw a mural or diorama, or construct models of the missions.

Application and Outreach Activities

The final type of postreading activities we list here is application and outreach activities. These include concrete and direct applications—cooking something after reading a recipe—and less direct ones—attempting to change something after reading about it in a story. For example, after fourth graders read *Brother Eagle, Sister Sky* written by Chief Seattle and illustrated by Susan Jeffers, they might decide they want to work out a plan to change students' attitudes and behavior with regard to the environment—at school, at home, and in the community. Similarly, eighth graders might collect food or clothing to donate to a shelter after reading a newspaper article about a homeless family. The more you can tie reading to the world outside of school, the more you will give purpose to reading and to school itself.

Student postreading presentations often include graphic or pictorial material.

Pause and Reflect 4.4

Considering the Components of Your Own Postreading Activities

At this point you have learned a good deal about postreading activities. Here is a chance to sketch and create your own. Identify the grade level you teach and the reading abilities and attitudes toward reading your students have. Next, consider what kinds of postreading activities you might engage your students in, and why. Then, create three or four postreading activities that are challenging but that your students can succeed at with your assistance. Finally, and this is the most important step, critically evaluate each of your activities and their appropriateness for the students you described. ■

Sample Postreading Activity

Again, postreading activities are those things you do to help students go beyond the text, to do something with the material they read, something that will help them see the relevance of reading, how it relates to their own lives and to the wider world around them. These activities will also help them remember better what they read, provide opportunities to express themselves in a variety of ways, and give them opportunities to see how others interpret selections. As was true with prereading and during-reading, postreading activities are determined by your students, the selection, and your purposes, and will grow out of and complement the prereading and during-reading activities.

The range of postreading options is limited only by your and your students' imagination and enthusiasm. Teaching Idea 4.3 is a sample postreading activity designed to follow students' reading and listening to parts of a challenging biography of an Oglala Sioux holy man.

Teaching Idea 4.3
Sample Postreading Activity for *Black Elk Speaks* by John G. Neihart

Students: Eighth-grade students of high reading ability who enjoy a challenge.

Selection: *Black Elk Speaks* by John G. Neihart. First published in 1932, this famous and sometimes controversial biography (which is available on the Web at http://www.blackelk speaks.unl.edu/index2.htm) records the life of Black Elk, an Oglala Sioux holy man, who was born in 1862 and lived into the mid 19th century. What makes the book controversial is that it is told in the voice of Black Elk himself, but scholars do not know how much of the story is actually Black Elk's and how much of it is Neihart's embellishments.

Purposes: To explore several themes and topics prompted by the biography and by so doing to better understand some of Black Elk's ideas and values and some ways in which they relate to the world of today.

Procedure: This is a difficult text, and eighth-grade students should not be expected to read all of its 200-plus pages or to understand it thoroughly. Yet with sturdy scaffolding, eighth graders can gain a good deal from it and may be motivated to read additional material on native Americans and their lives and beliefs. That sturdy scaffolding should consist of a variety of prereading activities and several sorts of during-reading activities. Depending on the time you have available, you can read some of the chapters to students, you can summarize some of the book, you can have students read some of the chapters in a print text, and you can have students read some of the chapters in the Web version of the text. Reading some of the text on the Web provides students with some variety and, more importantly, gives them access to frequent electronic explanations that they can get by clicking on highlighted words and phrases.

In this culminating activity, students work in five groups, each of which explores one of the themes and topics listed below, answering the questions posed and preparing a group presentation for the class. Here are the five themes/topics and the prompts for each of them:

History
- What is it?
- What are your personal views of history? Your favorite parts? Your least favorite parts?
- Do you think U.S. teenagers today have a good sense of their "personal history"? What, for example, do you know about your parents' backgrounds? About your grandparents' backgrounds?
- Try to think of at least one conversational historical issue.

Reflection and Silence
- Is personal reflection important to being healthy?
- How much time per day do you think people spend in reflection? How often during the day do people spend time in silence?
- Make some predictions comparing the reflection and silence of a Lakota medicine man with that of a current-day high school student.

Personal Impact
- Do you believe that one person can have a dramatic effect on the world? If so, how? Give examples.
- Do you believe that life is a random place, where things just sort of happen without reason? Can people control their own lives? Or are they being controlled by other people and the atmosphere that surrounds them? Find at least one example to support your ideas.

Connection
- Do your actions affect the lives of others? Can you isolate someone to the point where nothing they do will affect anyone else?

- How far-reaching are your actions? For example, is something you do here in your home state going to affect someone living in a neighboring state? Does every choice you make affect other people? Give at least one example to back up your claim.
- Find the meaning of the term *butterfly effect* and explain it to the class.

Visions and Psychic Powers
- Do you believe in people who claim to have psychic powers (for example, the ability to see into the future, to cure people, or to read their minds)? If so, do you have examples to support your idea? If not, how do you explain some of the rather mysterious things that they claim to do?
- In what way could a prophet or a psychic really influence a large group of people?
- Suppose the President of the United States got up this morning and said, "I had a dream that a huge earthquake will soon hit California; therefore, we must evacuate all of California's major cities." Would you believe him?

Requirements for the Group Presentations
- Each presentation will be 10 minutes.
- Each presentation should have an introduction that explains the topic and format of your material.
- Each presenter should have an outline of what he or she will say.
- Everyone in the group must participate.
- Give specific details and supporting evidence.
- Use a visual aid (poster, overhead transparency, or handout).

Give students enough time to prepare solid presentations, stressing that these are to be professional-quality presentations and that groups need to keep to their 10-minute limit. Following each presentation, give the class 5 minutes for questions and responses; this means that the presentations may take 2 days. After all the presentations have been made, critique them as positively as possible, making at least one positive comment and probably no more than one less-positive comment on each presentation.

A Comprehensive Scaffolded Reading Experience

In Teaching Idea 4.4, we outline a Scaffolded Reading Experience that takes students through the three phases of reading activities with a single selection. As you read the prereading, during-reading, and postreading activities, think about what is being accomplished in each. Does it pique student interest? Does it build prior knowledge? Are students given a chance to work with concepts or vocabulary before they meet them in the text? Do students know why they are doing a particular task? Are students being led to consider how a selection might relate to their lives? Are students being read to, or are they reading orally or silently? Are students focusing on certain elements in the text as they read? Are students given opportunities to respond to and interact with the text? Do the activities extend students' thinking about ideas, events, or characters? Are students being encouraged to make connections between text ideas and real life? Are students being given a chance to express themselves in a variety of ways—through art, writing, discussion, drama, outreach?

Concluding Remarks

Instructional scaffolding is one of the most powerful instructional approaches we know of. And the Scaffolded Reading Experience is a powerful and flexible approach

Teaching Idea 4.4
Outline of a Complete SRE for Cherylene Lee's "Hollywood and the Pits"

Students A class of average-ability seventh graders in a suburban setting. Most of the students in the school are white and middle class.

Selection "Hollywood and the Pits" by Cherylene Lee. The narrator of "Hollywood and the Pits," a Chinese American girl, recounts events from her life in the year 1968 when she was 15 years old. The story contains the details of her past, of her family—her mother, her grandmother, her sister, and her father—and of her own life as a child actress, when she was encouraged to be "The Chinese Shirley Temple." The story also contains details of the La Brea Tar Pits, an archaeological dig in the center of the city of Los Angeles that preserves the bones of animals dating back to the Pleistocene age. The narrator relates her fascination with the Tar Pits and explains how, as a teenager, she "breathed, ate, slept, dreamed about" the Pits. This fascination, however, came with a price. The narrator, who does not like to disappoint her mother, explains, "My mother thought something was wrong with me. Was it good for a teenager to be fascinated by death?"

The story addresses the questions of self-discovery and the responsibility of following a parent's wishes in a family and culture where filial piety is expected. As students read, they will meet a teenager who faces the conflict of wanting to please her mother but wanting, simultaneously, to pursue her own dreams of leading a normal U.S. teenager's life. As they read, students will be encouraged to consider and value their own lives and the freedom they are given.

Purposes (1) To introduce students to the social, family, and cultural aspects of a Chinese American family through reading activities,

(2) to develop an appreciation for the characters' points of view, (3) to develop a deeper understanding of the freedom of choice in U.S. culture, and (4) to consider the relevance of this teenager's struggle to lead her own life. (This activity was adapted from Cooke, 2002.)

Activities:
Day 1: Prereading Activities
- motivating activities (introduction to the La Brea Tar Pits using the Internet), *15 minutes*
- relating the reading to the students' lives (open-ended questions on what it would be like to live in Los Angeles and go to the Tar Pits), *5 minutes*
- building text-specific knowledge (explanation of the title and how the Tar Pits figure into the story), *5 minutes*
- pre-teaching vocabulary activity (expanded definitions of 10 words central to the story, along with the contexts in which they occur), *10 minutes*
- direction setting (directions to consider the Tar Pits and how they prompt conflict between the narrator and her parents), *5 minutes*

Day 2: During-Reading Activities
- oral reading by the teacher (teacher reads the first three pages aloud), *10 minutes*
- supported reading (focusing questions and a chart for students to complete as they read), *10 minutes*
- silent reading, *20 minutes*

Day 3: Postreading Activities
- class discussion (small- and large-group discussions facilitated by discussion guides), *30 minutes*

that applies the concept of scaffolding to creating lessons that assist students in understanding, learning from, and enjoying each and every selection they read. In this chapter, we have presented a number of fairly brief examples of SRE activities as well as one brief example of a complete SRE. If you want to examine some detailed and complete SREs, go to www.onlinereadingresources.com, where you will find more than 50 of them. You can consider these as examples, or you can print them out and use them with your students. We encourage you to make use of the site. Another complete SRE, this one created by social studies professor Patricia Avery for a history chapter about women's suffrage, is described in Avery and Graves (1997). We believe that this is a particularly strong SRE and an excellent example of what can be done to scaffold students' reading of expository text, and we encourage you to examine it.

In planning your own SREs, remember that when it comes to planning reading activities that are going to prepare, guide, and enrich your students' reading experience with a particular selection, you need remember only six things:

- students
- selection
- purpose
- prereading Activities
- during-Reading Activities
- postreading Activities

Once you have identified your *students'* concerns and interests, become familiar with the *selection*—its topics, themes, and vocabulary, and know your *purpose*—what you expect students to know, feel, or do as a result of reading the selection—then, you can begin selecting and planning *activities.*

Be enthusiastic and excited about the selection as well as the activities you have planned for fostering a successful reading experience for your students. Your enthusiasm will be contagious. Let your students in on why they are doing the activities, how these activities will help them learn something new, interesting, or exciting from their reading material, and how the activities will help them read for meaning and pleasure. Reading is a wonderful lifelong activity; and it is lifelong readers we are trying to make of our students.

■ EXTENDING LEARNING

1. There is one most appropriate Extending Learning activity for this chapter—actually creating an SRE, making a detailed lesson plan for teaching a particular short story, chapter, poem, or article. Whatever type of selection you use, choose a challenging one that requires a sturdy SRE. In the SRE you create, include the following elements.
   - description of the school, class, and students for whom the SRE is intended
   - list of objectives: List 2 to 4 major objectives for the SRE. If you like, you can also list some subordinate objectives, but we would not include more than four major ones.
   - discussion of the difficulty of the reading selection: Explain what it is about the reading selection that makes it challenging and worthy of the sturdy SRE you are creating.
   - detailed chronological description of activities. Provide a detailed description of the prereading, during-reading, and postreading activities you plan to use. Doing a thorough job of this is likely to require 5 to 10 pages.

- list of student materials. List both the available materials you will use and those you will construct yourself.

Once you have completed your SRE, reflect on it and critique it. Identify its strong points and note areas in which it might be improved.

2. Of course, actually trying out your SRE with a group of students is an extremely valuable experience, and an experience that we recommend highly if it is feasible for you. If you do try out the SRE, be sure to reflect and make some notes on what worked best, what worked less well, and anything that did not work well at all.

BOOKS FOR MIDDLE-GRADE READERS

Almond, D. (2004). *The fire-eaters*. New York: Delacorte.

Aronson, M. (2004). *John Winthrop, Oliver Cromwell, and the land of promise*. New York: Clarion.

Chief Seattle. Illus. by Jeffers, S. K. (1991). *Brother eagle, sister sky*. New York: Dial.

Clements, A. (1998). *Frindle*. New York: Aladdin.

Freedman, R. (1987). *Lincoln: A photobiography*. New York: Clarion.

Globe. (1993). *Native American biographies*. New York: Globe.

Goor, R., & Goor, N. (1990). *Insect metamorphosis: From egg to adult*. New York: Atheneum.

Haskins, J. (1992). *The life and death of Martin Luther King, Jr.* New York: HarperTrophy.

Hesse, K. (1997). *Out of the dust*. New York: Scholastic.

Jiménez, F. (1999). *The circuit*. Boston: Houghton.

Johnson, L. L. (2002). *Soul moon soup*. Ashville, NC: Front Street.

King, M. L. Jr. (1997). *I have a dream*. New York: Scholastic.

Krakauer, J. (1997). A bad summer on K2. In *Eiger dreams: Ventures among men and mountains*. New York: Anchor Books.

Krull, K. (1994). *Lives of the presidents: Fame, shame (and what the neighbors thought)*. San Diego, CA: Harcourt.

Lee, C. (1993). Hollywood and the pits. In L. Yep (Ed.), *American dragons*. New York: Harper-Collins.

Levy, E. (1997). *My Life as a fifth-grade comedian*. New York: HarperCollins.

MacLachlan, P. (1991). *Journey*. New York: Delacorte Press.

Meltzer, M. (1990). *Crime in America*. New York: Morrow Junior Books.

Naylor, P. R. (2000). *Shiloh*. New York: Aladdin Fiction.

Neihart. J. C. (1932). *Black Elk speaks*. Lincoln, NB: University of Nebraska Press.

Pinkwater, D. (2004). *Looking for Bobowicz: A Hoboken Chicken Story*. New York: HarperCollins.

Sorenson, M. (1997). *Danger marches to the palace:* Queen Lili'uokalani. Logan, IA: Perfection Learning.

Wu, W. (1993). Black powder. In L. Yep (Ed.), *American dragons*. New York: HarperCollins.

Yep, L. (Ed.). (1993). *American dragons*. New York: HarperCollins.

chapter 5

Teaching Comprehension and Study Strategies

Strategies help to make readers independent.

Suppose you are reading the newspaper and you come to a sentence you don't understand. What do you do? Perhaps you read on, hoping that the next sentence or two will make the meaning clear. Or, perhaps you reread the sentence or go back to the sentences preceding it.

Or, suppose it's Saturday and you have two tests coming up on Monday. You need to read a novel, three textbook chapters, and four journal articles. What do you do? You know you won't have time to read and study each in depth, so you must use some efficient approaches to understand and remember what you read. The novel you read quickly, skipping over lengthy descriptions and dialogue and concentrating on the basics of setting, plot, and characters. As you read, you look for recurring themes. When you finish, you might ask questions like, "Why was the protagonist so driven?" and "What was the author's main theme?" Before you read the chapters and articles, you might think about points your instructor emphasized; while you read, you might take notes or underline material relevant to these points; and, after your first reading, you might reread those sections that are most relevant to the course.

What you have done in both of these cases is to use reading strategies—deliberate plans that help you understand and recall what you read. In Chapter 4, we discussed ways in which you can help students understand, enjoy, and learn from individual selections they are reading. In this chapter, we describe ways in which you can assist students in internalizing strategies that they can use independently in understanding the variety of texts they read in and out of school. To use Tierney and Cunningham's (1984) terms, the topic of the last chapter was "learning from text," while that of this chapter is "learning to learn from text."

We have divided the chapter into three parts. In the first part, we define reading comprehension and study strategies, note some of their characteristics, describe key comprehension and study strategies, and give a brief example of each. In this part, we also consider some central concepts underlying the approach to strategy instruction suggested here. In the second part, we describe a powerful approach to teaching comprehension strategies and present an example of instruction that follows that model. In the third part, we describe several sequences of strategies that are widely recommended.

Reading Comprehension and Study Strategies

As defined by Pearson and his colleagues (Pearson, Roehler, Dole, & Duffy, 1992), reading-comprehension strategies are "conscious and flexible plans that readers apply and adopt to a variety of texts and tasks." Study strategies are similar to comprehension strategies, but differ somewhat in that comprehension strategies focus on understanding text, while study strategies focus on learning from and remembering information from text. Both comprehension and study strategies are processes readers engage in for the purpose of better understanding and remembering what they read. One strategy, for example, is determining what is important. Particularly when reading informational material to gain knowledge they need to use, readers must determine just what it is they need to learn. In the opening scenario of the chapter, we suggested that one way you might identify the important information in a chapter you are reading for a course is to consider which points in the chapter the instructor has emphasized. Another way would be to read the chapter introduction and summary before reading the entire chapter, and still another way would be to skim through the chapter seeing what was highlighted in the headings and subheadings before reading the chapter page by page. Readers who are adept at determining what is important in a reading selection have these and a variety of other strategies available, and they employ whichever strategies best fit each reading situation they encounter.

A large and robust body of research, which began well over 20 years ago and continues into the present, has clearly demonstrated that strategy instruction can be effective (see, for example, National Reading Panel, 2000; RAND Reading Study Group, 2002; Pearson et al., 1992; Pressley & Woloshyn, 1995; Rosenshine, 1995; Sweet & Snow, 2003). For all students, including English-language learners and students with special needs, strategies lead to independence in reading.

Characteristics of Comprehension and Study Strategies

In this section, we consider several characteristics of comprehension strategies, some of which are identified in Pearson's definition and some of which are not. As the discussion will reveal, these characteristics are not absolutes but vary from one situation to another.

Strategies Are Conscious Efforts. At least when they are initially taught, the strategies discussed here are conscious efforts that you ask students to deliberately engage in. For example, after teaching students how to make inferences while reading, you will sometimes ask them to make inferences about specific aspects of material they are reading, and they will sometimes deliberately pause as they are reading and realize that they have come to a point at which they need to make an inference. With practice and experience, however, some strategies are likely to become increasingly habitual and automatic; for example, readers will frequently make inferences without realizing they are doing so. Nevertheless, even well-learned strategies can be brought to consciousness and placed under the control of the reader.

Strategies Are Flexible. Flexibility and adaptability are hallmarks of strategies. The very essence of teaching students to be strategic is teaching them that they need to use strategies in ways that are appropriate for themselves and for particular situations. For example, the strategy of rereading can be used in a variety of ways: A student can reread the whole of a selection immediately after first reading it; she can reread *parts* of a selection immediately after first reading it, or she can reread the whole of a selection a week after first reading it. Whether one or another of these approaches to rereading is most useful will depend on the student, the selection she is reading, and her purpose in reading it.

Strategies Should Be Applied Only When Appropriate. Part of teaching students strategies is teaching them to apply a strategy only when the reading situation they face makes the use of a particular strategy appropriate. For example, the strategy we just mentioned, rereading, is often useful. However, if a student is reading a straightforward short story, understands it perfectly well, and is not preparing for a test of some sort, she certainly does not need to reread it. In fact, unless the student had some specific reason for rereading the story, rereading would probably be an inappropriate activity here. On the other hand, it almost always makes good sense to read software installation instructions several times before attempting to install new software.

Strategies Are Widely Applicable. Many strategies can be used across a wide range of ages, abilities, and reading material. For example, it is appropriate for a fifth grader to summarize Walter Dean Meyers' *USS Constellation: Pride of the American Navy*. It is appropriate for an eighth grader to summarize Jack London's "To Build a Fire." And it is appropriate for a graduate student to summarize the major tenets of the reader response approach to literature as they appear in something like Louise Rosenblatt's *The Reader, the Text, the Poem*.

Strategies Can Be Overt or Covert. Some strategies involve readers in creating some sort of observable product, while others involve mental operations that cannot be directly observed. Summarizing, for example, is a strategy that often results in a written record of what was read. Determining what is important, on the other hand, is a strategy that frequently does not result in the reader's writing anything. When you are initially teaching a strategy, you may frequently want students to produce an observable record of their use of the strategy so you know that they are able to use it. However, much of the time, the strategies students use will be solely mental processes.

Pause and Reflect 5.1

Identify a comprehension or study strategy that you use, and decide if your use of it is consistent with the five characteristics of comprehension and study strategies we described. It would be a good idea to do this in writing. ■

Key Comprehension and Study Strategies

In defining comprehension strategies and discussing some of their characteristics, we have mentioned several specific strategies. Here, we define and give an example of eight comprehension strategies and three study strategies that are particularly worth teaching.

Key Comprehension Strategies
- using prior knowledge
- asking and answering questions
- making inferences
- determining what is important
- summarizing
- dealing with graphic information
- imaging
- monitoring comprehension

Key Study Strategies
- surveying informational material
- taking notes on text
- making a study plan

Each of these strategies involves readers in actively constructing meaning as they read. Additionally, many of the strategies result in readers transforming ideas from one form to another or in their generating relationships among ideas, which are both activities that support comprehension and memory. For example, when readers summarize they must transform the author's text into something more concise, and when they make inferences they must relate information in the text to information they already know.

Using Prior Knowledge. When using this strategy, readers purposely bring to consciousness information that relates to what they are going to read or what they are reading. What readers are doing here is putting a set of schemata into place, establishing a framework for the new information they will encounter in the text.

Say, for instance, a fourth grader is perusing the library shelf and picks up a book titled *Mistakes That Worked* by Charlotte Foltz Jones. Before she begins reading the book, she thinks about what she knows about mistakes. As she thinks, she recalls mistakes she's made and mistakes others have made. But she really can't think of any "mistakes that worked." Thus, she begins to read the book with the realization that most mistakes don't work and that the book is going to present something different, some information on mistakes that have worked. The student is using her prior knowledge to set up expectations about what she might encounter in the text. When she reads about one of the mistakes that worked, she will be able to contrast it to her own mistakes, and making that contrast will help her both understand what she is reading and remember what she has read.

Asking and Answering Questions. Using this strategy, the reader poses questions prior to reading a selection or as she is reading it and then attempts to answer the questions while reading. Employing this strategy virtually guarantees that reading is an active process. It also serves to focus the reader's attention. A reader who has asked a particular set of questions will be particularly attentive to the information that answers those questions.

Consider a sixth grader preparing to read a chapter on nutrition in a health text. As the first step, she might survey the chapter and find these headings: Nutrients and the US RDA, The Seven Dietary Guidelines, Shopping for Groceries, and Preventing Disease Through Proper Diet. Then, she might pose one or two questions about each heading: "What are nutrients?" "What is the US RDA?" "What are the seven dietary guidelines?" "Do I follow them in my diet?" "Should I follow them?" "How is shopping for groceries related to nutrition?" and "Can a proper diet prevent all disease?" As she reads, the student will get answers to some of her questions, find that others are not answered in the chapter, and pose and answer additional questions. As a result of this active involvement, she is likely to learn a good deal.

Making Inferences. When readers apply this strategy, they infer meanings by using information from the text and their existing knowledge of the world, their schemata, to fill in bits of information that are not explicitly stated in the text. No text is ever fully explicit, and readers must constantly make inferences to understand what they are reading. By teaching students to make inferences, you are helping them learn to use their existing knowledge along with the information in the text to build meaning.

Suppose that a fifth grader is reading a science text and learns that woodchucks build deep burrows and huddle in them in large groups during the winter. Knowing that a fair number of animals hibernate, she might infer that woodchucks hibernate in their burrows. Knowing that ground temperature remains stable and reasonably warm at depths greater than 3 or 4 feet, she might further infer that woodchucks make their burrows deep in order to take advantage of this warmth.

Determining What Is Important. Making use of this strategy requires that readers understand what they have read and make judgments about what is and is not important. As Chambliss and Calfee (1998) explain in detail, most texts contain much more information than a reader can focus on and learn. Consequently, determining what is important is a crucial and frequently required strategy. Among other things, determining what is important is something students need to learn to do before they can summarize a selection. Only by determining what is important can students know what to include and what to exclude in a summary.

Sometimes, texts include direct cues to what is important—overviews, headings, summaries, and the like. In many cases, however, students need to rely on their prior knowledge to infer what is important in a particular selection.

For instance, while reading Julisa Velarde's story "Always Moving" in S. Beth Atkin's *Voices in the Field*, a collection of stories by the children of migrant farm workers, a seventh grader might think about the most important issues and events in the narrative and come up with the following set of important points:

- Julisa, whose parents are divorced, is always moving because her mom has to go where the lettuce-picking jobs are.
- When Julisa's mom goes to some jobs, Julisa and her younger sister Christina stay at one of their aunt's houses so they don't have to keep moving so much.
- Sometimes when Julisa moves she doesn't remember where she is. She misses her cousins and her friends.
- Julisa has gone to many different schools in many different towns, which is hard. She'd rather stay in one place and go to one school.
- Julisa's mother wants her daughters to do well in school, learn English, and keep studying hard so they can have good careers and houses of their own.
- Julia feels sad her mother has to work so hard. She wishes she had a job that was easier than working in the fields, that they had one home, and that her mom would always be there.

Together, these important points constitute the essence of Julisa's story.

Summarizing. Using this strategy requires students to first determine what is important and then condense it and put it in their own words. Brown and Day (1983) have suggested some basic rules for summarizing. Slightly modified, these include:

- deleting trivial or irrelevant information
- deleting redundant information
- providing a superordinate term for members of a category
- finding and using generalizations the author has made
- creating your own generalizations when the author has not provided them

The above list of important ideas from "Always Moving" constitutes a good summary of Julisa's story. By dropping less important details and focusing on the most important aspects of the story, the student was able to understand what Julisa was trying to communicate. An even briefer summary, one that focuses on the theme of the story, is also possible:

> Because Julisa's mother has to move to where the lettuce-picking jobs are, Julisa and her sister have to move often, too. This is hard for the family and causes problems for Julisa, such as having to change schools and missing her cousins and her friends. Julisa's mom wants Julisa and her sister to learn English and study hard so they can have good careers, not a low-paying and hard one like hers, and not one that makes them move all the time.

Dealing with Graphic Information. When they employ this strategy, readers give conscious attention to the visual information supplied by the author. Long before youngsters learn to read, they are drawn to and fascinated by the visual material books offer. Teaching them when, how, and why to use the illustrations, graphs, maps, diagrams, and other visuals that accompany selections will enable them to make optimal use of the visual aids texts often provide.

History texts, for example, almost always contain maps that include a legend to the symbols they employ. Students need to learn that maps usually have legends, the kind of information legends normally contain, where legends are typically placed, and how to interpret them.

Imaging and Creating Visual Representations. Using this strategy, readers create visual representations of text, either in their mind or by reproducing them on paper or other tangible forms. One kind of imaging occurs when readers visualize people, events, and places. Another kind of imaging consists of visually organizing key ideas in text in a way that graphically displays their relationships. The former type of imaging tends to be used with narrative material, while the latter works particularly well with expository text.

One imaging technique appropriate for middle-grade students is constructing semantic maps of key concepts. For example, a semantic map for a chapter on mountains in a geography text might look like that shown in Figure 5.1.

Note that both dealing with graphic information and imaging and creating visual representations can be particularly helpful for English-language learners, whose graphic skills may be much stronger than their English language skills.

Figure 5.1 **Semantic Map for Mountains**

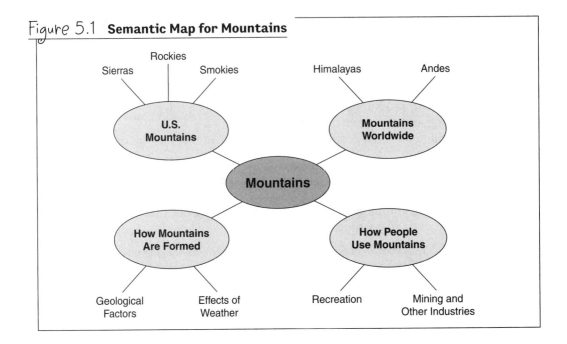

Monitoring Comprehension. Good readers are metacognitive; that is, they monitor their comprehension. Monitoring comprehension is a more general strategy than any of those discussed thus far. In monitoring comprehension, readers keep track of what they wish to gain from a text and of their understanding—or lack of understanding—of the text as they are reading. They then use whatever strategies they need to maintain or improve comprehension. You might think of monitoring strategies as the employer and the other strategies as the employees.

Readers who monitor their comprehension are asking these kinds of questions: "Am I understanding what the author is saying? What do I do if I don't understand something I'm reading? What could I be doing to understand better what the author is saying? Can I do something that will help me remember the material better?"

If, for example, you were reading along and realized that you did not really understand what you were reading, what would you do? What fix-up strategy would you use? In most cases, you would probably reread as much material as necessary in order to build meaning. While you were reading, if you realized there were words whose meanings were unclear to you, you might choose to look them up. If there were illustrations or other graphic material, you might look at those. At some point, you might consciously check your prior knowledge to see how what you already know fits information gleaned from the text. You might try to reproduce a visual image of the material in your head. In brief, you would do whatever was necessary to arrive at a satisfactory understanding of what you were reading. This, of course, is precisely what you want to prepare students to do.

Surveying Informational Material.   Surveying informational material and the next two strategies we describe here are generally referred to as "study strategies." This is so because they assist students in learning and remembering material. When surveying informational material, for example, the student approaches a text—perhaps a textbook chapter, an article in a magazine, or a part of a chapter or article—with the conscious realization that she needs to learn and remember some of what she is about to read. She also approaches it with the realization that understanding and learning are not likely to come without effort, and that having a plan of study will result in more efficient and more effective learning.

Consequently, before reading the article thoroughly, she first skims it. In doing so, she probably reads the introduction, the headings, and the summary or conclusion. Additionally, she may read the first paragraph following every major heading, which may be an overview of the upcoming section; and she may even read the first sentence of each paragraph. Surveying the text will, of course, take time, but it will yield two extremely valuable results. On the one hand, surveying gives the reader a good idea of the organization of a text, something critical to reading efficiently and to remembering material. Surveying also gives the reader some idea of the contents of the selection, making it possible for her to call up her prior knowledge of the topic and bring that to bear in understanding the selection, and increasing the likelihood that she can take the new information she gains from the selection and integrate it with her existing knowledge. We believe that the bottom line of surveying is very simple: If you want to read as efficiently as possible and are reading informational material in order to learn and remember it, then not surveying material before reading and studying it is just plain foolish.

Taking Notes on Texts.   As we just noted, surveying gives the reader a place to store new information gleaned from a text and therefore is a great aid to remembering what you read. However, for the vast majority of people—whether they are middle-grade students on their way to becoming mature readers or adults who are already mature readers—simply reading a text is not enough to foster lasting learning and remembering. When reading new and unfamiliar material and trying to learn and remember it, most people need to do something with the information. Taking notes is one of the most frequently used and frequently appropriate techniques for bolstering learning and memory.

As we teach students to take notes, three facts are particularly worth emphasizing. First, it is usually most appropriate to take notes only after you understand the basic content and organization of a text. This means you need to read a selection and consider its headings and subheadings before taking notes. Taking notes without a basic understanding of the content and organization of a selection is likely to result in notes that do not capture the key content of the selection. Second, notes should be taken in your own words, not by simply reproducing the words of the text. Taking notes in your own words forces you to process the meaning of the text and results in much better memory for it. Third, it is often appropriate to create some sort of two-phase notes, in which you capture the main points of the selection in one column and then comment on that content in a second column. Such two-phase

Note taking really pays off when studying expository material.

note taking is likely to result in better memory for the content, deeper understanding of it, and its being better integrated into existing schemata.

Making a Study Plan. Study activities like surveying and note taking require time, effort, and a plan that ensures that you commit the necessary time and effort. This means that you need to identify a place to study and a time to study, as well as make a real commitment to actually doing the studying necessary to learn whatever it is that you need to learn. Students have very different ways of effectively studying, but for most students studying soon after the initial learning in a quiet environment that lets them physically organize material and concentrate on it makes the best sense. Generally, you will need to work with students as individuals to find out where they are able to study best, when they study best, and under which condition they are best able to study. In many households today, finding a time and place to study is not easy, and of course studying outside of school is not the first order of business on many of today's students' agendas. Nevertheless, doing everything possible to motivate and assist students in studying is essential. Unless students take the time and effort to study a significant amount of time outside of school, they are unlikely to gain the knowledge and skills necessary to succeed in school and in the world outside of school. Moreover, studying outside of school is particularly important for those students who find school and schoolwork a challenge. Somehow, we as teachers need to muster the arguments and provide students with the motivation and the scaffolding that will make studying a regular part of their days and weeks.

The comprehension and study strategies described here will help students reach the goal of understanding, learning from, and remembering important aspects of what they read. In fact, they are crucial to students' reaching the goal of understanding, learning from, and remembering what they read. In learning these strategies, students are internalizing a way of reading and thinking that is active, critical, and reflective. Having learned this mode of thinking, students will be both able and inclined to engage in a variety of reading and learning strategies to understand, appreciate, and learn from what they read. Putting substantial amounts of time into helping students master these strategies and then continually reviewing them, giving students opportunities to use them, and prompting students to use them will be extremely beneficial for students. It should be noted that students will differ in the rate at which they learn the strategies that have been described. We believe it is more important for students to have a thorough understanding of fewer strategies than to have a superficial understanding of a larger number of strategies. While the ultimate goal is for students to have several strategies to apply, what is most important is that they are able to effectively use the strategies they have.

Pause and Reflect 5.2

The 11 comprehension and study strategies that we have described cover the vast majority of the strategies that need to be taught. However, there are certainly other comprehension and study strategies. Consider some other strategies that you use or are otherwise familiar with. Do you think some of these should be taught? If so, should they be taught in addition to those we described or in lieu of some of ours? ■

Concepts Underlying Our Approach to Teaching Strategies

Up to this point, we have discussed important characteristics of strategies and described eight key comprehension strategies and three key study strategies. In this section, we describe a number of concepts that underlie the approach to strategy instruction we suggest. We emphasize these concepts based on our own experiences and the work of a number of educators, including Deshler and Schumaker (1993), Dole, Brown, and Trathen (1996), Duffy (2002), Duke and Pearson (2002), Pressley (2000, 2002), Sweet and Snow (2003).

The Teacher's Mediational Role.   Because learning is a constructive process in which much of what the learner understands is actually constructed by the learner, it often happens that you explain or demonstrate one thing, but some students understand something quite different. In teaching a strategy, you must constantly be alert to how students are interpreting your instruction and be ready to assist students who get a bit off track. This means that after you discuss a strategy or demonstrate it to students, you need to question them or ask them to demonstrate their use of the strategy so that you can see whether they have appropriately interpreted the strategy and understand how to use it. If this reveals any misunderstandings, these should be cleared up before students internalize them.

Cooperative Learning.   Cooperative learning puts students with varying abilities and knowledge bases together so that they can provide scaffolding for each other as they work toward mastering strategies. In initially teaching a strategy, it usually makes sense to let students work together on the strategy before requiring them to deal with it individually. Thus, after you have explained and modeled a strategy such as summarizing, you might have students work in pairs or in groups of three or four as they make their first few attempts at summarizing material.

Authenticity and Quality of Texts. It makes good sense to have students learn to use strategies with the kinds of selections they will typically read. At the same time, during the initial stages of instruction, it will be useful to work with fairly short texts in order to focus students' attention. For example, it is often convenient to put a paragraph of text on an overhead so that you and the students can all see it as you discuss the strategy and how to apply it to the text. Later, of course, students need to work with increasingly lengthy texts. Regardless of whether shorter or more lengthy texts are used, remember that students will have difficulty applying strategies to text that they cannot adequately decode and read with some fluency. It is impossible to draw inferences, for example, from text that is not first comprehended at the literal level. Since the focus of instruction is strategy use, students should be working with texts that are not so difficult for them to decode that they will have no mental energy left for strategy application.

Multifaceted and Long-Term Instruction. Strategy instruction needs to be multifaceted and long term. What you are introducing, building, and nurturing are complex procedures, behaviors, and attitudes. These take time to develop, and develop differently in different students. If one approach does not work with a particular student or group of students, then another approach needs to be tried. Good strategy instruction also takes patience, commitment, flexibility, and a good dose of perspective and humor. Like many things that are worth having, strategies are often not easily acquired.

Promoting Positive Attitudes and Behaviors. As we just mentioned, strategy instruction promotes certain attitudes and behaviors. If you want your students to use strategies, they need to be motivated to use them. They must understand how using strategies will help them achieve their goals. You can achieve this in part by frequently specifying the utility of the strategy you are teaching and of those that students have already mastered. Students must also learn that, although strategies do require substantial amounts of time and effort, they do not require unreasonable amounts of time and effort. You can help them learn this by thoroughly preparing them to use the strategies you ask them to use and by allowing a good deal of class time for them to work with strategies, particularly with strategies they are just learning.

Connecting Success to Strategy Use. Strategy instruction should also include prompting students to connect their performance gains to their having used strategies. Let us say that an eighth grader, Julie, an aspiring ballerina, comes up to you one morning quite excited. She has just read *On Pointe* by Lorie Ann Grover. Prepared for Julie's usual lengthy, detailed retelling, you are surprised when she says.

"The girl in *On Pointe,* Claire, has studied dance for 10 years. She's working so hard to be a professional dancer—her dream—and then, when she tries out for the City Ballet Company, she doesn't make it—she's too tall! She feels like her life is over until she figures out she doesn't have to be in a company to dance—she's a dancer and can dance anywhere."

Because of the animation in her face and voice, you know this book has made a special connection with Julie. "I think this story had special meaning for you, Julie, which is wonderful," you tell her. "Also, do you know what you have just done . . . besides making a personal connection with this story? You've used the summarizing strategy. You've told everything important about the story in just a few sentences. Summarizing can help you better understand and remember a lot of what you read."

Practice and Feedback. If students are going to get better at a strategy, they need to practice it in a way that allows you to evaluate their use of the strategy and give them feedback about how they are doing on it. Moreover, they need many opportunities for practice and feedback, and these opportunities need to extend over considerable periods of time.

Review. When learning something complex such as comprehension strategies, students need to be given many opportunities to review and solidify what they have learned. Thus, part of your plan for strategy instruction should include systematic review of the strategies you teach. Ideally, students need opportunities for review in the days, weeks, months, and even years that follow their initial experiences with a strategy.

A Powerful Approach to Teaching Strategies

Over the past two decades, a substantial body of theory and research has supported two approaches to teaching strategies—*direct explanation of strategies* and *transactional strategies instruction* (Sales & Graves, 2005). Direct explanation of strategies has been repeatedly validated and endorsed over the past two decades (e.g., Duffy, 2002; Duffy et al., 1987; Duke & Pearson, 2002; Graves, Juel, & Graves, 2004; National Reading Panel, 2000; Pearson et al., 1992; RAND, 2002; Sweet & Snow, 2003). Direct explanation of strategies is a very explicit, step-by-step approach. Usually, teachers use carefully prepared materials specifically designed to facilitate students' learning the strategy, and carefully preplanned lessons. A typical unit designed to initially teach a strategy might last from several days to several weeks. It begins with the teacher doing the bulk of the work, explaining the strategy, noting its importance, modeling it use, and the like. Then, gradually, the instruction progresses from a situation in which the teacher does most of the work to one in which students assume primary responsibility for use of the strategy.

The basic components of explicit instruction are listed below. Following these steps is a powerful, efficient, and effective way to initially teach a strategy.

- An explicit description of the strategy and when and how it should be used
- Teacher and/or student modeling of the strategy in action

- Collaborative use of the strategy in action
- Guided practice using the strategy with gradual release of responsibility
- Independent use of the strategy (Duke & Pearson, 2002)

However, relying exclusively on direct explanation to teach a strategy may result in a problem. Used by itself, direct explanation may be too artificial and too separated from the ongoing activities of the classroom. Students may learn to use the strategy during the special periods set aside for strategy instruction but then fail to use it when they are reading at other times of the school day and at home.

In response to this problem, Pressley and his colleagues developed transactional strategies instruction. It too has been described and researched in a number of studies (e.g., Brown, Pressley, Van Meter, & Schuder, 1996; Pressley, 2000, 2002; Pressley et al., 1992; Reutzel, Fawson, & Smith, 2003) and found to be effective. Like direct explanation, transactional strategies instruction includes direct explanation as part of the initial instruction on strategies. However, compared to direct explanation, transactional strategies instruction is much less structured, and the period of directly teaching the strategy is likely to be brief. Moreover, transactional strategies instruction is introduced as part of the ongoing reading activities in the classroom when the occasion arises for students to use a particular strategy. This means that the instruction cannot be preplanned and special materials that would facilitate teaching it cannot be prepared in advance. As we just noted, there is solid evidence that transactional instruction is effective. However, there is also clear evidence that relatively few teachers can and do learn to use transactional strategies instruction (Pressley & El-Dinary, 1997; Pressley, 2002). Because it is an on-the-fly approach and not supported by a specific curriculum and instructional materials, teachers have found it very difficult to work transactional strategies instruction into the school day.

In the approach described in this chapter, which is modeled on that described by Sales and Graves (2005), we have combined these two types of strategy instruction and modified them in several ways. One way in which we have modified them is to include more deliberate and carefully planned instruction in initially teaching the strategies than is typically used in transactional instruction and to include more review, rehearsal, integration, and constructivist activities than are typically used in direct explanation. Another way in which we have modified them is to include more direct attention to motivation and engagement than is often included in either sort of strategies instruction. In particular, we emphasize the importance of really selling the strategies to students.

In illustrating the approach, we first describe the components that make up the first 2 days of instruction. Next, we consider how instruction proceeds over the course of a 3-week unit. After that, we explain the constructive nature of good comprehension strategy instruction. Finally, we discuss the types of review and followup activities that are needed to make a strategy a tool that students spontaneously use. Although instruction will vary somewhat with different strategies, different students, and different age groups, the general plan presented is widely applicable.

Teaching Idea 5.1
Promoting Strategy Use

Learning to use strategies is challenging work, and students need to be motivated and convinced that taking the time and effort to learn to use strategies is worth it. Outline a brief pep talk you can use to persuade students that learning a particular strategy is important. Also, construct a large and colorful poster advertising that strategy to display and refer to when you teach it.

Instruction for Determining What Is Important

Over time, some readers more or less automatically recognize and can identify the important ideas stated in a text. But this kind of strategic reading—distinguishing between important and supporting ideas—takes time and practice and, for most students, explicit instruction. A sample for the first 2 days of instruction for the strategy Determining What Is Important is described on the pages that follow.

The First Day's Instruction. The activities presented in this section are designed to be used with sixth graders on the first day of instruction for the strategy Determining What Is Important. The students have had some experience with the strategy in previous grades, but this is the first time it will have been formally taught. Recently, students have been having difficulty discriminating between important ideas and less important details in their science and social studies books, and so this is an opportune time for instruction in this particular strategy. The first day's instruction includes four different components—motivation and interest-building, teacher explanation, teacher modeling, and large-group student participation with teacher mediation.

Motivation and Interest Building (*about 15 minutes*). As in any learning, motivation is essential, and motivation is particularly important in strategy instruction because learning and using strategies is hard work (Almasi, 2003). For readers to employ this or any other strategy takes concentration and work, so readers need to perceive some sort of reward for their effort. Students need to know something is in it for them. That *something* will vary from student to student and text to text. Teaching Idea 5.1 will give you some ideas and practice at advertising a strategy of your teaching.

To capture students' attention and build interest in reading the text that will be used in the instruction—*Case Closed: The Real Scoop on Detective Work* by Milton Meltzer—introduce the Determining What Is Important Strategy with a gamelike activity. The activity described here vividly illustrates that it is easier to remember words and phrases if they are associated with an over-arching idea. The categories and words chosen for this example are from *Case Closed*—an expository text

Figure 5.2 **Categorized Words and Phrases**

weapons	crime solvers	evidence
gun	forensic scientist	blood
knife	lab technician	fingerprints
rope	FBI	hair
candlestick	investigator	bullet
lead pipe	detective	DNA
poison	cop	torn piece of fabric

that will interest most sixth graders. The categories are—murder weapons, evidence, and crime solvers. The details that support these categories are rope, knife, lead pipe, poison, gun, candlestick, blood, fingerprints, DNA, hair, bullet, detective, forensic scientist, lab technician, cop, and FBI. Before the activity, duplicate the words (but not the figure titles) from Figure 5.2, Categorized Words and Phrases, on blue paper and the words from Figure 5.3, Randomly Arranged Words and Phrases, on green paper.

Before introducing the book and beginning the game, write the word *detective* on the board and discuss what detectives do and what sorts of skills they need. End the discussion by pointing out that detectives need to remember details because they might be valuable clues. Detectives also need to be able to sort out the things that might be important to a case from unimportant information.

Divide the class into two teams—the green team and the blue team. Tell students you are going to give each team member a sheet of paper with same words printed on it. The object of the game is to read the words as if they were clues at a crime scene—trying to remember as of them as possible. Students will have 15 seconds to silently read the words. At the end of 15 seconds, they will turn their papers over.

Distribute the sheets of paper—blue for blue team and green for green team—columns of words facing down. When all students have their papers, ask students turn them over and read them. After 15 seconds, tell students to stop reading and turn papers face down. Next, tell students they have 1 minute to write down as many words as they can remember on the back of their sheet of paper. After a minute is

Figure 5.3 **Randomly Arranged Words and Phrases**

evidence	forensic scientist	fingerprints
gun	blood	detective
knife	rope	weapons
FBI	poison	lab technician
bullet	crime solvers	investigator
lead pipe	DNA	candlestick
hair	cop	torn piece of fabric

up, have students count the number of words on their paper and circle that number. Collect the papers and tally the numbers for each team. The students will be surprised to discover that the blue team remembered far more words than the green team—even though the same words were on both the green and blue sheets.

Ask students how is it that all the students in blue group remembered more words: Are they really that much smarter? Would they really make better detectives?

Teacher Explanation (*about 10 minutes*). Put both lists on an overhead and compare them, leading students to deduce that those reading the blue list remembered more words because the words are grouped in categories. Explain that, in most of the reading they do in subjects like science and social studies, the information is organized around a particularly important idea and supported by details. Determining what that important idea is helps a reader remember and understand the information better.

At this point, ask students about the reading they have been doing in science and social studies, and discuss some of the challenges they have faced. One of the challenges likely to come up is that informational books cover a lot of information and it is hard to remember all of it. Explain that the strategy they will be working on for the next several weeks—Determining What Is Important—will help them to better understand and remember what they read. Tell students that learning and using this strategy will take some work at first, but that it is a strategy that will improve their understanding and remembering, and make reading more worthwhile and fun in the long run.

Teacher Modeling (*about 5 minutes*). Reveal more about how the strategy works by writing a sentence such as the following one on the board:

> After a Monet painting, valued at more than half a million dollars, had been missing from the Chicago Institute of Art for nearly two years, Sid Spade, a long-time private detective for the Spying Eye Detective Agency, finally cracked the case, using his highly successful method of "track 'em and crack 'em."

Read the sentence aloud, and model the thought processes you might go through in identifying the most important information in the sentence.

> Let's see, what is the main idea the author is communicating in this sentence? The topic seems to be the Monet painting. No, on second thought I think the more important idea is Sid Spade. And what is the most important information about Sid? Cracking the case sounds pretty important. (Circle the phrases *Sid Spade* and *finally cracked the case* on the board.) The other information—that he's a long-time detective for the Spying Eye Detective Agency and he used his track and crack method—are interesting, but not as important. (Cross out *a long-time private detective for the Spying Eye Detective Agency* and *using his highly successful method he said of "track 'em and crack 'em"* on the board.) What other detail about Sid and the case is important? Hmmm. Well, I think the fact the case he cracked was a missing Monet painting is part of the important information. (Circle the words *Monet painting* and *missing*.) The details

Figure 5.4 **Details about the Importance of Observation in Detective Work**

- skilled observation makes detectives successful
- training wasted if not skilled observers
- when first go to crime scene don't know what might be important—scrap of cloth, cigar ashes, button, Lincoln penny
- value of odds-and-ends may only become clear as investigation proceeds
- an overlooked critical clue may mean the crime will go unsolved
- keen observation very important when crime scene investigation begins

about the Monet painting—that it was worth nearly half a million and had been missing from the Art Institute for two years are interesting, too—but these details support the more important idea that the case of the missing Monet was solved and Sid Spade the one who solved it. (Cross out *valued at more than half a million dollars, had been* missing [missing is circled, not crossed out] *from the Chicago Institute of Art for nearly two years.*)

Once you have explained the strategy and modeled it, check to see if students were following you by asking a few of them to explain the strategy and note why it is worth knowing.

Large-Group Student Participation and Teacher Mediation (*about 10 minutes*). Put a paragraph from one of the students' social studies or science texts on the overhead and read it aloud. The paragraph should be one in which the important information stands out. The sample paragraph below is taken from *Case Closed.*

> The power of observation is what makes detectives successful, too. All their specialized training would be wasted if they were not skilled observers. Think about it for a moment and you can see why. When detectives arrive at the scene of the crime, they don't know what may turn out to be a vital clue. Could it be this scrap of cloth? These cigar ashes? This button? That Lincoln penny? The value of such odds and ends as clues may become clear only as the investigation proceeds. Overlook the critically important clue and the crime might go unsolved. That's why keen observation is so important when investigation of the crime scene begins. (Meltzer, 2001, p. 10)

Ask students what the paragraph is mainly about (observation in detective work). Next, ask them how they determined this. (Everything in the paragraph talks about detectives observing things, picking out clues.) Have students supply the details about the importance of observation in detective work that are given in the paragraph, and write these on the board as shown in Figure 5.4.

After you have written the details students have suggested on the board, ask them, "Which information in the paragraph is the most important?" Explain that all of these details say something about observation and detectives, but there is one general idea that is most important, possibly the idea that the author really wants to get across. Help students determine the most important idea by asking questions such as these about each of the details listed: "Is this the most important idea in the

Figure 5.5   **Most Important Idea and Supporting Details
on the Importance of Observation in Detective Work**

Observing clues is very important in detective work,
especially at the beginning of crime scene investigations.

- skilled observation makes detectives successful
- training wasted if not skilled observers
- when first go to crime scene don't know what might be important—scrap of cloth, cigar
  ashes, button, Lincoln penny
- value of odds-and-ends may only become clear as investigation proceeds
- an overlooked critical clue may mean the crime will go unsolved
- keen observation very important when crime scene investigation begins

paragraph?" "Do the other ideas support this one?" "Do you think this is the main thing the author is trying to tell you?" Have students suggest one sentence or phrase that expresses the main idea of the paragraph, such as, "Observing clues is very important in detective work, especially at the beginning of crime scene investigations."

After students have agreed on the most important idea, revise the chart on the board to show the most important idea with its supporting details underneath it as shown in Figure 5.5.

Thus far, this introductory session has lasted about 40 minutes. In most classrooms, it would be a good idea to move to another topic at this time and continue the strategy instruction the next day. Teaching Idea 5.2 will give you practice at modeling your own thought processes.

The Second Day's Instruction. The second day's instruction on the strategy Determining What Is Important includes five different components—review with teacher modeling, large-group student participation with teacher mediation, teacher modeling and guided practice, guided practice and pair-share, and group-share with teacher response and mediation.

Teaching Idea 5.2
Modeling Your Thought Processes

Learning to use strategies effectively is not an easy task for students. Moreover, effectively teaching strategies is not an easy task for teachers. One of the most challenging parts of teaching strategies is modeling your own use of the strategy as part of the instruction. Reread the sentence about the missing Monet painting and the teacher's modeling of the thought processes she goes through in determining the most important information in the sentence on page 121. Then find another passage that you can use to model what you go through in determining the most important information in that passage. Finally, create a modeling script for your own passage similar to the one on page 121.

Review with Teacher Modeling (*5 minutes*). Very briefly review the first day's lesson, discussing what strategies in general are and what the specific strategy of determining what is important is. Explain again that what readers do when they use this strategy is focus on the most important information and let the less important details fade into the background. Model your thought processes as you determine what is important in a short text, probably the paragraph that you ended yesterday's lesson with. Motivate students by reminding them how helpful the strategy will be for understanding and remembering what they read. Talk about how much of the social studies and science material they read contains a great deal of information. If they can focus on only the most important information, they will reduce the amount they need to learn and remember.

Large-Group Student Participation with Teacher Mediation (*10 to 20 minutes*). Work together with students to determine the most important idea in a few additional paragraphs in the same book. Call on students to determine what is most important in each paragraph and to explain how they determined that the information they selected is the most important. On the board, create a visual display similar to the one you did for the paragraph used on the first day of instruction. If students seem to understand the strategy, move to the next step. If not, do some further explaining and modeling.

Teacher Modeling and Guided Practice (*about 10 minutes*). Once large-group questioning indicates that students have a basic understanding of the strategy, they need a chance to practice it. Since they have only worked with paragraph-length selections thus far, they should continue with paragraph-length selections in this practice session. Also, since the selections used thus far have been ones in which the important information stood out clearly, the practice paragraphs should also clearly reveal the important information.

Duplicate two paragraphs from students' science or social studies text or a nonfiction trade book such as *Case Closed*, the selection used in Day One's instruction. Leave space after each paragraph for students to jot down the paragraph's most important idea.

Read the first paragraph aloud as students follow along. After you finish reading, model the thinking you would do to determine what seems the most important information in the passage. Using a transparency, model how you would jot down a sentence that expresses this main idea. Have students write that same sentence on their papers beneath the paragraph.

Guided Practice and Pair Share (*about 10 minutes*). Next, read the second paragraph on the sheet. When you finish ask, "What is the most important thing to remember and understand in this passage?" Give students a few moments to think about their answers. Have them turn to a partner (these have been designated in advance) and share their ideas. Then read the same paragraph aloud again, asking students to listen for the most important information. Have students write down the information they think is the most important to remember and understand.

Group Share with Teacher Response and Mediation (*about 10 minutes*). Invite students to present the important information they found in the passage and discuss how they determined this was the crucial information. Monitor their responses carefully and provide feedback and clarification as necessary.

This would conclude the first two days of instruction and practice with the strategy. The remainder of the unit is discussed in the next section. How effective the lessons are will depend, to a large measure, on how lively the instruction is and how motivated, engaged, and attentive students are. Also, it's important to note that the instructional periods will vary greatly with the age and maturity of the students. For example, while most fourth graders may be able to attend to a teacher presentation for only 20 minutes, many eighth graders may be able to attend for 30 to 40 minutes.

Overview of a Unit

A typical unit might last 3 weeks. Although instruction should continue to include a number of the features of the first day's instruction, it should gradually change as students become increasingly competent with the strategy. Here are some of the major ways in which it changes.

Subsequent Instructional Periods Become Shorter. During the first few days of instruction, the instructional periods should be quite lengthy, perhaps lasting 30 minutes or so. After the first few days, the periods of instruction get shorter, with those at the end of the unit perhaps lasting 15 minutes.

Instruction Becomes Less Concentrated Each Week. During the first week, students should work on the strategy nearly every day; then, with each successive week, they should work on it less frequently. For example, during the first week there might be 4 days of instruction, during the second week 3 days, and during the third week 2 days.

Students Do More of the Work. Particularly on the first day of instruction and to a lesser extent in the first few days of instruction, the teacher bears the burden of much of the work. In other words, the teacher heavily scaffolds instruction. Teacher explanation, teacher modeling, and teacher response and feedback occupy a significant amount of the time. Increasingly, however, the teacher should gradually release responsibility for completing the strategy to students. More and more time is spent on students actually working with the strategy. Also, perhaps after the first week or so, students move from working in pairs to working independently at least some of the time.

Texts Become Longer and More Challenging. In addition to students doing more of the work themselves, over time they need to work with increasingly lengthy and more challenging texts. On the first few days of instruction, students might work with paragraphs; next they might work with one-page texts; then, eventually, they will work with typical chapter-length texts. Similarly, on the first few days, students would work with selections in which the important information stands out prominently, that is, selections in which important information is cued by titles, headings, or topic sentences. Later, they would work with material in which the important information is less obvious, material more typical of much of what they will read.

Strategies Are Used on Authentic Tasks. Since the purpose of students learning strategies is for them to use the strategies as part of their normal reading experiences, they need to be given increased opportunities, prompts, and encouragement to employ the strategies outside of the context of specific strategy instruction. Such opportunities can be pointed out during class time devoted to reading; during class time devoted to other subjects, such as social studies and mathematics; and when the strategies are likely to be useful for work done outside of class. For example, almost any written report requires that students determine what is important in the material they read for the report.

Students Are Encouraged to Use the Strategies Independently. Once students reach the point where they can routinely use the strategies when you prompt them to do so, you need to repeatedly encourage them to use the strategies without your prompting them. Much of the time, when students set out to read something or encounter a comprehension problem in what they are reading, you will not be there to suggest what strategy they can use to read effectively or to remedy the problem.

The Constructive Nature of Good Strategy Instruction

Conveying the constructivist, interactive, and flexible nature of good strategy instruction is difficult on paper, and we want to be certain that our description of strategy instruction thus far has not left some of you thinking of it as rather rigid and teacher centered. Good strategy instruction is neither rigid nor teacher centered. In Figure 5.6, we emphasize this by comparing teacher-dominated instruction to constructivist instruction.

Review and Followup Activities

If students are to become permanent strategy users, their use of the strategy needs to be encouraged and nurtured beyond the initial unit of instruction. Three types of followup are important.

One- or Two-Day Formal Reviews. It seems appropriate to have one or two formal reviews of the strategy following initial instruction. By formal reviews, we mean 30- to 45-minute instructional sessions in which renewing students' understanding and competency with the strategy is the main topic of the lesson. Assuming that initial instruction in the strategy took place early in the school year, the first review might be given in November and the second review in February or March.

Figure 5.6 **Teacher-Dominated and Constructivist Strategy Instruction**

A Portrait of Teacher-Dominated Instruction	**A Portrait of Constructivist Instruction**
The teacher lectures and the students listen.	The teacher and the students interact, with modeling, scaffolding, and discussion prominent.
Children assume the role of passive, rather than active, participants.	Children assume the role of active participants.
It is as if the knowledge the teacher has can be transmitted directly to the students.	It is understood that the knowledge the teacher has cannot be transmitted directly to the students.
There is little discussion and debate.	There is considerable discussion and debate.
Teachers do very little on-the-spot diagnoses of individual students' understanding and progress.	Teachers frequently make on-the-spot diagnoses of individual students' understanding and progress.
The instruction proceeds at a predetermined rate and sequence that is dictated by the curriculum.	The instruction proceeds at a rate and sequence that is dictated by the students' needs and progress.
Lessons are often scripted.	Lessons are not scripted.
All students are expected to proceed at the same rate.	Students are expected to proceed at their own rate.
Skills are emphasized at the expense of understanding.	Understanding is emphasized as strategies are developed.
Students are rarely informed about the purposes of the strategies taught.	Students are always informed about the purposes of the strategies taught.
Little, if any, attention is given to developing students' self-monitoring and self-regulation skills.	Developing students' self-monitoring and self-regulation skills are central concerns.

The descriptions here are modified forms of descriptions originally written by Brown and Campione (1990) and Pressley, Harris, and Marks (1992).

More Frequent Mini-Lessons. In addition to the 30- to 45-minute formal reviews, occasional 5- to 10-minute mini-lessons should be given when the materials students are working with seem applicable to use of the strategy and a short review seems needed.

Frequent Suggestions to Use the Strategies. Finally, whenever the materials students are using lend themselves to use of a strategy that has been taught, students can be given a brief reminder that the strategy may prove useful.

Widely Recommended Sequences of Strategies

In addition to using individual strategies such as those discussed thus far, good strategy users employ sequences of strategies—several individual strategies routinely used as a set—to understand and remember what they read. Three sequences of strategies—the K-W-L Procedure, Reciprocal Teaching, and SQ3R—have been widely recommended for students to use when their goal is to learn from and remember informational material. In the next several sections, we briefly describe each of these sequences and then discuss procedures for teaching them.

You'll need to closely observe students to know how much review they need.

The K-W-L Procedure

The K-W-L Procedure, developed by Donna Ogle (1986), can be used as a teacher-directed procedure for guiding students through a particular selection or taught to students as a strategy for them to use independently (Carr & Ogle, 1987). Since this chapter deals with strategies, here we are primarily concerned with teaching K-W-L as a strategy that students can use independently; however, you can also use it in teacher-led instruction. The procedure consists of three major steps: What I **K**now, What I **W**ant to Know, and What I **L**earned.

What I Know.   The first step includes two stages. To begin, students consider the topic of the selection and list what they already know about it. Then, they categorize the information they listed and note other categories of information that they expect to learn something about as they read. For example, if the topic is horses, one student might list that horses are expensive, take a lot of care, are a lot of fun, and are used for racing and recreation. Given this list, she might generate categories for which she has some information—Uses of Horses, Advantages Owning Horses, and Disadvantages of Owning Horses—and categories in which she expects to find information—Types of Horses and the Origins of the Modern Horse. Note that this step of listing what is known and identifying categories of information can be completed in small groups. Also, when K-W-L is used as a teacher-led procedure, this is a group brainstorming activity in which the teacher solicits responses and writes them on the board.

What I Want to Know.   The second step follows directly from the first. Based on the information the students already have and the categories in which they expect to find additional information, they list areas in which they would like further information. Even when K-W-L is used as a group or teacher-led activity, students are encouraged to construct personalized lists of what they want to learn from their reading. For example, having considered the issue of how much horses cost and thinking at least vaguely about getting one, the student may decide that getting information on the cost of horses is her major interest in reading the passage.

What I Learned. The third step is for students to record what they have learned. Additionally, students are encouraged to consider some things they wanted to learn about the topic but did not learn from this particular selection and to pursue their interest further through additional reading. For example, the student who wanted to know about the cost of horses may find that the selection contained very little information about current costs and that she needs to go to the classified section of a newspaper in order to find current prices. Again, if the procedure is being used in small groups or by the whole class, individual students are encouraged to create their own lists of what they learned and what they still want to learn and to pursue additional reading in order to gain the information they are seeking.

Reciprocal Teaching

Reciprocal Teaching, developed by Palincsar and Brown (1984), is a small-group procedure in which students work together to learn how to actively glean meaning from informational texts. The procedure employs five strategies: reading, generating questions, clarifying issues, summarizing, and making predictions. At first, the teacher or some other more experienced reader serves as the leader of the group, taking the primary role in carrying out the strategies and modeling them for others in the group. The central purpose of the strategy, however, is to get all students actively involved in using the strategies. Thus, from the beginning, responsibility is increasingly handed over to the students in the group, and eventually students work without the aid of the teacher.

Reading. The text is divided into short segments, initially a paragraph or so in length, and the leader reads the first segment aloud.

Questioning. Once the segment has been read, the leader or other group members generate several questions prompted by the passage just read, and members of the group answer the questions. For example, after reading the opening paragraph of Seymour Simon's *Oceans,* one question a student might ask is, "How is the earth different from any other planet in the solar system?" to which another student might respond, "It's the only planet with water on its surface."

Clarifying Issues. If the passage or questions produce any problems or misunderstandings, the leader and other group members clarify matters. For example, in continuing to work with *Oceans,* a student might point out that the earth is different from other planets in a number of ways. Other members of the group might agree, but then point out that the book's topic is oceans and therefore the presence of water is being emphasized, not planets.

Summarizing. After all the questions have been answered and any misunderstandings have been clarified, the leader or other group members summarize the segment.

Predicting. Based on the segment just read, segments that have preceded it, and the discussion thus far, the leader or other group members make predictions about the contents of the upcoming section. The sequence of reading, questioning, clarifying, summarizing, and predicting is then repeated with subsequent sections.

Reciprocal Teaching is one of several sequences of strategies that center on collaborative work. For recent information on Reciprocal Teaching and for information on two other collaborative strategies—Questioning the Author and Collaborative Reasoning—you may want to read Palincsar (2003).

The SQ3R Method

The SQ3R Method was originally described by Robinson in 1946 and is probably the best known and most frequently recommended sequence of strategies for use in content-area classes. The sequence consists of five steps: surveying, questioning, reading, reciting, and reviewing. This sequence is certainly not something students should use with all material, and it is probably more appropriate for seventh and eighth graders than for fourth and fifth graders. However, for serious study of informational material students want to learn and remember, it is a very useful technique.

Surveying. The first step of the SQ3R method is to survey the article or chapter, considering the title, introductory paragraphs, headings and subheadings, and concluding paragraphs. Any graphic overview and other pictorial information should also be surveyed. As a result of their survey, students should have a good idea of what types of information the selection contains and how it is organized.

Questioning. The second step is to return to the first section of the selection and formulate a question that is likely to be answered in that section. If the selection contains section headings, then this step consists largely of turning the headings into questions. The purpose of posing questions is to focus students' attention and give them a definite purpose for reading.

Reading. The third step is to read the first section, attempting to answer the question posed. If that question is not answered in the section, then students need to formulate another one and answer it.

Reciting. The fourth step is to recite the answer to the question posed. If possible, the question should be answered in the students' own words and without looking back at the selection. At least with difficult or lengthy material, it is a good idea to have students write out their answers. After questioning, reading, and reciting with

Teaching Idea 5.3
Eliciting Students' Knowledge about Comprehension and Study Strategies

The noted psychologist David Ausabel once said this about teaching and learning. "If I were to reduce the whole of educational psychology to a single statement it would be this: Ascertain what the child knows and teach accordingly." This is extremely good advice; it is advice that is particularly important when working with children from other cultures and whose native language is not English; and it is advice that we would also give. One of the best ways to ascertain what students know is to ask them. Get together with a small group of middle-grade students and talk with them about what they know about the K-W-L Procedure, Reciprocal Teaching, SQ3R, or other comprehension and study strategies. If it is not possible to get together with middle-grade students, talk to a group of your classmates instead.

the first section of the selection, students repeat these steps with each of the remaining sections.

Reviewing.   The last step is to review the material learned, that is, again answer the questions posed. This should initially be done as soon as the article or chapter is concluded. Then, in order for the material learned to be remembered over time, it should be periodically reviewed. Teaching Idea 5.3 suggests one way of finding out what students know about various strategies.

Teaching Sequences of Strategies

We recommend that these sequences of strategies be taught using the same procedure that we described for teaching individual strategies. Initially, teach each of them in a fairly concentrated unit in which teaching the strategy is the main order of business. Begin with explicit instruction to the class as a whole or a relatively large group of students. Provide motivation, explain the strategies, model them, solicit student participation from the large group and provide mediation as necessary, have students practice them in pairs or small groups, and have the small groups share their work and again provide mediation as necessary. Finally, gradually give students the responsibility for using the strategies independently and provide periodic review and encouragement to use the strategies in a variety of authentic situations.

Pause and Reflect 5.3

In our Concluding Remarks section, we note that determining just which strategies to teach and when to teach them is something you will need to decide because of differences in students, schools, and curricula. However, assume for the moment that you can decide on which strategies to teach and when to teach them. List those you would teach at each of grades 4 through 8 and explain why you chose each of them. ∎

Concluding Remarks

Reading-comprehension strategies are "conscious and flexible plans that readers apply and adopt to a variety of texts and tasks" (Pearson et al., 1992). Study strategies are similar but focus more on learning and remembering information from text. There are a dozen or so comprehension and study strategies that are particularly worthwhile for students. The approach we recommend for teaching these strategies is a constructivist version of direct explanation: This approach includes an explicit description of the strategy and when and how it should be used, teachers and students modeling the strategy and using it together, guiding students as they practice with the strategy, and gradually releasing responsibility for independent use of the strategy to students. In addition to individual strategies, there are several sequences of strategies that deserve instruction. These include the K-W-L Procedure, Reciprocal Teaching, and SQ3R.

The information presented in the chapter provides you with a powerful approach to teaching strategies, but one very important task remains: You need to decide which strategies to teach. Which strategies you teach will, in some cases, be determined by your school's curriculum. More often, however, identifying strategies to teach will be left up to you. In this case, we have a definite recommendation: Teach a few strategies well rather than many strategies less well. Comprehension strategies are complex procedures and they need to be learned well if they are to be of real use to students. Teaching either one or two strategies a year is a reasonable goal. In choosing which one or two to teach, we suggest that you teach those that your students appear ready to learn and that can be used frequently in dealing with the selections students read in your classes.

This brings us to the crucial matter of who should have the responsibility of initially teaching strategies. That could be the reading teacher or the language arts teacher, or it could be a shared responsibility of teachers in several content areas. Whoever gets the assignment, the initial instruction must be robust, and followup and review activities need to occur in all content areas. If comprehension strategies are going to be used in all content areas, and they certainly should be, then they need to be encouraged and reviewed in all content areas.

Whatever strategies you teach and wherever they are taught, remember that learning the strategy itself is not the primary goal of strategy instruction. Comprehension strategies are the means to an end—the end being students understanding, enjoying, and remembering what they read.

■ EXTENDING LEARNING

1. One very useful experience that will help you understand and appreciate the nature of good comprehension strategy instruction is to observe a teacher who is doing an excellent job of teaching comprehension strategies. The first task here, of course, is to identify such a teacher, and we cannot be of a lot of assistance in helping you do so. However, we can and do suggest that you make every attempt to locate an effective strategy instructor and then observe him or her teaching and afterwards talk to him or her about her teaching. Potential

sources for locating teachers are your university instructor, your cooperating teacher, other teachers you know, and your classmates.

2. A second useful experience in coming to really understand strategy instruction is to study quality materials that are used in teaching strategies. One very strong program for teaching comprehension strategies, and a program very much in keeping with that described here, is titled *Making Meaning* (Developmental Studies Center, 2003). *Making Meaning* teaches most of the strategies described in this chapter and provides program information and teaching materials for grades K–6, with two volumes devoted to each grade level. We recommend that you get a copy of Volume 1 (which contains both a general overview of the program and a number of specific lessons) for grade 4, 5, or 6. Once you do, study it carefully, and compare the instruction suggested there to that suggested in this chapter. You will find a lot of similarities, but you will also find some differences. Also, you will be able to examine a number of specific examples of the concepts discussed in this chapter.

   Another set of professionally prepared materials you might like to take a look at is *Reading Explorations* published by PLATO Learning (2002). *Reading Explorations* is a reading comprehension strategies program for fourth- through sixth-grade students presented on an interactive CD. Eight of the nine strategies discussed in this chapter are taught. The instruction is fairly brief. Also, there are limits to what can be done on a computer: Most notably, unlike a skilled teacher, a computer cannot listen to students' responses, figure out just what they need, and provide it. Still, you will certainly gain some insights about teaching strategies from examining the program.

3. Probably the best single experience you could have in order to fully understand and appreciate the nature of good comprehension strategy instruction is to prepare a short unit of strategy instruction and actually present it to a class. If you do so, we recommend that you choose something simple—perhaps the Questioning step of Reciprocal Teaching or the Surveying step of SQ3R—and teach it in a 2- to 4-day unit. If possible, get someone to observe and critique your unit, and whether or not you can get an observer, be sure to critique it yourself and reflect on what when well, what did not go as well, and what you learned from the experience. Admittedly, this is a very difficult assignment that demands a lot of your time and an available classroom. But it will be a powerful learning experience and well worth the time and effort you expend.

■ BOOKS FOR MIDDLE-GRADE READERS

Atkin, S. B. (1993). *Voices from the field: Children of migrant farmworkers tell their stories.* New York: Little, Brown.

Glover, L. A. (2004). *On pointe.* New York: Margaret K. McElderry Books.

Jones, C. F. Illus. by John O'Brien. (1991). *Mistakes that worked.* New York: Doubleday.

London, J. (1998). *The call of the wild; White fang, and To build a fire.* New York: Modern Library.

Meltzer, M. (2001). *Case closed: The real scoop on detective work.* New York: Orchard Books.

Meyers, W. D. (2004). *USS Constellation: Pride of the American Navy.* New York: Holiday.

Simon, S. (1990). *Oceans.* New York: Morrow.

Chapter

6

Teaching Literature

Sharing books by reading and talking together promotes engaged reading.

A group of seventh-grade students, two boys and five girls, are sitting around a table, talking. Their classmates are doing the same at five other tables, and the room is noisy, but not chaotic, while students discuss Richard Peck's *The River Between Us*. It seems, from the conversation, that this was a thought-provoking and popular choice. Adam comments on how the book moved from a World War I setting to the Civil War and back again. Tia agrees that it was a bit confusing at first, but they all agree that they thought that Peck's setting changes were effective. Tia comments, "But I did love the end, you know, finding out about Howard's real grandparents and all that. That was really cool the way he did that."

Mary agrees, adding, "It was a real surprise, but then it made you think back about what happened to the characters and how it made a difference if they were black or white. And then the end makes you think, so what? Why does it matter so much anyway?"

The group goes on to talk about race and the way concerns about race influence the lives they lead, the things that happen in school, and even racial profiling by police, a current topic in local newspapers and on local radio and television talk shows. After small-group discussion time, Ms. Paul, the teacher, spends the last few minutes of class asking about the discussions of each group, and posing ideas for the class as a whole to consider. One group discloses that they talked about how sometimes books make you question things you thought you knew, and Ms. Paul repeats their idea, then asks the students to consider the question, What are books for?, as they write in their journals, promising that they'll talk more about this tomorrow.

Although not all of them are fluent, grade-level readers, these students are engaged, motivated readers who have spent time reading and talking about a book. They have written responses as they read, had several small-group discussions, done some written exercises that their teacher has given them, and have just finished the story, listening as their teacher read the last chapter aloud, following along in their own copies. Because they are used to thinking and talking about literature and have done so as a group for the preceding 5 months, they are comfortable sharing their ideas. Today the group took a major step; they moved from a consideration of an individual book, to thinking about literature as a whole. Their perceptive teacher seized on their comments to pose a big question for them to consider: How do we use literature? What function does it serve?

How *do* we use literature? As discussed in Chapter 1, people used to think that literature was there for readers to read carefully enough to discover the author's intended meaning, but now it is clear that readers bring a great deal of themselves to the act of creating meaning with the text. The students in Ms. Paul's classroom, like students in thousands of other classrooms, were aesthetically engaged with a well-told story, reading it in the company of others, and thus able to talk with others about the meanings they were creating. They were also using the story to transform the way they think about the world. Although Ms. Paul shaped and guided their experiences with this story, she did so with care, leaving a great deal of room for them to respond in their own way, and to respond over time as they worked together to absorb Richard Peck's words and ideas and construct from them their own literary experience.

When you teach from the perspective of transactional theory, as Ms. Paul does, you offer students the opportunity to engage with texts, work as active readers, and transform their ideas. Simultaneously, you develop engaged, responsive readers. The freedom to guess, to pursue ideas, to follow hunches, and to present partially formed thoughts helps students learn how to read with gusto and pleasure. Knowing that they won't be wrong, that there is no single right answer, frees students from the constraint of having to understand a particular text just as the teacher understands it. This freedom, coupled with the need to think about their reading that comes with it, encourages students to be engaged readers.

In this chapter we consider how to develop engaged, responsive readers through sharing good books and setting tasks that ask students to think about what they read. We discuss the role of peers in a response-centered classroom, and how discussion and other oral language activities such as drama play a central role in the development of a community of readers. We then present ideas for helping students develop their literary understanding by helping them make connections between books and their lives, as well as across books. We close with suggestions for helping students learn about nonfiction, narrative fiction, and poetry.

Developing Engaged Readers

Engaged readers are knowledgeable about books because they have had many opportunities to explore books. Readers need multiple experiences with books that will entice them. In Chapter 3 we discuss how to select adolescent literature to foster engaged, responsive reading. Selection is, however, only the beginning. Just as students need many good books from which to choose, they need time to browse—to dip into books and to talk with more knowledgeable others, both teachers and peers, about the opportunities that good books offer. They need time to engage in reading, thinking about and responding to books in the company of others. In *You Gotta BE the Book*, Wilhelm (1997) describes the powerful results that engagement in reading can create with both fluent and struggling readers. This kind of teaching demands a focus on the students themselves—what they are doing or not doing as they read—and an unwavering belief that all students can be engaged readers, if they know what the rewards are.

Sharing Good Books

Good readers know how to select books that they can read and enjoy. These readers understand what they like and how to find it. Usually, they frequent the library, have books at home, and have read widely. This experience allows them to make good decisions when they select books to read. Even these good readers, however, need help when selecting books, especially when they've reached adolescence and can stand in the middle of a well-stocked library and complain that there "aren't any good books" to read! Reluctant readers generally do not have experience in selecting books, and often need help finding a book that they can be successful with and can enjoy. Help for both kinds of readers can come from teachers who have an extensive knowledge of adolescent literature, and of their students. When you know your students, their interests, experiences, and abilities, then you can suggest books that might engage them, and sometimes you might be right. It's difficult to select a book for another person, but offering an array of books increases the chances that any given reader will find something of interest, especially when those books are both well-written and compelling.

Well-written books are important for several reasons, not the least of which is that they are also often the most interesting. Second, hearing and reading well-written text allows adolescents to develop both their oral and written language. The language in books is carefully structured and infinitely varied; thus students are exposed to a wider range of well-crafted language than they would encounter in the classroom or at home. All students, including English-language learners, benefit from reading well-written books. Third, the ideas in books also provide students opportunities for thinking about their world in new ways, and from new perspectives. The opportunity to participate in the experiences that literature brings them also increases students' schemata for viewing the world and learning. The more ideas and experiences they are exposed to, the more they have to bring to their classroom experiences.

Compelling literature—stories, poems, and nonfiction that capture the imagination and stir the soul—creates in students a desire to read. Wanting to know what happens to a character, making the echoes of a poem a part of our own memories, or being fascinated by a vividly described bit of reality all propel readers to read and read more. Books that present ideas, issues, and information that interests adolescents, that invite engagement, discussion, and even argument, help to create avid readers.

Giving book talks, in which teachers or students promote a book by describing what they found compelling about the text without giving away too much of the content, is one way to introduce students to books. Effective procedures for doing this are described in Teaching Idea 6.1. Creating a book review file is another. Biographical information followed by brief, one- or two-line comments can be put on index cards and filed in some meaningful organization. If you have classroom access to a computerized data base, use that. When students are at a loss for something to read, they can browse through the review file, reading the comments of others until they find something that looks interesting to them. Each subsequent reader adds comments.

As we discuss in Chapter 2, reading aloud is also a very effective means of getting students engaged in reading and introducing them to books that they might otherwise miss. Effective teachers read aloud for a few minutes each day. Hearing a fluent reader reading with emotion and expression helps students to engage with the text; it might also be the only model of fluent reading that students have the opportunity to experience. Reading aloud is an effective way to introduce an author, genre, theme, idea, or concept. Many teachers have developed a collection of picture books that allow them to introduce popular themes or teach particular literary concepts. Reference books such as *Using Picture Storybooks to Teach Literary Devices* (Hall, 1990) make it easy to locate these books. Poetry, of course, begs to be read aloud, and effective teachers do so frequently, not waiting to introduce poetry until National Poetry Month in April, but sharing it with their students frequently, if not daily. There are also a significant number of short story collections, such as those

Teaching Idea 6.1
Giving Book Talks

1. Select a small number of books—5 to 10— that you can talk about in 5 to 10 minutes. Make sure these are books that have a good chance of engaging your students, either by thinking about what you know about your students' reading preferences and interests, or by consulting the Young Adult Choices list in the November issue of the *Journal of Adolescent and Adult Literacy.*

2. Prepare a brief, less than 1-minute advertisement for the book. Make it enticing. Starting with "This is a book about . . ." is not enticing. Beginning with "Have you ever wondered about what it would be like to realize one day that you were a clone?" is enticing. Mention the main characters' ages and names, briefly describe the setting, if it's important to the story, and tell the main events of the plot, up to the climax. Be sure that you do not reveal the ending. Tape this brief talk, written out on a small index card if you need it, to the back cover of the book.

3. When you are ready to present your book talks, hold up each book, cover facing the students. Tell them the title and the author, linking it to other books by the same author or that connect in some way that they might have read. Then do your book talk and go on to the next book.

4. If you allow students time for questions at the end, be sure to hold up each book as they ask questions about it.

5. Be sure students know where to find the books you've just talked about.

listed in Chapter 3, that are aimed at an adolescent audience and allow teachers to introduce contemporary authors to students.

Some teachers begin a unit of study by reading aloud from a book or books that the class will be reading, asking students to read along in their own copies. Sometimes, reading a chapter or two aloud is enough to get students started reading on their own. At other times, you might decide you want to ensure that all of your students have the same reading experience—that is, hearing you read rather than reading themselves. In this case, you might want to read the entire book, having students follow along in their texts. For some, this is a wonderful opportunity to experience a text that might be too difficult to read alone. Of course students can do this by simply listening, but having a book in hand allows them to process the words as well. This is another positive aspect of reading aloud, as it allows students to share in a reading experience regardless of reading ability. This shared experience in the classroom is a resource that both students and teachers can draw from as they read, write, and talk about other books. A community of readers offers students the opportunity to enrich their own ideas and build on the experience of others.

Carefully selecting books that students are assigned is another opportunity to help students engage with reading. Assigned texts should serve a function. Perhaps you are selecting books to illuminate particular literary concepts, or to facilitate development of a theme the class is pursuing, or to provide opportunities for particular kinds of reading practices. Whatever the reason, books that are written with an adolescent audience in mind are often more effective at promoting engaged reading than are more classic, adult-oriented texts.

Pause and Reflect 6.1

Think about your favorite books, either current favorites or favorites from the middle grades. Why did you like them so much? How did you discover them? What did you do when you finished reading them? ■

Reading Good Books

Good books aren't enough. As we discuss in Chapter 2, time to read in class for a variety of purposes also promotes engaged, responsive reading. Giving students time to read, whether self-selected or assigned reading, provides time for them to get interested in what they read. Even 10 minutes can whet the appetite, and, once intrigued, students will find it easier to continue reading outside of the classroom. Students understand that teachers give time to the things they value. If you value reading, then demonstrate that by giving students time to read.

Having a balance between self-selected and teacher-selected reading is also important. Reading self-selected texts for individual purposes helps students make reading a part of their lives. In addition to asking students to read, helping them discover good books, and giving them time to read in class, by helping your students set goals for their independent reading and assess their reading experiences in light of those goals, you make their independent reading a more purposeful activity. So does asking your students to demonstrate their comprehension of the books they are reading independently, through a variety of activities that allow them to share their understanding with their peers. Without purposefulness, students can lose sight of why they are reading. Many teachers find that periodic book conferences, in which teacher and student sit down to discuss what the student is reading, helps them keep track of their students' progress, as we discuss in Chapter 9, and helps students do so as well.

Setting a quota of books to be read in a certain time frame isn't creating purposefulness. Rather, it often pushes readers toward books that don't challenge them in any way. Not surprisingly, students with a quota look for short books; they can read these books quickly. This doesn't help them learn to make good, deliberate choices, nor does it provide opportunities to really engage with what they are reading. Without goals and accountability, struggling readers might select books that are impossible for them to read and comprehend. These readers might look as if they're reading, and might even *be* reading, but they won't be getting as much value out of their independent reading experience as they could. An extrinsic reason for reading and understanding text can help students develop the habit of reading so that eventually their intrinsic motivation to read is all they need.

Figure 6.1 **Questions About Literature/Comprehension Strategies**

- **Predicting:** What do you think this book is about? What will happen next? What will X do to Y? How will Y feel? Who will solve the problem?
- **Interpreting/Inferring:** Why did X do that? How does X feel? Why does X feel this way? Why is the illustration the way it is?
- **Connecting:** What other story does this remind you of? Has anything like this ever happened to you? Do you ever feel this way? Do you remember when? Would you have acted like this? Felt like this?
- **Evaluating:** Should X have acted this way? Who was right, X or Y? Do the illustrations help to tell the story? What do you like/not like about the illustrations? What do the illustrations tell you? Does the author use interesting words? What do you like/not like about X? Why did this story make you feel this way?
- **Creating images:** What does it look like when X happens? How do you think Y looked just then? What does the setting look like?
- **Confirming:** Were you right when you were thinking about what would happen? Did X respond the way you thought X would?
- **Questioning:** Why do you think the author had X do this? Why was the story set in Y?
- **Summarizing:** What are the big ideas in the story?
- **Generalizing:** How do the big ideas relate to what you know about life? Do all people feel this way? Do all people act this way? If they did, what might the world be like?

Students need time to read assigned texts, as well. Time spent reading in class can become part of the rhythm of a school day or week, as it does in classrooms, like Ms. Paul's, that are organized around book clubs. In the Book Club approach to teaching reading using literature or trade books, the pattern is often that of (1) brief, direct instruction or demonstration by the teacher, followed by (2) time for reading, followed by (3) time for writing about what has been read (either free or guided response), followed by (4) time for talking in small groups (book clubs), followed by (5) whole-class discussion, sharing, and summarizing. We explore the opportunities that this structure brings in Chapter 10.

Reading Strategically

Comprehension and engaged reading go hand in hand. Not only do engaged readers know how to select books that they can read and enjoy, they are also strategic readers who know how to monitor their comprehension and apply strategies that enhance their understanding. Often, people think about comprehension as one dimension of reading and literary response as another, but this is not the case.

Higher-level questions, which we discuss in detail in Chapter 7, are those that require students to predict, construct images, monitor understanding, summarize, interpret, generalize, and connect with other knowledge and experience. They are questions that ask students to evaluate and generalize. In short, they are questions that ask students to think, not just memorize, and to which there are multiple right answers. These kinds of questions not only help students think about literature, but also use effective comprehension strategies. Figure 6.1 shows how questions about literature are, in fact, also sound comprehension questions.

Many descriptions of the processes that a reader employs during an aesthetic engagement with text include actions that reflect the employment of good comprehension strategies. For example, engaged, comprehending readers make predictions, revise hypotheses, form inferences, and create images, all of which describe readers who are engaged in the secondary world of story, connecting with characters, and creating a virtual experience that allows them to think about their lives. If they are reading expository nonfiction, they construct conceptual understanding by forming hypotheses and confirming or disconfirming them. In either case, they fold their reading into what they already know and have experienced.

Reading Responsively

Responsive readers understand their own responses, recognizing what aspects of a text trigger certain responses in themselves. Purves, Rogers, and Soter (1990, p. 31) suggest the following to teachers who want their students to become responsive readers:

- Provide students with as many different books as possible.
- Encourage students to respond to as many books as possible.
- Encourage students to respond as fully as they are able.
- Encourage students to understand why they respond as they do.
- Encourage students to tolerate responses that differ from theirs.
- Encourage students to explore agreement and disagreement in responses.

We have already discussed providing books and time. As transactional theory suggests, readers who are engaged with texts are actively working toward a point, if reading expository nonfiction, or evoking a secondary world of story, if reading narrative fiction. Good teaching helps students become more adept at these processes.

To become more adept, students need the opportunity for broad, unencumbered responses, or free response, in which they explore their often inchoate ideas in whatever fashion they care to. Asking them to think, talk, or write about "whatever they want to say" about a book gives them the opportunity to focus on whatever is most salient to them. Wilhelm (1997) argues that it is important that teachers ask students to not only think, talk, and write, but also to engage in artistic and dramatic responses. It is known that good readers visualize. Struggling readers, he found, often need to learn to visualize what they are reading. The teacher can tell them to, which doesn't do much good, or can structure opportunities for them to respond through art and drama that will allow them to literally see what they are reading.

What you choose to ask students to do will depend on your goals for the activity and the type of text your students are reading. Recall the differences between the way you read narrative fiction or poetry and the way you read expository nonfiction. Meaning in nonfiction, the presentation of information and concepts, is more easily verified and more widely shared than in narrative fiction or poetry. When you read nonfiction to discover the point, to take away information to use in the real world, then you are dealing with meaning that can be agreed on and verified with reference to the real world. If, for instance, you are reading a nonfiction book about the galaxies, the information presented in the book can be evalu-

Teaching Idea 6.2
Creating Varied Response Options

Through writing, such as:

- in a response journal to open-ended prompts such as, "What I noticed about this book was . . ." or "The question I'd most like to ask the author is. . . ."
- in a response journal to specific prompts that ask students to consider particular aspects of the book such as, "The reason the main character did [a particular action] is that . . ." or "If this story were told from the point of view of the brother it would change in the following ways. . . ."
- through writing a script for reader's theatre that allows only characters' dialogue and narrator's voice—no facial expressions or actions.

Through talking with peers about the book, such as:

- discussing reactions to events or characters
- sharing connections with other books
- sharing connections with life
- discussing confusions and asking for clarifications

- reliving the text by retelling parts that especially affected the readers
- planning for reader's theatre, drama, or choral reading

Through drama and choral reading activities that ask for:

- recreation of a scene
- invention of dialogue
- extending the action beyond the story boundaries
- interpretating a poem or event through creative oral reading

Through visual art such as:

- reflecting the mood through painting
- illustrating a chapter or scene through painting
- creating a collage that reflects student response
- creating cutouts and using them to retell parts of the story

ated against known facts and other sources, author qualifications can be checked, and judgments about clarity and organization can be made. If, on the other hand, you are reading a science fiction novel from an aesthetic stance, open to an "horizon of possibilities" (Langer, 1995) that you know to be fictional, to be plausible but not actual, then your response can be much more idiosyncratic. Activities and tasks that follow the reading of fiction and poetry therefore have to be more open-ended, to accommodate the secondary worlds that readers are creating. Other open-ended questions such as "What does this book remind you of," "How does this story make you feel," or "What is most important about this text," offer students the opportunity to respond freely within a given framework. Other activities and tasks, such as those in Teaching Idea 6.2, offer more opportunities for response.

When reading and responding in the aesthetic vein, Benton and Fox (1985, p. 18) suggest giving middle-grade students a series of questions that push them to articulate their thinking as they read, beginning with the basic question: "What is going on in your head while you are reading (or listening, or viewing)?" Then, working within the framework of processes including picturing, anticipation and retrospection, interaction, and evaluating, he suggests the following as prompts or questions:

- What pictures do you get in your mind when . . .
- How did these present circumstances arise?
- What do you think will happen next and why?
- How do you think it will all end?
- What do you feel about this character/setting/event?
- What/how do you feel about the way the story is being told?

When these questions and others like them are used as writing prompts, they allow students to explore their own understanding before sharing it with others. Writing before discussing can help students discover what they think, and give them something interesting and at least partly articulated to bring to the conversation.

Many teachers find it most effective to ask students to respond in writing on a regular basis. These responses might be guided by questions or formats that you require, or be more open-ended. Writing, even briefly, after reading gives students time to articulate their thoughts, to pose questions, make judgments, and speculate. While keeping a response journal for every book that is read can soon become an onerous task and certainly discourages students from reading quickly, asking students to write in a variety of ways as they respond to what they read, and giving them time to do so in class as well as at home, exposes them to new ways of thinking about books even as it allows them to use writing to learn.

Simultaneously with asking students to tell what they are thinking and feeling, effective teachers also encourage them to explain their answers: What is it in the text that makes you think this? Whether students have read fiction or nonfiction, this return to the text to support personal opinions, ideas, guesses, and hunches helps students understand their own responses, and why they respond as they do. It also offers them the opportunity to share those responses with others, to discuss, argue, and learn from and with their peers.

Pause and Reflect 6.2

The next time you read a book or poem, write down what you are thinking and feeling as you read. You can do this whenever a thought or feeling occurs during reading, or wait until you finish reading a section or chapter. Then read over your responses and look back at what you've just read. Think about what it was in the text that triggered a particular response. Then think about what it was in your life that caused you to respond as you did. ■

Developing a Community of Responsive Readers

Avid readers often talk about books with others, inquiring about what a friend, or even a stranger, is reading, sharing information about favorite books and authors with others. Students can do this in the classroom. Just as students will learn which of their peers shares their taste in books when they read the comments of others, so, too, will they learn from talking with others about books. Both formal and informal discussions of books offer opportunities for students to learn about authors and titles that they might enjoy. These discussions also offer students the opportunity to learn how to conduct literary conversations, and to learn how varied readers respond differently to the same text. These conversations also offer English-language learners the opportunity to use informal oral language, in either their first language or English, in a supportive context.

Through interaction with other readers, students learn to see the similarities and differences among responses. A classroom that reflects the principles of transactional theory is one in which students are as supportive of others' responses as they are secure about articulating their own responses. They learn to value the responses of others as a means of broadening and deepening their own. And they begin to understand how the texts they read allow both common and individual responses. This happens when students are taught how to have productive literary conversations, or discussions with their peers, and then allowed to have them on a regular basis.

Talking About Books

Talking about books is an important part of learning. The underlying social nature of reading and responding is built up through talk. Students learn more and have more ideas and opportunities for thinking about what they read when they talk about books with each other. These conversations can be one on one, in small groups, and with the whole class. Effective teachers usually provide opportunities for all, varying the structure to suit the task at hand.

Although most students are quite adept at having conversations with others, having a conversation about a school topic, in the classroom, and at a particular time, is not quite the same as casual conversation on the school bus or at home. The topic is academic, focused on a book; the classroom is a more formal place than most other venues that students encounter; and the discussion is usually bounded by time. Furthermore, over the years students have learned the artificial pattern of school discussions in which the teacher asks a question, a student responds either voluntarily or having been called upon, and the teacher evaluates the student's answer, then asks another question to continue the cycle. This recitation, referred to as the IRE pattern—initiation, response, evaluation—is controlled by the teacher (Cazden, 1988; Mehan, 1979). In fact, two of the three turns in this pattern are for the teacher. This does not resemble a conversation, and is not a true discussion, but this is what students have learned to expect. They need to be given both permission and guidance to have the kinds of conversations that lead to engaged, responsive reading. True conversations:

- focus on an idea that is truly open for discussion
- are open to all reasonable arguments
- are open to any participant who is open-minded
- have an open time limit, open outcomes, and open purposes and practices
- do not have to end with consensus (Dillon, 1984)

Although an open time limit is not possible in the confines of the school day, the other conditions for true discussion are attainable. In these conversations, teachers both *coach,* demonstrating to students the kinds of behaviors that are appropriate

Figure 6.2   **Guidelines for Effective Discussions**

Teacher behavior:

- Don't ask too many questions, and ask questions that are brief and clear. Spend more time listening than you spend talking.
- Wait at least 15 seconds after you have asked a question before you ask another. If you're asking questions that require students to think, they need time to do it.
- Listen to what the students are saying and ask questions that encourage them to expand on their answers.
- Ask questions that require students to infer, predict, hypothesize, evaluate, connect, and monitor their own understandings.
- When asking open-ended, higher-level questions, accept a variety of answers and encourage several students to respond to you and to each other.
- Give children the opportunity to ask their own questions, of you and of each other.

A middle-grade class developed the following guidelines for their own behavior after talking as a group about productive discussions, engaging in several large- and small-group discussions, and listening to one of their discussions that had been audiotaped. Their rules were:

- Ask real questions.
- Listen carefully to each other.
- Acknowledge what someone has just said instead of skipping over it.
- Don't laugh at different or unusual ideas.
- Be honest about your opinions.
- Stick to the subject.
- Talk to each other, not just to the teacher.

and effective, and *scaffold,* offering support for tentative ideas by requesting elaboration, summarizing students' comments, and asking students to respond to what their peers are saying (O'Flahavan, 1995). These discussions are marked by little teacher talk, with students talking to and with each other as they offer their ideas and opinions about what they are reading. When the teacher does talk, it's to help manage the conversation or ask a real question, one without a known answer. This reversal of teacher role, from authoritative interpreter to questioning reader, changes the tenor of the discourse.

Asking "Why did X do Y?" presupposes that the one right answer is knowable, and that you know it. Saying, instead, something like, "I've been wondering why X did Y. What do you think?" or even simply, "Why do *you* think X did Y?" signals to students that there are multiple answers to the question. Hynds (1992) points out the importance of asking real questions—questions that you can't answer. The talk then moves from a recitation of already known facts to an exploration of the horizon of possibilities, always returning to the text to support, refute, or amend answers. Real conversations about books can flourish when good questions are coupled with positive responses to thoughtful answers and invitations to other students to respond. (Hynds, 1992). Figure 6.2 presents some guidelines for good discussions that can help you and your students talk with each other, whether in pairs, small groups, or whole-class configurations.

Often teachers ease their students into book discussion groups by having whole-class discussions in which they model effective behaviors, comment on effective behaviors, and encourage students to think and talk about effective behaviors. For instance, in one of our own classes it became apparent that students—most of them with degrees in English—needed to learn how to have productive conversations about books. Guidelines, based on those developed by the Cooperative Children's Book Center at the University of Wisconsin, Madison, were distributed and posted; among them were the following dictates:

- Look at every book for what it *is*, rather than for what it is not.
- Make positive comments first. Try to express what you liked about the book and why.
- After everyone has had the opportunity to say what they appreciated about the book, talk about any difficulties you had with a particular aspect of the book. Try to express these difficulties as questions, or "I wonder" statements, rather than declarative judgments on the book as a whole.
- There is no single right answer or correct response.

Learning to approach a book for what it is, rather than for what the reader wanted it to be, allowed these skilled readers to read beyond their own personal preferences and understand and appreciate a wide variety of literature. These guidelines, modeled, pointed out, and insisted upon by the teacher, greatly improved the discussions.

When good discussion behavior is explicitly taught, students quickly come to understand exactly what they ought to do during a book discussion. Even so, many students need more structure, especially when they are beginning to work in small groups. In this case effective teachers set a task, an outcome, for groups to accomplish. Tasks should suit the material being read and discussed. They might range from an answer to a previously posed question, the development of a summary of important ideas or events, a description of character motivation, a prediction, a listing of important facts, or a graphic of underlying structure, to a dramatic sketch or choral reading. Whatever the task, having a focus helps students develop the habit of productive conversation about books.

Of course being able to stay on task, ask good questions, and listen respectfully to each other is not sufficient for good conversations to occur. Certainly the book under discussion needs to be a book worth talking about. Books for adolescents that explore problems that are important to adolescents abound, and selecting books that will provoke strong reactions is one way to ensure good conversations. But even with the best book, the best questions, and expert teacher guidance, sometimes conversational groups fail to work well together. Lewis (2001) reminds us that what students have to say and how they say it is profoundly influenced by their social context. Power relations within groups can silence some members while granting license to others. Sometimes groups have to be dissolved and reconstituted in order to allow access for all.

Furthermore, some students will simply not be comfortable talking in groups. Although small groups allow for more participation than whole-class discussion does, some students will continue to more fully reveal their responses in writing rather than orally. Even though they may not contribute to the conversation, however, doesn't mean that they are not learning as a result of the conversation. Sometimes an assignment that asks students to revisit an initial written response in light

Working together on choral reading gives students an opportunity to explore literature and engage in an important oral language activity.

of a subsequent discussion will allow you to see how discussion influences even the quiet onlookers.

Drama, Choral Reading, and Other Oral Presentations

Other activities that help students develop their responses in the company of their peers involve various types of presentations. Oral presentations, with or without the use of technology, drama, and choral reading, offer students the opportunity to build on their individual responses in a group situation that is focused on an organized outcome. These activities require sound understanding of text, careful planning, and the use of articulate and relatively formal talk to present ideas to others.

Oral presentations build on exploratory writing and discussion and require a more formal use of language to present. Both individuals and groups of students can plan and create oral presentations that allow them to present their ideas about what they have read. While poster board and markers are still effective visual prompts to such presentations, schools with adequate computer access can encourage students to work together to, for example, create a PowerPoint presentation, access websites for authors and share that information, or create other technologically enhanced ways of sharing books with others. New technologies offer engaging ways for students to go beyond the standard book report while also gaining experience in effective use of technological capabilities. Presentations are especially effective when sharing information gleaned from nonfiction texts in any curriculum area, benefiting both the presenter and the audience.

Activities such as drama and choral reading are also effective, as they require students to discuss a book or poem with a group of others in order to plan their pre-

Teaching Idea 6.3
Planning and Presenting Dramatic Enactments

Drama can be pantomime, in which meaning is conveyed solely through facial expressions, movements, and other body language. Students can re-enact a scene, following the text as exactly as they can. Students might do a dramatic reading, or interpretation of a story or scene. They can also venture into improvisation, going beyond the story line into supposition. They can also engage in role-playing, in which they assume a role and interact with others who are also in role. Whatever the choice of dramatic activity, students first need to:

- Reread the story or scene to be enacted, noting the sequence of events
- Discuss the personalities and motivations of the characters
- Decide how the characters might sound
- For improvisation and role playing, decide what kinds of things characters might do, based on the character traits they have identified

Finally, students:

- Present their drama to an appropriate audience

sentations. Thus students spend time talking about, for example, plot structure, character development and motivation, style, mood, tone, and meaning. Discussions of poetry often focus on the relationship between meaning and sound, and the way the poet has used poetic devices. Once planned, these activities are presented as a cooperative group with a common goal. Stronger readers support weaker ones and everyone has the opportunity to use language in a more formal fashion. These activities also support English-language learners as they learn the vocabulary, syntax, and rhythm of a story or poem through repeated practice in a supportive environment (Fergusun & Young, 1996; McCauley & McCauley, 1992). Teaching Idea 6.3 presents steps for groups of students planning dramatic enactments. We discuss choral reading in Teaching Idea 3.3. In these activities, students are using oral language to learn with and from each other, as they are learning about literature and how it works.

Developing Literary Understanding

Engaged readers in a transactional classroom also develop in literary understanding (Purves, Rogers, & Soter, 1990). Students learn to consider how all sorts of books work—structures, genre characteristics, and literary devices—as they are developing an awareness of style and voice, mood and tone. Through wide reading they also develop an awareness of literature as a whole, as an art. Creating connections among the books they read allows them to understand the intertextuality that supports literature even as they are learning how to make similar connections between literature and their own lives.

This kind of classroom is created when students have (1) opportunities for broad, unencumbered literary experiences that result in their own personal responses (reading without an assignment to produce something in particular); and (2) a teacher who guides their reading and responses, helping them comprehend text, see patterns, make connections, draw conclusions, relate literature to their own lives, and read and respond critically. Both unencumbered and guided reading and responding are supported by reading, writing about, and talking about texts with both peers and teachers.

Making Connections

Helping students make intertextual connections among books and between books and their own lives is a powerful way of helping them see the value of literature in their lives. It often takes only a few questions or activities that ask students to make these connections for intertextuality to become a frequent focus of thought and conversation. There are several kinds of intertextual connections that readers make: text to text, life to text, and text to life.

Demonstrating how you make connections among texts by mentioning other books that you have read, either as a class or as an individual reader, that are similar to or different from the current book in some way helps students see that effective readers do make connections among texts. If you have organized your curriculum around themes, concepts, or genres, and if you are reading aloud to your class, these intertextual connections are easy and natural to make. Asking students questions that nudge them to think of other texts encourages them to develop the habit of doing so.

The same is true for making connections with their own lives. A bit of talk about your own connections to your own experiences, or tasks that ask students to do the same help them think about their literary experiences in light of their lived experiences, and to think about their life experiences in light of knowledge and insights gained through reading. This is what Langer (1995) describes engaged readers doing when they step out of their reading to think about life. Students understand and respond to texts through their own experience, and it's important to help them understand that their sense of who they are influences what they think as they read. Engagement with fictional narratives and poetry offers students opportunities to rethink their lived experiences, considering them in new ways because of their encounters with books. Engagement with nonfiction allows students to evaluate new knowledge in light of what they already know, and to increase their personal storehouse of knowledge about the world. This is the transforming power of literary experience—the chance to think about beliefs, values, attitudes, opinions, and understandings in relation to what we are reading.

Other Ways to Learn about Literature

What else can middle-grade students learn about literature? By the time they get to the middle grades, many students, those who have been in literature-rich classrooms in the primary grades, actually know a great deal about literature, but often don't know how to articulate it. They are positioned to learn how books work and how to think and talk about what authors do. Readers begin in what Early (1960) called "unconscious enjoyment," easily delighting in their encounters with books. Sometime during the middle grades, students develop "self-conscious appreciation" (Early) of the literature they read. They have an increased understanding of characters and their motivations, cause-and-effect structures in plots, various kinds of conflicts, and an increased interest in language. Thus the middle grades are the perfect time to help young readers begin to move toward "conscious delight" (Early), in which they come to understand why they respond as they do, are able to articulate how literature works, and begin to expand their reading repertoire beyond earlier, safe boundaries.

The focus of your students' literary learning will depend on the demands of the curriculum or, if you have the freedom to choose, what you think your students need to know. If you see that they are responding positively to books with especially engaging characters, then you might want to focus on how authors develop characters. Selection depends on the focus of instruction, perhaps literary elements such as strong settings, metaphoric language, or a particularly effective expository structure. Beach (1997) suggests that, along with engagement with text and making connections, teachers might want to ask their students to describe aspects of text such as characters or style, to interpret symbols, characters' actions or intentions, and themes, and to judge the characters as well as the quality of the text. Activities that ask students to do these tasks help them become more deeply involved with what they read and push them to reflect on their reading experience.

Many teachers chose to structure their teaching through a focus on literary genres, and connect their reading and writing instruction through genre study. Buss and Karnowski's *Reading and Writing Literary Genres* (2000) offers good suggestions for working with upper elementary and early middle-school students in this manner. Studying the defining aspects of a particular genre and some of the exemplary works within the genre acquaints students with literary structures and conventions, allows them to compare texts and consider judgments in light of genre conventions, and to build their knowledge of the world of literature. In Chapter 3 we define and describe the genres and subgenres that make up adolescent literature.

Middle-grade students are ready to build on their tacit knowledge of genres, figuring out the rules that govern each genre, and how genres differ from one another. Genre study can help students increase the breadth of their literary experience, introducing them to books they might not read otherwise because they prefer a different genre. It can also help them understand why they have the preferences they have and why they respond as they do. Genre study is easily linked to writing; as students are engaged in studying the attributes of a particular type of text, they can be encouraged to experiment with those attributes in their own writing.

Genre study may be especially important in relation to nonfiction. Most of the writing that students are required to do as they progress through school is expository, and because of a school literary diet that is usually primarily narrative, students have fewer good models on which to base their knowledge of effective expository writing. Studying how various writers convey information can help students learn techniques that will benefit them as they write themselves.

Author study, or an in-depth exploration of a particular author's craft, also links reading and writing. Individuals or small groups of students can select an author of interest, or the teacher can focus on one author with the whole class. For example, the teacher might read aloud from *Roll of Thunder, Hear My Cry,* Mildred Taylor's Newbery Award–winning saga of the life of an African American family in

Mississippi during the Great Depression. Small groups could be reading different books by Taylor that also chronicle the life of the Logan family. Some writing and discussion prompts, whole-class lessons, and assignments can focus on Taylor as an author, who she is as a storyteller, how she writes, why her writing is effective, and how her work is distinct from the work of others.

Whatever you choose to focus on, you can plan reading experiences and written tasks and activities that add to the more open-ended experiences that you offer students, giving students prompts for writing in response logs that ask them to explore what you want them to notice. You can give them discussion prompts that focus them on particular topics and ideas in small group-discussions, even as you plan questions for whole-class discussion that lead your students to a greater understanding of literature.

Activities and tasks that ask students to explore how literature works not only teach them about literature, but also help them discover what it is about particular books that engages or confuses them, what they like and dislike, and what authors do to guide and constrain their readers. This kind of work can also open new worlds of reading for students as they discover new interests, new authors, and new genres.

Teaching Nonfiction

Students might know when a piece of nonfiction is clearly organized, but they might not be able to tell you how the facts are arranged to form a concept, how the illustrations illuminate facts and concepts, or how the author's direct address to the reader engages interest. By systematically noticing and evaluating the accuracy, organization, design, and style of nonfiction texts, students can become more critical consumers of the information presented in these texts. Reading nonfiction offers a perfect opportunity to teach students how to detect bias, compare the quality of information across texts and authors, and to recognize the difference between fact and opinion. Reading nonfiction also offers opportunities for teaching and employing comprehension strategies that are especially relevant to reading expository nonfiction. Working in the classroom with some of the many outstanding examples of nonfiction that are available today can also help students develop a taste for excellence and a more selective stance. Content-area teachers who use appropriate nonfiction to supplement the textbook can do the same, using this as an opportunity to help students become both more adept readers and more critical consumers of information in the particular content area.

There are many ways to approach exploring nonfiction with middle-grade students. One of the prime considerations is to find nonfiction that engages readers. This is actually more difficult to do than selecting narrative fiction or poetry because engagement with nonfiction seems to be closely linked to personal interest. Not surprisingly, students who are interested in a particular topic are more likely to enjoy reading about that topic than are students who are not interested in the topic. However, there is a plethora of nonfiction picture books that are brief, visually and verbally engaging, and easy to understand; you can use these initially to help students understand what questions to ask and how to evaluate nonfiction texts. There are

Students learn a great deal about the world around them when they read the engaging nonfiction that is available to them.

also professional resources that will give you ideas about activities as well as exemplary titles to explore, such as Bamford and Kristo's *Making Facts Come Alive: Choosing Quality Nonfiction Literature K–8* (1998) and noted nonfiction writer Milton Meltzer's powerful *Nonfiction for the Classroom: On Writing, History, and Social Responsibility* (1994).

Content-area teachers who use nonfiction are also concerned with finding engaging books, but have the added challenge of finding those specific books that match the topics in their curriculum. School and public libraries have reference materials such as *Children's Books in Print* that are arranged by subject. *The Horn Book Guide,* published biannually, reviews virtually all new books published each year, listing nonfiction by discipline (social sciences, language, science, history, etc.) and by topic (astronomy, botany, immigration, modern history, etc.) within each discipline. Resources such as these make it easy to find books that might fit students' needs within any content area.

Language arts and content-area teachers who work with nonfiction find that an interesting classroom activity is to compare expository nonfiction with narrative nonfiction. In the past 10 years, narrative nonfiction has increased in availability. This type of nonfiction capitalizes on young readers' interest in and familiarity with narrative structure and uses a narrative frame to present information. Unlike narrative fiction, however, the primary aim of narrative nonfiction is the presentation of information and the development of concepts and understanding. *Expository* nonfiction, on the other hand, uses a more traditional expository structure to present information and guide the reader in building concepts. Comparing these two very distinct structures in terms of effectiveness, accuracy, and scope can help students develop their critical reading ability.

Teaching Narrative Fiction

Students often come to the middle grades well aware of how stories work. For years, they have been talking about what happened in a story, who it happened to, and, perhaps, why. They are more than ready to look closely at many aspects of narrative fiction. They can consider character development, exploring how an author creates characters that are so vivid that they seem real, using the tool of literary language. Students are also ready to read and explore plot structures that are more complex than the temporal sequences of events that mark most narrative fiction for younger readers. Parallel plots, flashbacks, and open-ended structures are well-represented in fiction for adolescents. Middle-grade readers can also consider the unity of character and action—how who a character is influences the events of the story which, in turn, influence the development of the character. Middle-grade students can explore the author's style, looking at structural patterns, word choice, figurative language, and rhythm. They can consider point of view and how that influences their responses. They can discuss the mood and tone of a piece of fiction, and the voice in which it is written. They can explore whether and how setting is integral to a story, and how an author makes a setting come alive.

The first step in deciding what to teach is to look at the literature you are using, and to read it with an eye to what the author does well. Peterson and Eeds (1990) suggest that when teachers focus on literary elements as they read, they are better equipped to build on tentative understandings that their students might advance in discussions. They are also better equipped to develop discussion questions and response prompts that will help students learn how texts work. As you read, ask yourself about the character development, plot structure, unity of character and action, role of setting, point of view, stylistic devices, and mood and tone of the piece—and take notes about what you notice. This will enable you to respond to questions and comments that students might put forth during discussions. You also can create some open-ended questions that ask students to notice the most notable aspects of the writing. Keep track of the terms you are using, perhaps on a chart or an overhead, as you talk about books, and create a literary glossary with your students, complete with definitions and examples from your reading. Using picture storybooks can also help you highlight literary devices. It is often easier to recognize and understand how these devices work in the relatively short texts of picture storybooks than in longer texts.

Along with learning about the literary devices that authors employ to create narrative fiction, middle-grade students can also begin to explore some basic literary theories and critical perspectives that allow them to understand texts in a particular way. Soter's excellent book, *Young Adult Literature and the New Literary Theories: Developing Critical Readers in Middle School* (1999), offers clear descriptions of basic theoretical perspectives followed by extended examples of response to particular texts. Appleman's book, *Critical Encounters in High School English* (2004), while focused on the teaching of English in grades 9–12, offers excellent suggestions that can be adapted for the middle grades.

Thinking about text in terms of its literary qualities, as described above, arises from *rhetorical criticism*, which considers how readers, texts, and authors work in relation to one another (Soter, 1999). Considerations of how an author develops a character, uses a particular point of view, or structures a plot—and how this, in turn, influences a reader—arise from the rhetorical tradition and are frequent in contemporary middle-grade classrooms. Other critical perspectives on texts allow students to begin to understand the complexities that surround the writing, reading, and marketing of books.

Psychological criticism is focused on the motivations and relationships involved in writing and reading a text. Questions about character motivations, intentions of the writer, and relations between characters and reader all explore literature from a psychological perspective. Exploring a text in this fashion allows students to think about what they are reading in a new way. The same is true for approaching texts through *feminist* and *cultural* critical perspectives. Considering how being a woman influences both the reading and writing of texts, how males and females are presented in a text, and how the author writes from a masculine or feminine perspective helps students see texts in light of gender.

Cultural criticism can also be introduced to middle-grade readers through questions about authenticity in the representation of particular cultures. Conflict or consonance between readers' values and the cultural values presented in a book help students begin to consider how cultural knowledge and dispositions affect the writing and reading of books. Cultural criticism has become particularly important as our access to a rich array of culturally diverse books has increased. These books often challenge the stereotypes and beliefs of readers, creating a resistance to the experience that is presented (Beach, 1997), yet it is crucial that students read and think about books that reflect the diverse cultures that make up the fabric of North America and the world (Galda & Cullinan, 2002, 2006). Cultural criticism gives teachers and students another tool with which to explore response.

The ways to approach teaching narrative fiction are almost as varied as the fiction itself, and many books offer excellent suggestions. *Teaching Literature in Middle School: Fiction,* is part of the Standards Consensus Series published by the National Council of Teachers of English (1996). This useful volume is a collection of previously published material, mostly from a database of classroom-practice materials, that relate to teaching to state standards regarding narrative fiction.

Teaching Poetry

Most middle-grade students have had experience with poetry units across their school careers, and it is beneficial to set aside a particular block of time in order to explore poetry as a genre, but it is equally important to treat poetry as part of the fabric of everyday classroom life. Many effective teachers read poetry aloud frequently, casually discussing poetic devices that create particular effects and linking how a poem sounds to what it means. When the focus then turns to poetry and how it works, students can build on this experience with poetry and its vocabulary.

Effective teachers link poetry study across reading, writing, and oral language opportunities, gathering poems that feature a focal poetic element or form (see Chapter 3) and exploring those poems as a class by posting the poem on an overhead and discussing it. Asking, "What do you notice in this poem?" is a good way to get students engaged in discussing a poem, and easily leads to a more focused, teacher-directed discussion. After the class discussion, students can be encouraged to find other poems that are examples of the focus of the lesson, to copy them into poetry journals or to share them with others. They can also be challenged to try to write a poem that displays the particular qualities or techniques they have been discussing. Often, a choral reading experience, described in Chapter 3, allows students to explore how a poem's sound relates to meaning, and is a powerful aspect of poetry study. Sloan's (2003) *Give Them Poetry! A Guide for Sharing Poetry with Children K-8*, Heard's (1998) *Awakening the Heart: Exploring Poetry in Elementary and Middle School*, and Livingston's (1991) *Poem-Making: Ways to Begin Writing Poetry* are among the many excellent resources for teachers planning a study of poetry.

Concluding Remarks

Teaching literature is a complex, exciting, and sometimes daunting process. Students vary widely in terms of reading ability, preferences, experience, and motivation. Inviting your students to become engaged, knowledgeable readers through sustained encounters with good books is a powerfully effective way to teach. Providing well-written, thought-provoking books in a variety of genres and across reading levels, time to read in class, time to respond individually, and time to discuss books with peers allows students to build on their personal responses and the responses of others as they grow as readers. Time for direct instruction and demonstrations by the teacher is also crucial to the development of knowledgeable readers. Classroom structures that support students with time and access to good books, and teachers who are engaged and knowledgeable readers themselves, eager to share their enthusiasm and expertise with their students, help adolescents develop their interest in and enthusiasm for reading.

Probst (2004) suggests that there are five kinds of literary knowing. Through extensive, safe, meaningful encounters with excellent literature, students can begin to develop:

- knowledge about the self
- knowledge about others
- knowledge about texts
- knowledge about how contexts influence meaning making
- knowledge about how they create meaning as they read

Your students can learn how to use literature as both mirror and window, if you provide models, instruction, practice, social structures, and support for them to do so. They can come to understand the literary tools that authors use to create powerful books if you are deliberate in your instruction, anchoring it in the books students are engaged by. Your students can learn that who they are—the sum total of life experiences, interests, and understandings—and their reasons for reading, constitute a context that influences how they create meaning, and that this meaning will differ across readers, if you allow them to talk freely about the books they are reading. And they can learn to be metacognitive about how they read—what they do as they immerse themselves in the world of a story, the emotional space of a poem, or the conceptual content of nonfiction—if you teach them to be aware of what they are doing and thinking. If you do this, your students will have a very good chance of becoming engaged, responsive readers who will develop the life-long habit of reading.

EXTENDING LEARNING

1. There is a public perception that students need to read the classics rather than what is called adolescent literature. Think about what you have learned about adolescent literature in Chapter 3, what you have learned about motivated and engaged reading in Chapter 2, and what you have learned about teaching literature in this chapter. Write a letter to parents or administration in which you argue your position.

2. Select a particular genre, author, or nonfiction subject that you enjoy, and identify books that you would include in a study of these books in the middle grades. Develop an annotated bibliography, including a set of questions for writing prompts or discussion, along with other activities that would help your students understand the conventions of the genre, the characteristics of the author as a writer, or the presentation of subject matter.

3. Select a book that you particularly enjoy and think you will want to use in a middle-grade classroom. Read it again, taking notes on the aspects of the text (see Chapter 3) that you think your students could learn about. Then devise a series of questions, activities, and response strategies that would help middle-grade students explore that particular text.

BOOKS FOR MIDDLE-GRADE READERS

Peck, R. (2003). *The river between us.* New York: Dial.
Taylor, M. (1976). *Roll of thunder, hear my cry.* New York: Dial.

chapter

7

Fostering Higher-Order Thinking and Deep Understanding

Succeeding in the 21st Century requires higher-order thinking and deep understanding.

Cathy Koontz had always wanted to become a high school teacher. In college, she majored in history and minored in political science, and her dream was to teach these subjects to eleventh- and twelfth-grade AP classes. As a member of the debate team in high school, she developed a real respect for thoroughly understanding topics and creating well-crafted arguments based on that understanding. She believed that helping high school students learn and reason in ways that would make them competent and contributing members of society would be a tremendously rewarding pursuit.

Then, while she was observing in several middle-school classrooms during her first methods course, Cathy was struck by the range of understanding and reasoning skills she observed and by the range of assistance with higher-order thinking and deep understanding that different teachers provided. In the classrooms she observed, some students understood many topics deeply and were already adept and even sophisticated thinkers. They could identify a problem, investigate it thoroughly, break it into logical components, and pursue a chain of reasoning that led to valid conclusions. Unfortunately, other children in these same classrooms never seemed to engage in these sorts of activities. Not only could they not identify a problem, break it into logical components, and come to understand it thoroughly, but they seemed to have no interest in doing so. In fact, they seemed to have little knowledge or interest in most of the topics discussed in their classes. Moreover, and worse yet, many teachers seemed to do little to promote their students' thinking and understanding.

These observations led Cathy to an abrupt shift in her career plans. She switched to a middle-school track, did her student teaching in a middle school, and developed a particular interest in teaching higher-order thinking and fostering understanding in young thinkers in the middle grades. On graduating, she took a position as a sixth-grade teacher, believing that higher-order thinking and deep understanding can and should be nurtured, even in the wild and wooly world of the middle school.

We can indeed foster significant thinking and understanding in middle-school students, and we need to work diligently with all students and in all classes to assure that we do so. In this chapter, we take up two powerful approaches— fostering students' higher-order thinking and promoting their deep understanding of topics. Not only are these approaches closely related, they are also synergistic. Students can only engage in higher-order thinking when they think about topics they understand well, and the more thoroughly students understand a topic—the richer their schemata for the topic—the better their higher-order thinking will be. Thus, we need to teach students how to think, and we need to give them the raw material of thinking—deep understanding of topics—that will enable them to use and hone their thinking skills.

Fostering Higher-Order Thinking

We define higher-order thinking quite broadly. A number of authorities have contributed to our understanding of the concept. These include philosophers such as Ennis (1985), psychologists such as Bransford and Brown (2000), Resnick (1987), and Sternberg (1998), and critical-thinking proponents such as Costa (2001). We have gleaned valuable information and insights from these and many other experts on thinking. Based on this information and these insights, in this section of the chapter, we define higher-order thinking and describe two taxonomies of thinking skills that we believe will guide you as you teach content in such areas as literature, social studies, and science, and simultaneously develop your students' thinking and reading proficiency.

Just What Is Higher-Order Thinking?

After noting that higher-order thinking resists precise definition, Resnick (1987) lists some key features of higher-order thinking. Although lengthier than a typical definition, Resnick's list does an excellent job of capturing the full meaning of the concept, and we therefore present all of it here.

- Higher order thinking is nonalgorithmic. That is, the path of action is not fully specified in advance.
- Higher order thinking tends to be complex. The total path is not "visible" (mentally speaking) from any single vantage point.
- Higher order thinking often yields multiple solutions, each with costs and benefits, rather than unique solutions.
- Higher order thinking involves nuanced judgments and interpretation.
- Higher order thinking involves the application of multiple criteria, which sometimes conflict with one another.
- Higher order thinking often involves uncertainty. Not everything that bears on the task at hand is known.
- Higher order thinking involves self-regulation of the thinking process. We do not recognize higher order thinking in an individual when someone else calls the plays at every step.
- Higher order thinking involves imposing meaning, finding structure in apparent disorder.
- Higher order thinking is effortful. There is considerable mental work involved in the kinds of elaborations and judgments required. (p. 3)

Consider for a moment an assignment that is likely to engender this sort of thinking. Suppose your school is in a residential neighborhood of a large city, and your seventh graders are working on a 3 week unit on improving the urban environment. As one of their assignments, they are to investigate public housing and consider ways in which it might be improved to better the lives of the residents and the community more generally. Here are just a few ways in which this project engenders the sort of thinking Resnick describes: The thinking required is indeed nonalgorithmic; there is no formula students can follow to complete the task. In fact, it is not even clear where to begin. Should they begin at the library, by visiting public housing, by talking to city officials? The thinking is also complex, with the total path not visible at the onset. Students, for example, may interview some of the public housing residents and get ideas for their investigation they had never thought of. And their work may yield multiple solutions that require judgments. Would housing designed to attract both low-income and middle-income residents be an improvement over the existing complexes, which include only low-income residents? Would one- or two-story housing be an improvement over the high rises typical of public housing? If so, what would be the costs of one- or two-story housing? Two costs, for example, would be the need for more land and, in all probability, less green space available. We could continue listing ways in which the project would lead to the sort of thinking Resnick describes, but we believe that our point is clear: Projects such as this one, and many other activities students undertake in middle schools, can engender higher-order thinking. Significant amounts of what students do in school—in reading literature and content-area material and in other parts of the curriculum—should involve higher-order thinking. We suggest that you keep these features of higher-order thinking clearly in mind as you work with students, and repeatedly ask yourself if you are engaging students in this type of thinking.

Pause and Reflect 7.1

Consider a learning activity you experienced yourself that involved higher-order thinking. Or consider a teaching activity you have used that involved higher-order thinking. List the features of Resnick's characterization of higher-order thinking that you or your students are likely to have engaged in while completing that activity. ■

A Taxonomy of Higher-Order Questions

The approach to fostering higher-order thinking that is probably most frequently recommended and strongly endorsed by both common sense and recent theory and research is asking higher-order questions (Beck, McKeown, Hamilton, & Kucan, 2001; RAND Reading Study Group, 2002; Taylor, Pressley, & Pearson, 2002). While Resnick's characterization suggests what constitutes higher-order thinking, it does not list specific kinds of higher-order questions. For that, we recommend *A Taxonomy for Learning, Teaching, and Assessing* (Anderson & Krathwohl, 2001). This is a considerably enlarged and updated version of Bloom's *Taxonomy of Education Objectives* (1956), which has been the standard guide to types of thinking and questioning for nearly 50 years. Below is a simplified version of Anderson and Krathwohl's taxonomy, taken from Online Reading Resources (www.onlinereading resources.com). The definitions of the first six types are taken from Anderson and Krathwohl. The last definition reflects a mixture of their thinking and our own.

- **remembering:** retrieving relevant knowledge from long-term memory
- **understanding:** constructing meaning from instructional messages, including oral, written, and graphic communications
- **applying:** carrying out or using a procedure in a given situation
- **analyzing:** breaking material into its constituent parts and determining how the parts relate to one another and to an overall structure or purpose
- **evaluating:** making judgments based on criteria and standards
- **creating:** putting elements together to form a coherent or functional whole, reorganizing elements into a new pattern or structure
- **being metacognitive:** being aware of one's own comprehension and being able and willing to repair comprehension breakdowns when they occur

It is not the case that all of these types of questions need to be asked with every selection students read. However, all of them need to asked over time, all of them need to be asked frequently, and we need to be particularly careful to avoid asking only lower-level questions—those that demand only factual knowledge—because classroom observations have revealed that all too many teachers fall into the trap of doing so.

Here are examples of each type of question, taken from a story you all know— "The Three Little Pigs":

- **remembering:** *What did each of the three little pigs build their houses from?*
- **understanding:** *Why isn't straw a very good building material?*
- **applying:** *Suppose you had to build a house. What material would you build it with?*
- **analyzing:** *In what ways is a brick house better than a straw or stick house?*
- **evaluating:** *What do you think of the first little pig's decision to build a straw house? Why do you think this?*
- **creating:** *What are some things the first little pig might have done to make his house safer from the wolf?*
- **being metacognitive:** *When you learned that we were going to read the story of the "Three Little Pigs," how difficult did you think it would be? Why did you think this?*

And here is another example, this one from a popular middle-grade history text. The text is "Mom, Did You Vote?" a chapter on the origins of women's suffrage in Joy Hakim's textbook, *War, Peace, and All That Jazz* (2002).

- **remembering:** *About when did Alice Paul begin her campaign for women's suffrage?*
- **understanding:** *Why were women denied the vote when the United States was first formed?*
- **applying:** *Identify some sort of social injustice that exists today, and consider ways in which tactics used by the suffragists might be used to improve the situation or draw attention to the problem.*
- **analyzing:** *Which of the suffragists' approaches do you think was the most effective? Why do you believe that?*
- **evaluating:** *Do you think the suffragist did the right thing in mounting their protests? Why or why not?*
- **creating:** *Suggest some tactics the suffragists did not use that might have been effective.*
- **being metacognitive:** *Think about your own attitude toward women having the vote, and consider how your attitude might affect your reading and understanding of the chapter.*

Not all these types of questions need to be asked, or should be asked, with every selection, but over time students should get plenty of opportunities to work with all of them. Additionally, we do not want to leave the impression that exactly how you classify questions is the issue here. Many questions might be placed in several different categories of the taxonomy, and that is fine. What is important is that you ask many sorts of questions, and that a significant number of these be higher-order questions. Teaching Idea 7.1 gives you a chance to practice doing this.

An Additional Perspective for Considering Questions

The other source that we have found particularly useful in choosing questions to ask is Sternberg's work on what he calls a "triarchic theory of intelligence" (Sternberg,

Teaching Idea 7.1
Writing Questions Illustrating Anderson and Krathwohl's Taxonomy

Identify a middle-grade narrative text widely used by students like those you work with or are planning to work with, and write a set of questions on the text exemplifying each of the seven types of questions identified by Anderson and Krathwohl. Now identify a middle-grade expository text, and write a set of questions exemplifying each of the seven types of questions Anderson and Krathwohl identified.

1998; Sternberg & Spear-Swirling, 1996). The central thesis of Sternberg's theory is that there are three basic kinds of thinking: analytic, creative, and practical. He defines these three sorts of thinking thusly:

- Analytic thinking involves analyzing, judging, evaluating, comparing and contrasting, and examining.
- Creative thinking involves creating, discovering, producing, imagining, and supposing.
- Practical thinking involves practicing, using, applying, and implementing. (Sternberg & Spear-Swirling, p. ix)

As Sternberg notes, schools typically focus on analytic thinking and largely neglect the other two sorts. This, he argues, is very unfortunate because all three sorts of thinking are important, both in the classroom and beyond it. We very strongly concur, and we suggest that as you create questions and plan other activities, you frequently make it a point to involve all three sorts to thinking.

Here are examples representing each of Sternberg's three sorts of thinking, again taken from "The Three Little Pigs":

- **analytic thinking:** *Why isn't straw a very good building material?*
- **creative thinking:** *What are some things the first little pig might have done to make his house safer from the wolf?*
- **practical thinking:** *Suppose you had to build a house. What material would you use?*

And here are examples representing each of Sternberg's three sorts of thinking, based on "Mom, Did You Vote?":

- **analytic thinking:** *Which of the suffragists' approaches do you think was the most effective? Why do you believe this?*
- **creative thinking:** *Suggest some tactics the suffragists did not use that might have been effective.*
- **practical thinking:** *Identify some sort of social injustice that exists today, and consider ways in which tactics used by the suffragists might be used to improve the situation or draw attention to the problem.*

As you can see, with both texts the examples of Sternberg's three sorts of thinking are three of the seven questions we asked to illustrate the use of Anderson and

Krathwohl's taxonomy. The two systems overlap. However, we believe it is useful to consider Sternberg's scheme as well as Anderson and Krathwohl's in order to avoid putting too much emphasis on analytic thinking, which happens too frequently in many classrooms. Additionally, in Chapter 6 we included yet another perspective on higher-order thinking which we believe is important to consider. Obviously, we consider higher-order thinking an extremely important facet of a literacy curriculum for middle-grade students.

Whatever system you use to remind yourself to ask higher-order questions, there are several considerations to keep in mind. The first is to repeatedly engage students in higher-order thinking. The second is to involve all students in higher-order thinking—accomplished readers and less skilled ones, native-English speakers and English-language learners, and both regular and special students. The third is to foster students' understanding of topics so that they have something to think about. We turn now to this topic—teaching for understanding.

Teaching for Understanding

As Perkins, one of the major architects and advocates of teaching for understanding, notes, "understanding enables a person to perform in a variety of thought-demanding ways . . . [to] explain, muster evidence, find examples, generalize, apply concepts, analogize, represent in a new way, and so on" (1993, p. 13). Understanding is clearly one of the principal goals of education for all students and at all levels. As Perkins and his colleagues (Perkins, 1993; Blyth, 1998; Wiske, 1998) emphasize, to teach for understanding we must go beyond simply presenting students with information and ensure that students:

- retain important information
- understand topics deeply
- actively use the knowledge they gain

The reader who has attained an understanding perspective consciously seeks understanding and uses the knowledge she gains through reading. Of course, everything we have discussed in this book thus far has understanding as an ultimate goal. But here we treat understanding as a specific goal. There is a good deal of evidence that we should do so.

As pointed out by authorities such as Resnick (1987), Prawat (1989), Perkins (1992), Wiggins and McTighe (1998), the RAND Reading Study Group (2002), and Guthrie (2003), expectations of schooling and the level of knowledge and skills that our society requires have risen dramatically in recent years and will continue to rise, perhaps even more dramatically, in the future. These same authorities and empirical data, such as that produced by the National Assessment of Education Progress (National Center for Educational Statistics, 2004) and reports such as *The Twin Challenges of Mediocrity and Inequality* (Sum, Kirsch, & Taggert, 2002), indicate that few American students—and in particular few students of color, students living in poverty, and English-language learners—are performing at the advanced levels that full participation in our society demands. Teaching for understanding can change this.

Some Key Attributes of Teaching for Understanding

Thus far, we have defined understanding, emphasized the importance of having understanding as a goal of instruction, and noted that too few students are reaching adequate levels of understanding. We turn now to explaining what teaching for understanding looks like, and we begin with a dramatic example of what it is not. The example, taken from an observer's field notes as he observed a fifth-grade class (Prawat, 1989), is from a mathematics lesson rather than reading a reading lesson, but we use it here because it is such a telling example of how instruction sometimes goes astray. Here are the observer's notes:

> The focus of this lesson is on multiplying decimals. Prior to assigning students a series of seatwork problems, Miss Jones is working through two problems on the board. One example involves money—$32.45 x 0.5. The teacher repeats the algorithm that students are going to use in doing these problems: First, multiply as you would with whole numbers. Second, count the number of places to the right of the decimal point in the top number, then count the number of places to the right of the decimal point in the bottom number. Add these together, and place the decimal point so that the product contains this number of places.
>
> Most students seem to understand the procedure and are anxious to get started, when one little boy raises his hand. He has a perplexed look on his face. Suddenly he blurts out, "This doesn't make sense. You started with 32 dollars and 45 cents and ended up with 16 dollars and whatever cents. You multiplied by that number [0.5], how did you get *less*? Two other children agree that it does not make sense.
>
> At first the teacher thinks she has made a computational mistake, so she works the problem again. It soon becomes obvious that this is not the problem. The little boy thinks that the product should be bigger, not smaller, than the number that is multiplied. The teacher is at a loss about how to handle the question. She repeats the algorithm, explaining to the class, "I'm just teaching the computational way. What I'm looking for now is for everyone to understand where to place the decimals." The little boy shakes his head, still confused. The teacher assigns the problem set. (pp. 316–317)

In talking to the observer after the lesson, Ms. Jones noted that she moved on despite the boy's confusion because she was already a chapter behind and needed to finish the book by the end of the year—a very frequent problem teachers face and one we will address shortly. She also noted that the immediate goal was for students to get the basics, that she didn't have time for the "fancy stuff," and that "later on, at the junior high level, it'll start to make sense to them" (Prawat, 1989, p. 317).

From the teaching for understanding perspective, this won't do. If at all possible, the concepts and procedures that students are learning need to make sense to them *as they are learned.* In fact, it is only when things make sense that there will be any real learning. In this particular instance, then, the teacher might have stopped, done her best to understand the little boy's (we'll call him Tom) confusion, and attempted to clarify the situation. The following scenario suggests one alternative.

Ms. Jones: You know, Tom, I think I see what you mean. Often, when we multiply we do get numbers that are larger. For example, if we multiply 6 x 2, we get 12. And what do we get if we multiply 6 x 3?

Tom: 18

Figure 7.1   **Four Key Attributes of Teaching for Understanding**

It takes time.
It requires focus and coherence.
It involves negation.
It is highly analytic and diagnostic in nature.

Ms. Jones: That's right. If we multiply a number by 2 or 3 or anything larger than 1, we get a larger number. But what if we multiply by 1? What do we get then, Tom?

Tom: Let's see. If we multiply 6 x 1, we get 6; and if we multiply 12 x 1 we get 12. I think when we multiply anything by 1 we get the same number.

Ms. Jones: That's right. When we multiply a number by 1, we get the same number. And when we multiple anything by a number larger than 1, we get a larger number. Now comes the tough part. What happens when we multiply a number by something smaller than 1? Say we multiply 6 by .5. What happens then, Tom?

Tom: Hum, 5 x 6 is 30, but there's a decimal point so it is 3.0. This time the number gets smaller. I think I see. When we multiply by a number smaller than 1, even though we are multiplying our answer gets smaller.

Next, Ms. Jones summarizes what Tom has said. She then orally gives some problems with multipliers larger than 1 and multipliers smaller than 1 to other students in the class. She repeats the generalization so that everyone understands.

Of course, even doing everything that Ms. Jones did in this scenario does not guarantee that all her students will understand. However, it certainly makes their understanding more likely, and it is almost certainly a better solution than simply continuing with the planned lesson when some students are confused.

This revised math lesson illustrates a critical principle: Your goal virtually always ought to be that students understand whatever you are discussing. Despite the press of time, despite the need to cover the curriculum, despite the well-planned lesson you're aching to get on with, when students do not understand, you need to stop what you are doing and do your very best to help them understand.

Perhaps the most basic characteristic of teaching for understanding is that it takes time. Prawat (1989) suggests three additional key attributes. The four key attributes of teaching for understanding are listed in Figure 7.1.

We have already discussed and illustrated the first key attribute of teaching for understanding, the fact that doing so takes time. In fact, it takes a good deal of time. However, the time is well spent because when teachers don't teach for understanding the knowledge students acquire is fragile, inert, of little or no use in solving real problems, and soon gone.

Because teaching for understanding requires more time, it also demands focus and coherence. If you are going to spend a good deal of time on something, you had better be sure just what it is you are spending time on. Similarly, if you are going to spend a good deal of time on a topic, it needs to be coherent—to you as the teacher and to the students as the learners. Thus, for example, if you are dealing with narratives and focusing on plot, it is important that both you and the students understand that you are focusing on plot, understand what plot is, and understand why you are focusing on plot.

In order to assure coherence—assure that what you are doing makes sense to students—you are frequently going to have to negotiate meaning with students. That is, you need to discuss the meaning of the text with them and insure that everyone is interpreting it similarly, or at least understanding each other if they are interpreting it differently. As noted previously, the process of making meaning is a constructive one; meaning does not simply spring from a text to the reader's head. Readers must grapple with a text, manipulate ideas, shape them, and interpret them if they are to derive significant learning from what they read. What the reader gets from reading depends heavily on the sum total of her experience and on her unique intellectual makeup. No two readers or listeners will construct exactly the same meaning from a particular text or discussion. Thus, in situations in which you want students to construct the same meaning or very similar meanings, you will often need to engage in negotiation—a give-and-take discussion in which students and their teacher talk through a topic, often rereading a text and listening to what the other is saying about it, attempting to understand what each other is saying, and attempting to come to some agreement on the meaning.

This sort of negotiation is nicely shown in the following excerpt provided by Beck and her colleagues (2001), in which a teacher and several Pennsylvania students negotiate the meaning of a fourth-grade Pennsylvania-history text. The passage the group is considering describes some insights George Washington had about the willingness of the French to relinquish their holdings in Pennsylvania.

> Washington gave the governor's letter to the French leader. No one knew this, but Washington made a drawing of the fort. Washington saw that the French planned to make war on the English. At last, the French leader gave Washington a message for the governor. He said that the French would not leave Pennsylvania. (Wallower & Wholey, 1984, p. 41)

Teacher: So, what's the author's message here?

Kalondah: That, um, the French aren't gonna leave Pennsylvania. And they just plan to keep it.

Teacher: The French plan to keep it for themselves. What's the author say to make Kalondah think that?

Deandre: They were planning to stay, and I think that they're bound to have a war.

Teacher: Deandre said that they were bound to have a war. Hum. What do you think gave Deandre that idea?

Kristen: Because the governor knew that, um, the French were staying because, um, I think he knew that the French wouldn't just let the English have it without having a war.

What is important to recognize here is how the teacher's prompts serve to focus the discussion, get several students involved, and help the students come to some consensus on the meaning of the passage.

Negotiating meaning requires hard work on your part and on your students' part.

Finally, teaching for understanding is both analytic and diagnostic. That is, the teacher needs to analyze students' responses in an effort to determine what they are thinking, decide whether or not there is a problem of understanding, and, if there is a problem, diagnose its nature and come up with a solution. Suppose that the social studies passage just discussed had produced these responses.

Teacher: So, what's the author's message here?
Kalondah: That, um, Washington wants to make war on the French.
Teacher: Now, why do you say that Kalondah?
Kalondah: Well, because he made a map.
Teacher: That's true. He did make a map, and he might have made it because he wants to make war on the French. But we don't really know that. Can anyone suggest another reason he might have made a map?
Deandre: Maybe he didn't want a war. Maybe he just thought that the French might want a war, and he wanted a map just in case, in case they made war so he could fight back.
Teacher: Now what Deandre said is certainly possible. And what Kalondah said also make sense. The truth is, we're not sure what Washington's plans are yet. He might want a war, or he might just want to be prepared in case the French start a war, or he might have other plans. We'll have to read further and see if we can learn more.

Here, the teacher has tried to find out what caused Kalondah to make the inference she did, how other students are interpreting the passage, and what the passage actually does and does not reveal. And the results of his analysis and diagnosis is the very reasonable conclusion that the class will need to read further to find out more about just what is going on. We believe that many discussions of

Figure 7.2 **A Four-Part Framework for Teaching for Understanding**

Generative Topics
Understanding Goals
Understanding Performances
Ongoing Assessment

text will take a form much like this, as students and teachers delve into texts and their interpretations of them in the quest for true understanding.

In the next three sections of the chapter, we present three specific approaches to teaching for understanding.

Teaching for Understanding Units

Perkins's (1992, 1993) major approach to Teaching for Understanding is with thematic units that follow a specific framework, that might last 2 to 4 weeks to allow students the time to reach true understanding, and that give students many opportunities to establish links between the many concepts necessary to really understanding something. Perkins' framework, shown in Figure 7.2, has four parts. Here we define each of these parts, elaborate on each, and give an example or two of each.

Generative Topics. Generative topics are topics that are central to the subject area students are studying, accessible to students, and connectable to many other topics both in the subject matter and in other areas. Generative topics can be concepts, themes, procedures, historical periods, theories, ideas, and the like. For example, in the field of literature, *plot* is a generative topic. Plot is central to the study of literature, plot is an important element in many types of literature and in many individual pieces of literature, and plot exists outside of literature. Historical episodes—for example, the Civil War period—basically follow a plot, as do our lives. As another example, consider the field of history. *Cause and effect* is a concept central to much of history, and like the generative concept of plot, cause and effect also exists in areas outside of history. In fact, many if not most fields of study—science, humanities, and art, for example—deal with cause and effect. As still another example, consider the idea of *beauty*. Beauty is a central concept in art and literature, of course, but beauty also plays an important role in life and even in science. Frank Press (1984), former president of the National Academy of Sciences, once spoke of the discovery of the double helix that broke the genetic code as not only rational, but beautiful as well. Finally, consider the topic of *health*. Health can be considered a part of science, but it is also a part of social science; there is of course psychological health as well as physical heath. Of course, health can also be related to government—as when a powerful world leader becomes ill; and it can be related to a myriad of other areas, including people's daily lives. A few additional examples of generative topics for middle-grade students and some of the many aspects of those topics are listed in Figure 7.3.

Figure 7.3   **Some Possible Generative Topics for Middle-Grade Students**

Plot—in life, in literature, in history, the elements of plot, what makes a good plot

Strife—causes of strife, results of strife (war, violence, hardship, strife in families, strife in school)

Friendship—personal friendships, great friendships in history, friendships celebrated in music, making friends, losing friends, keeping friends

Courage—in literature, in science, in history, in sports, in war, in our lives

Working with highly generative topics whenever possible is important because teaching for understanding takes time. If you are going to spend a good deal of time on a topic, and that happens when you teach for understanding, you need to carefully choose topics that are important themselves, that connect to many other topics, that students can access and appreciate.

Understanding Goals.   One problem with generative topics is that they are often too broad. Beauty, for example, could be studied in any age, in any medium, and in almost any field. Even though understanding units may last 2 to 4 weeks, the time available is obviously not infinite, and a teacher almost always needs to select one or several parts of broad generative topics to deal with and some specific goals to be achieved. For example, one possible understanding goal for sixth graders studying the idea of beauty might be for students to understand that people's idea of physical beauty has changed over time, that the ancient Roman's idea of beauty differed from that held by Italians during the Renaissance and from that held by Italians today. Another possible understanding goal for these sixth graders might be that they will understand that the idea of physical beauty also differs from culture to culture and even from individual to individual.

Or consider again the generative topic of health, and assume that the students under discussion are eighth graders. Eighth graders cannot understand health in the same depth as an M.D. or a scientist working for the National Institutes of Health, but they can certainly understand a great deal about health. They could, for example, understand and profit from studying some aspects of nutrition. In this case, one understanding might be that students learn the six types of food described in a contemporary food pyramid (grains, vegetables, fruits, dairy, proteins, and fats). Another might be that they understand what foods help keep them healthy. And another might be that they become more knowledgeable consumers, learning about the labels on packaged food. This line of thinking suggests one aspect of useful understanding that deserves more attention than it often gets—the affective component of understanding. It is not nearly enough for eighth graders to *know* about nutrition and the labels on packaged food. They also need to *care* about these matters. If you are going to spend considerable time and effort on the topic of nutrition, one of the major goals should be for students to develop healthier eating habits.

Another generative topic was recently used by Jamie Gutterman (2004) for developing sixth graders' understanding of Greek and Roman Mythology. The unit provided students with in-depth knowledge on the topic over about 3 and a half

Figure 7.4   Lessons from a Sixth-Grade Understanding Unit on Greek and Roman Mythology

Lesson	Topic
One	Introduction to Mythology
Two	The Who's Who of Mythology
Three	A Personality Profile of the Olympians: Part I
Four	A Personality Profile of the Olympians: Part II
Five	Some Comparisons to Historical World Leaders
Six	Enduring Mythology
Seven	Pandora's Box
Eight	Designing a God or Goddess
Nine	The Six Pomegranate Seeds
Ten	Introduction to the Trojan Horse
Eleven	The Trojan Horse
Twelve	The Trojan Horse Readers' Theater: Part I
Thirteen	The Trojan Horse Readers' Theater: Part II
Fourteen	Archeology and Mythology
Fifteen	Cumulative Assessment of the Unit

weeks. Here we use a lightly modified version of her unit as an example for discussing the remainder of Perkins' four-part format. An outline of the unit is shown in Figure 7.4. As the titles of the lessons suggest, the unit dealt with a variety of topics—including the nature of mythology, characteristics of the gods, specific myths, and links between mythology and the historic and contemporary world. This is indeed a significant set of topics and issues, and we would expect some significant learning and understanding from the 3-week unit.

Understanding Performances. In Perkins' four-part framework, students demonstrate their learning and understanding in what he calls "understanding performances." Understanding performances are things that students do that require them to understand whatever it is you are teaching. Thus, when students complete an understanding performance, they demonstrate that they have, in fact, understood. During the 3-week mythology unit shown in Figure 7.4, students took part in a number of understanding performances. Fairly early in the unit, students began completing a matrix that listed the gods on one axis and their functions, attributes, domains of influence, personalities, and relationships to other gods on the other axis. As the unit progressed and students read more and learned more, they added to the chart. Later in the unit, after they designed their own gods, they made a mural illustrating the characteristics and wrote a brief explanation of how their mural represented their god and how their god was like and unlike the mythological gods. Finally, for their cumulative understanding performance, they completed the cumulative understanding performance shown in Figure 7.5.

Note that this cumulative performance is just one in a series of performances students engaged in throughout the unit; they did not wait until the end of the unit to demonstrate their understanding. This is a very important feature of teaching

Figure 7.5 **Cumulative Understanding Performance of the Mythology Unit**

This cumulative understanding performance is intended to connect modern day "gods" to the ones studied in the unit. The work will require the students to think about the connections they can make to contemporary figures and determine characteristics that will elevate the contemporary figures to god-like status on Mt. Olympus. The procedure is as follows:

1. An envelope containing photographs of the following modern personalities is passed around the room. Students are asked to each take one photo. Included in the photographs are George W. Bush, Johnny Depp, Snoop Doggy, Jennifer Lopez, Randy Moss, Saddam Hussein, Kevin Garnett, Ricky Martin, Usher, Britney Spears, Beyonce, Donald Trump, Tom Cruise, Michael Jackson, and others.

2. Working with a partner, students will use their photographs to create a new god to join the other twelve on Mt. Olympus. They will share their new god's characteristics, qualities, and attributes with their classmates in brief oral presentations after completing the following activities:

   a. Write a paragraph describing the personality and special characteristics of this person as a Greek or Roman god.

   b. Write an additional paragraph citing the qualities and attributes they assign to their photograph god.

   c. Write a paragraph describing the role this god had during the Trojan War and how it affected the outcome of the war.

for understanding units. Students should be engaged in understanding performances throughout the period that they are studying a topic.

Ongoing Assessment. The last part of Perkins' four-part framework, ongoing assessment, is very closely related to the understanding performances. Just as students should be engaged in understanding performances throughout the unit, students and teachers should be engaged in ongoing assessment throughout the unit. Of course, one of the things that teachers assess is students' understanding performances—for example, whether their matrices of gods and their characteristics were accurate representations of what they had studied. If some students are unable to complete the matrices, then they need feedback and some reteaching, and they need the feedback and reteaching early on so that they do not continue through the unit with their misconceptions about the nature of the gods causing confusion. Each of the later understanding performances offers additional opportunities for ongoing assessment, and for feedback and reteaching if needed. However, ongoing assessment is not limited to understanding performances. At all points in the unit and with all activities—reading, individual conferences, small-group discussions, writing, or other events—it is important to constantly be assessing whether students are understanding, and to constantly be ready to assist students in reaching understanding if they are experiencing problems. As Perkins and Blythe (1993) put it, "To learn for understanding, students need criteria, feedback, and opportunities for reflection from the beginning of and throughout any sequence of instruction" (p. 7).

Summary Comments on an Understanding Perspective. Certainly all teachers want to teach for understanding. You obviously would not want to teach for

Teaching Idea 7.2
Outlining a Teaching for Understanding Unit

Outline a Teaching for Understanding Unit for a particular grade level. Choose a generative topic, state one or more understanding goals that fall under that topic, describe at least two understanding performances that students could engage in as they were engaged in the unit, and explain how you could provide ongoing assessment very early in the unit and periodically throughout the remainder of it. Do this in writing, and make it just as specific and concrete as you can.

misunderstanding or teach with the goal of students' forgetting whatever you were teaching. Yet, in all too many cases, misunderstanding and forgetting take place. Teaching for Understanding is hard. But by keeping the attributes of Teaching for Understanding—time, focus and coherence, negotiation, and frequent analysis and diagnosis—clearly in mind and by employing the four-part framework—generative topics, understanding goals, understanding performances, and ongoing assessment—in situations where it is appropriate, students' understanding is a goal you can reach. See Teaching Idea 7.2 for practice.

Pause and Reflect 7.2

One of the key attributes of teaching for understanding is that it takes time, more time than is often allotted to topics in school. Take a moment and think about a fairly difficult concept that you understand quite thoroughly. Now think back and try to remember what you did to come to understand the concept—when you were first introduced to it, how you were first introduced to it, what you did to initially learn it, how you refined and extended your learning of it, when and how you actually made use of the concept. Now consider the total amount of time you put into mastering this difficult concept. Share your recollections of what you did to learn the concept and the time it took you to do so with a classmate, and see if the classmate will share a similar recollection with you. ■

Jigsaw Cooperative Learning

Jigsaw is another powerful approach that can be used in teaching for understanding. Jigsaw is an easily implemented technique that puts students in the position of becoming experts in some part of a domain and then sharing their expertise with others in the class. It is a particular type of cooperative learning, an approach which has been shown to produce some extremely positive results in a variety of cognitive and affective areas (Johnson, Johnson, & Holubec, 1994; Slavin, 1987; Tierney & Readence, 2005) and which has been particularly recommended for English-language learners (Gersten & Baker, 2000). Research has demonstrated that students in cooperative groups showed superior performance in academic achievement, displayed more self-esteem, accommodated better to mainstreamed students, showed more positive attitudes toward school, and generally displayed better overall psychological health. Students in cooperative groups displayed better interpersonal relationships; and these improved interpersonal relationships held regardless of differences in ability, sex, ethnicity, or social class (Johnson & Johnson, 1989). Moreover, cooperative learning has been shown to be successful in teaching students how to resolve conflicts (Johnson & Johnson, 2002).

Jigsaw was developed and investigated by Aronson and his colleagues (Aronson, Blaney, Stephan, Sikes, & Snapp, 1978; Aronson & Patnoe, 1997). Using the Jigsaw approach, a class of 30 or so students work in five heterogeneous groups of six or so students each on material that the teacher has broken into subtopics for each student to work on. Here are the major steps of the approach.

Steps in Using Jigsaw

1. Each student in a group learns one part of the material being studied, becoming the expert on that topic. For example, in studying a particular state, one student in each group might investigate cities in the state, another in each group investigates the state's agriculture, another its industries, and so on.
2. After studying her section individually, the member of each group who has studied a particular subpart of the topic gets together with the four members from other teams who have studied the same subpart.
3. The five students in each of these expert groups discuss their subtopic, refining their knowledge about it.
4. The experts return to their own groups and teach their classmates about their sections. Because classmates afford the only opportunity for students to learn about sections other than their own, students are necessarily interested and motivated to attend to each other's presentations.
5. Students take individual exams on all of the material, both the material they taught to others and material they learned from others.

Jigsaw, of course, must be used in a situation where a subject can be broken into subparts for students to teach. With that single proviso, the procedure is widely applicable. One excellent use of Jigsaw is in peer response to writing. In a class of 30 students, five groups of six students can each identify and become "experts" in a particular aspect of writing. Suppose, for example, that sixth-grade students were working on expository writing over a period of a month or so. One group might become experts in introductions to expository essays, focusing on such matter as the clarity of the introduction and whether it provided an adequate overview of the paper. A second group might become experts on the body of the paper, focusing on whether the body supported what was said in the introduction. A third group might deal with conclusions, focusing on their clarity and the extent to which they were appropriate for what was said in the body of the paper. A fourth group might become experts on transitions between paragraphs and sentence structure, looking for complete sentences and for clarity and variety in the sentences used. And a final group might deal with punctuation and spelling, checking to ensure that punctuation and spelling followed acceptable conventions.

Students write their papers individually; then each paper written by the members of a group is checked by all members of the group, with each member focusing on his or her specialty; then each paper is revised by the original writer. This procedure lets all students become authorities in at least one aspect of writing, gets

Teaching Idea 7.3
Planning a Jigsaw Activity

Identify a topic from a reading methods course that would work as a jigsaw topic. Identify the five or six subtopics that you would assign to the expert groups, and write out the assignments for each group. Estimate the time the expert groups would need to work on their subtopics and the time the experts would need to teach what they have learned to their groups. If possible, use the Jigsaw procedure with your classmates in your methods class. Finally, whether or not you actually use the procedure, get together with a classmate and discuss the costs and benefits of using Jigsaw.

all members of each group substantial feedback, and is very likely to result in better second drafts than if only one student had responded to each paper.

As another example of a topic with which Jigsaw could be used, consider the seventh-grade unit on improving the urban environment that we discussed in the first section of this chapter on Higher-Order Thinking. Here, the Jigsaw groups could be organized by topic rather than by skill as they were with the writing example. One group might become experts in public housing, a second on public transportation, a third on health, a fourth on low-cost recreation available, a fifth on prices at grocery and department stores in the city, and a sixth on job opportunities. As in all Jigsaw projects, the students have both a base group and a subtopic group; they work in the subtopic group becoming experts in a particular areas, and then they come back to their base group and share their information. Since each of the base groups will eventually have the same information, you need to come up with a culminating activity that does not result in students hearing the same message again and again. Written reports from each group are one possibility. But there are others. For example, one base group might present an oral report, another do a skit, another make a collage, another create a brief short story centered in the urban environment, and still another present an action plan for improving conditions.

Jigsaw can be used in a wide variety of situations, it can be easily implemented, and it can be very effective in fostering true understanding. We think it merits a good deal of use in middle-school classrooms. For steps in planning a Jigsaw activity, see Teaching Idea 7.3.

Pause and Reflect 7.3

Identify a topic for a middle-grade class that would work well with Jigsaw. Identify the five or six subtopics that you would assign to the expert groups, and write out the assignments for each group. Estimate the time the expert groups would need to work on their subtopics and the time the experts would need to teach what they have learned to their groups. Finally, get together with a classmate and discuss the potential benefits and the potential risks of using Jigsaw with middle-grade students. ■

Figure 7.6   **Knowledge as Design Questions**

What are the purposes of the topic?		What is the structure of the topic?
	The Four Design Questions	
What are some examples of the topic?		What are some arguments for and against the topic?

Knowledge as Design

Knowledge as Design is a simple and straightforward yet very powerful discussion framework that you and your students can use to fruitfully investigate almost any topic. It was first described by Perkins in 1986 and has been refined and further developed since that time (Perkins, 1994). Like each of the instructional procedures discussed in this chapter, it is fully consistent with the contemporary model of reading we discuss in Chapter 1, particularly the constructivist perspectives on instruction.

Two basic principles underlie Knowledge as Design. The first principle is that considering the design of a topic—the relationship between its structure and its purpose—fosters meaningful and even insightful discussion about almost any topic. The second principle is that learning is a consequence of thinking. If you can get students actively thinking about a topic, then they will be learning about that topic. Knowledge as Design suggests that students can productively answer the four questions about a topic or object shown in Figure 7.6. Answering these questions as a group gives students the opportunity to share what they know about the topic and come up with a rich set of information on it.

As we said, the procedure is simple and straightforward, as you will see in the following scenario. Olivia Martinez, a fifth-grade teacher, began by identifying the topic *television shows* that grew out of students reading *The TV Kid* by Betsy Byars. The class then took up the four design questions one by one, engaging in what Perkins calls a *Design Conversation*. Finally, the class worked toward some sort of closure. Here is a small sample of the many responses these fifth graders generated in discussing the topic of television shows.

Purposes of Television Programs

Ms. Martinez: What are some of the purposes of TV shows? Why do we have TV shows? Why do you watch them?

Students: They're fun. They're exciting. It's something to do. It's better than homework.

Structure of Television Programs

Ms. Martinez: How are TV shows organized? What are they like? What are the parts of them?

Students: They're different. Some are an hour, and some are half an hour. They have commercials. They're on every week. Some are on every day.

Examples of Television Programs

Ms. Martinez: What are some examples of TV shows? What are some shows that you know?

Students: Cartoons. "Monday Night Football." "Fear Factor." "NCIS."

Arguments For and Against Television

Ms. Martinez: What are some good things about television shows, some things you like?

Students: They're exciting. They're fun. They give you something to do. The good guys win. They let you forget your troubles—like homework.

Ms. Martinez: What are some arguments against television, maybe some things you think or maybe some things your parents think.

Students: The ads, there're too many adds. Reruns. There's a lot of shooting. They rot your brain. Sometimes the stuff's not for kids.

Quite obviously, these fifth graders know a lot about television. Using the design conversation has enabled them to get what they know out on the table where the whole class can think about it and see what it means.

At this point, we will consider each of the three parts of a design conversation—choosing a topic, the design conversation itself, and closure—in slightly more depth.

Choosing a Topic. The first step in using Knowledge as Design is, of course, to choose a topic. Although Knowledge as Design can be used with virtually any topic, like each of the approaches we consider in this chapter it is most appropriately used with topics that are worthwhile and justify students spending time delving into them. Additionally, in order to ensure students' success with the procedure when they are first learning to use it, it is a good idea to initially choose topics that are concrete, that students know a lot about, and that students are likely to be interested in. The *television shows* topic obviously meets the criteria of being concrete, something students know about, and something they care about. And, when you consider that U.S. students watch an average of something like 4 hours of television a day and that carefully considering the topic might make them more selective in their viewing—just might even convince some of them to cut down their viewing so they have more time for reading—then it also meets the criterion of importance.

Once you choose a topic, it's a good idea to see if it will work as a design conversation before giving it to students. To do so, simply jot down one or two purposes, the structure of the topic, one or two examples, and some arguments for and against the topic. Figure 7.7 shows the responses we came up with from very briefly brainstorming the topic of *television shows.*

If the topic seems to work for you, try to think how it will work for students. Think about some of your students, what they know, and how they are likely to respond to each of the design questions. If it seems as if your students will be able to answer the design questions, then you have probably chosen a good topic.

Figure 7.7   **Our Responses When We Considered Television Shows as a Possible Topic for a Design Conversation**

	Television Shows
Purposes:	entertainment, information, persuasion
Structures:	half hour show, hour shows, mini-series
Examples:	nightly news, football games, Joan of Arcadia, reality shows, commercials
Arguments For:	informative, engaging
Arguments Against:	mindless, addictive, celebrating poor taste

One other thing to think about as you consider topics is just when to use design conversations. Design conversations can be useful before students read, to activate or build background knowledge and interest in the reading. They can be used after students read, to summarize, synthesize, and share information. Or they can be used at both points to accomplish all of these goals and to let students compare what they knew before they read and what they learned from reading.

Leading a Design Conversation. Once you have chosen the topic and are confident it will be a useful one for your students, the next step is to lead students through the four design questions. Frequently, the question— "What are the purposes of the topic?"—is the one asked first. However, this does not need to be the case. You might also begin by asking about the structure of a topic or asking students to give some examples of it. Wherever you begin, the procedure usually works best if you get all of the students' responses on one design question before going on to another one. You will want to keep a record of students' responses, and that can be done on the board or on an overhead with a template that provides convenient spaces for students' responses to each of the questions. A completed record, which Perkins calls a Design Conversation Worksheet, is shown in Figure 7.8.

As you are asking the questions, it is very important to do everything possible to promote an open discussion and encourage students to volunteer answers. This means treating all students' answers with respect by acknowledging partially correct responses and avoiding criticism. It also means being sure all students have opportunities to respond, and seeing that students treat each other with respect. In Chapter 6, we gave several guidelines for effective discussions. Many of these apply to design conversations.

Something else to consider as you conduct the design conversation is that the four categories of questions should be thought of in broad terms, not narrow or limiting ones. The *purpose* question, for example, can be thought of as a question about *goals, objectives, functions,* or *aims.* In asking about purposes, you are asking "What is it for?","What does it do?", or "What can we accomplish with it?" Similarly, the *structure* questions can be thought of as a question about *organization, features, materials,* or *parts.* In asking about organization, you are asking "How is it organized?", "What does it look like?", "What is it made of?", "What are it's parts?", and "How

Figure 7.8 **Design Conversation Worksheet on Monarchies as a Type of Government**

Purposes
  kings and/or queens rule the country, not the citizens
  royalty make decisions
  way of keeping order in a nation

Specific Examples
  England
  Norway
  Denmark
  Monaco

Structure
  positions are usually inherited
  the royal family keeps control for possibly generations
  the royalty live in palaces
  usually the royalty are wealthy

Pro Arguments
  clear pattern of authority
  people in the country maybe like all the royal ceremonies and traditions
  visitors can tour the palaces
  the royalty can be a symbol for the country

Con Arguments
  can create a problem with human rights
  the people can't decide for themselves
  what happens if the royal family breaks the rules—like the Prince and Princess get divorced?

Conclusions
  maybe this type of government doesn't fit today's world as well as it did in the olden days
  maybe monarchies aren't as powerful as they used to be

is it put together?" Interpreting each of the design questions broadly allows you to use the procedure with a very broad range of topics.

Closure. The third step of Knowledge as Design, *closure*, gives students the opportunity to synthesize the information they have produced, connect it to their existing knowledge, search for insights, and draw conclusions. One matter to consider as you think about closure is how long design conversations should generally be. Their length will vary considerably, depending on the topic, your purpose, your students, and how the conversation progresses. One conversation might last 5 minutes, another 20 minutes, and another most of the period.

With most topics, there are a variety of directions that closure can take. With the topic of television shows, for example, students might compare television to other forms or entertainment—reading, radio, movies, and live theater. They might also compare watching television to doing other activities—working on hobbies, reading, participating in sports, and completing schoolwork. Certainly, since so many U.S. students watch so much television, you might be inclined to work toward closure that critically evaluates the value of watching television or at least raises the possibility that watching somewhat less television might be something to consider.

Continued Work with Knowledge as Design. In working with Knowledge as Design, it is essential to choose topics that are relevant to students—what's going on in their lives, what they're reading about, what they're interested in. As students become increasingly competent with the procedure, you can introduce topics from subject areas that will further challenge students' imaginations and thinking abilities. Figure 7.8, which we previously showed to illustrate the format of a design conversation worksheet, illustrates the responses eighth graders gave on the topic of monarchies before beginning a unit on types of government.

In your initial work with Knowledge as Design it is a good idea to work with topics that are concrete and that students know a lot about. As students become increasingly competent with the procedure, you will find that they can also use Knowledge as Design with more abstract topics and topics they are not as familiar with.

Shown below is an excerpt from a design conversation the sixth-grade students in Mark Pallota's social studies class had on the topic of voting. The topic grew out of their reading about Rosa Parks, particularly Chapter 14, Voting Rights, in *Rosa Parks* by Kai Friese. Students were asking the question, "What's such a big deal about voting, anyway?" This particular class had been engaging in design conversations throughout the year and knew the procedure well, so one student, Mike, suggested they have a design conversation on the topic. The following scenario also illustrates an instance in which the conversation leader, in this case, Mike, begins the conversation with examples.

Examples

Mike: OK, we're going to talk about voting. What do we know about voting? Let's start with some examples: What have you voted for? What about your parents or other people—you know, adults—what are some examples of what they vote for?
Jordan: Last week we voted for what new books we wanted for our class library.
Lisbeth: Friday we'll vote for a new class president.
Honing: My parents get to vote for president, mayor, governor, people like that, in government. Also laws, in the U.S. when you're eighteen you can vote for laws and stuff like that.

Purpose

Mike: (after collecting a few more examples): Good. OK, now let's look at these voting situations, you know, why are people voting for books, people, etc.? Marla, would you write down what people say about voting purposes?
(Marla writes student responses on the board.)
Seth: People feel good because they have a say. Like with the library books. Even if your book doesn't win, at least you had your say.
Jana: Before we vote for class president, there will be campaign speeches. Then Ms. B. will let us argue about who will be the best president. Maybe that way we'll choose the best one. If we couldn't vote, if Ms. B. just chose a president, it would be just her opinion.
Carlos: OK, you know if you're voting between two things, like this Friday when the election is just between Jena and Kari? Even if a few people are not happy with who wins, most people are—at least the ones who voted for the winner!

Keep Knowledge as Design discussions on track by using the board to record students' responses.

Structure

Mike: (after collecting a few more purposes): Good list of purposes, I'd say. Now, what about the structure of voting; you know, what is voting like? What are some of its important features?

Jana: Each person gets a single vote.

Paul: You vote secretly.

Seth: Someone is in charge of counting the votes.

Arguments

Mike: Cool. Let's explore the arguments one at a time. Why does each person get one vote? How does that help voting fulfill its purpose?

Carlos: People would be mad if some others got more than one vote and if people were left out, they might not go along with the decision.

Seth: Yeah, but some people do get left out. Kid's don't get to vote, not for U.S. president, anyway.

Mike: Right. Sometimes there are rules about who gets to vote. Like being a certain age, for instance. That's another characteristic of voting. Thinking of the arguments again, why are there such rules?

This dialogue on voting illustrates only a part of the conversation. A full design conversation on voting might consume half an hour or more. But we hope this example is sufficient to show a class dealing with a challenging topic from the curriculum, show students learning a good deal about voting, and illustrate how the teacher learns a lot about what students do and don't know about the topic as the conversation progresses.

Teaching Idea 7.4
Designing a Design Conversation

Choose a topic for a design conversation that might work with middle-grade students. Remember, design conversations need to deal with topics familiar to the students. This could be something that is common knowledge, such as something having to do with the school or community, or it could be a topic the class has been reading about. Once you have a topic, fill out a Design Conversation Worksheet like that shown in Figure 7.8 (p. 180) with responses that middle-grade students might make. Finally, reflect on the responses you have shown and consider the extent to which they represent the sort of thinking you would expect from middle-grade students. To the extent that they do not, modify them to make them a more authentic example of how middle-grade students are likely to respond.

As the dialogue on voting reveals, as students become increasingly familiar with Knowledge as Design, they become able to work with the procedure without the teacher's leadership. Mark Pallota comments on his students conducting their own design conversations.

> Once they understand the procedure well, I have my students work in small groups, perhaps with several groups each working on part of a general topic and then sharing their knowledge. When students work with Knowledge as Design in groups, it's important that they record their responses so they can review the knowledge they have produced and share it with others. I like to reproduce the design conversation worksheet as a handout. This provides students with an excellent place to record their conversations and helps guide them in asking the design questions.

In concluding this section on Knowledge as Design, we want to say a word about how frequently you might find the procedure useful for dealing with the content you consider in your classroom. Our general thought here is that you and your students may choose to use it fairly frequently, often including a design conversation in conjunction with the reading that students are doing in such areas as history, science, and health. As we have already noted, these discussions can occur both before students read about a topic and afterwards. If you hold design conversations before students read a selection, it will need to be with topics students know something about, and in many cases it will be appropriate to complete the conversation after students have read the selection and gained additional information and insights. Of course, just how often you use the procedure depends on some of the same factors that you consider in planning scaffolded reading experiences—your students, the topics you deal with, and your purposes. How frequently you use Knowledge as Design also depends on what other discussion and thinking procedures you use in your classroom. Still, because Knowledge as Design is broadly applicable, because it is easy to use, and because it can lead to powerful learning about a number of topics you and your students investigate, it is certainly a candidate for frequent use. Teaching Idea 7.4 contains steps for creating design conversations.

Concluding Remarks

Fostering higher-order thinking and teaching for understanding are two extremely important goals of education at any level, and they are critically important for middle-grade students as they begin increasingly intensive and deeper study of increasingly complex topics. Fortunately, we know a good deal about each of these topics. Resnick has provided a rich description of the nature of higher-order thinking, Anderson and Krathwohl have created a powerful taxonomy of questions, and Sternberg has created a simple yet very useful scheme that describes three sorts of questions. A number of authors have described the nature of understanding, why understanding is important, and key attributes of teaching for understanding. Three very useful approaches to teaching for understanding are the use of Understanding Units, Jigsaw Cooperative Learning, and Knowledge as Design. Additionally, it is important to remember that fostering higher-order thinking and teaching for understanding go hand in hand. You can't do higher-order thinking without a deep understanding of topics.

In concluding this chapter, we want to note that we consider it one of the most important ones in the book. Reading and responding to literature and content-area material gives students myriad opportunities for thinking. Teaching for understanding and fostering higher-order thinking—giving students the knowledge and skills they need to succeed in school and in the world beyond school—is a goal all teachers must value highly. Regardless of the subject matter you teach or the skills and backgrounds of your students, you must help all students understand topics deeply and become competent in higher-order thinking.

■ ▬▬▬▬▬▬▬▬▬▬▬ **EXTENDING LEARNING**

1. Identify three classes, tell the teachers you would like to observe their teaching and that you will tell them just what you were looking for after your visit, and get permission to observe their classrooms. Construct a coding sheet with the heading Higher-Level Questioning and with four columns below that. Label the first column Types of Questions and list in it the seven levels of Anderson and Krathwohl's taxonomy. Label the columns to the right Class 1, Class 2, and Class 3 (you can put in teachers' names once you identify the actual classes you will visit). Observe each classroom for an equal amount of time, spending at least 1 hour in each of them. Tally the types of questions and assignments used in each class on your observation sheet. Don't be overly concerned about how you classify the questions and assignments. The main thing you are trying to do is to distinguish between *remembering*, which is not a higher-level category, and the other six categories. Once you have finished your responses, tally them and write a brief statement for yourself about how much higher-level questioning seems to be taking place in each of the classrooms. Meet with the teachers and discuss your findings if they would like to learn about them, but be very tactful, and remember to share with the teachers that not many classrooms include a lot of higher-level questions.

2. Arrange a meeting with a middle-grade teacher and discuss the notion of teaching for understanding generally. Ask if he or she is familiar with the term "Teaching for Understanding" and the general point of view it represents. If the term and the concept are familiar, ask how he or she interprets Teaching for Understanding, what sort of job he or she thinks schools in general are doing in assisting students to develop deep and useful understanding, and what he or she is doing to teach for understanding. Also ask about what he or she sees as the barriers to Teaching for Understanding, and about how these barriers might be overcome. If the teacher is not familiar with the term or the concept, explain it as fully as you can. Then, go ahead and discuss the other matters we have listed here as much as possible.

3. Identify a class or small group of middle-grade students. Create a Jigsaw or Knowledge as Design activity that you can introduce and complete in a single period of an hour or so. Try out the activity with the students. This is probably the most time consuming of the activities we have suggested here because you have to identify a class or small group, thoroughly prepare for your teaching, and then do the teaching. However, it is also one of the most beneficial, because it gets you directly involved in teaching. Be sure to take some notes immediately afterwards so that you have something to refer to the next time you use the procedure.

BOOKS FOR MIDDLE-GRADE READERS

Byars, B. (1976). *The TV kid*. New York: Viking.
Friese, K. (1990). *Rosa Parks: The movement organizes*. Boston: Sliver Burdett Press.
Hakim, J. (2002). *War, peace, and all that jazz*. New York: Oxford University Press.
Wallower, L., & Wholey, E. J. (1984). *All about Pennsylvania*. Harrisburg, PA: Penns Valley Press.

chapter

8

Vocabulary Instruction

Vocabulary knowledge serves as the foundation for success in both reading and writing.

Like most children, Danzell said his first word when he was about 1 year old. Like many children, by the time he entered first grade, Danzell had achieved a substantial oral vocabulary, and he could read a few words. Also like many children, Danzell's reading vocabulary grew rapidly during the elementary years. But unlike many children, sometime during his elementary years, Danzell developed a keen interest in words. He underlined words in the books he read, grew to love word games, pestered his teachers and parents about the meanings of new words he encountered, and bought his own pocket dictionary. By the time he entered eighth grade, Danzell had a reading vocabulary of well over 30,000 words, and he actively used much of this vocabulary in his talk and his writing.

I f all students were like Danzell, vocabulary instruction would be an easy task. But few students are like Danzell, and many will need all the assistance we can give them if they are to develop the broad and deep vocabularies so necessary to success in and out of school. Moreover, even students with rich and powerful vocabularies and a keen interest in words will profit for developing still broader and deeper knowledge about words. Fortunately, we know a great deal about how to foster children's vocabulary development. This chapter describes a curriculum and a number of instructional options for bolstering all middle-grade students' vocabularies.

Several considerations are particularly important to keep in mind as you begin planning a vocabulary program: First, the vocabulary-learning task is enormous. Estimates of vocabulary size vary greatly, but a reasonable estimate based on a substantial body of recent and rigorous work (Anderson & Nagy, 1992; Anglin, 1993; Nagy & Anderson, 1984; White, Graves, & Slater, 1990) is this: The books and other reading materials used by school children include well over 100,000 different words. The average child enters school with a very small reading vocabulary, perhaps 100 words. Once in school, however, a child's reading vocabulary is likely to soar at a rate of 3,000–4,000 words a year, leading to a reading vocabulary of something like 10,000 words in fourth grade and 30,000 words in eighth grade.

Second, the fact that there are far more words to be learned than we can possibly teach is not an argument that you should not teach any of them. Both instruction on individual words and instruction that promotes students' ability and propensity to learn words on their own are very worthwhile.

Third, many children of poverty enter school with small vocabularies and lag further and further behind their middle class counterparts as they progress through school. It is especially important to find ways to bolster the vocabularies of these students (Becker, 1977; Biemiller, 2001; Hart & Risley, 1995; National Reading Panel, 2000, RAND Reading Study Group, 2002). For similar reasons, bolstering the English vocabularies of English-language learners is critically important (Nation, 2001).

This chapter presents a comprehensive plan for vocabulary instruction, one broad enough to include instruction for children who enter school with small vocabularies, for English-language learners, for children who possess adequate but not exceptional vocabularies, and for children who already have rich and powerful vocabularies.

A vocabulary program likely to really assist children in the enormous and varied tasks they face in building rich and powerful vocabularies must, of course, be a powerful and substantial one. Yet at the same time, it must not constitute an inappropriately large part of the curriculum. The program we describe here—one based on more than 20 years of work on vocabulary learning and instruction (Graves, 2006)—respects this fact and is designed to provide direct instruction on words, to promote independent word learning, and to kindle students' interest in words. It has four components:

- providing children with frequent, extensive, and varied language experiences
- teaching individual words

- teaching students strategies for learning words independently
- fostering word consciousness

In the remainder of the chapter, we deal with each of these in turn.

Providing Frequent, Extensive, and Varied Language Experiences

The language experiences referred to in the heading are, of course, listening, speaking, reading, and writing. Listening is the earliest of these skills that children begin to master; almost all children being to understand some of what they hear long before the end of their first year. If they are fortunate, children hear a huge volume of language well before they enter school. They hear their parents or other caregivers talking all the time, they hear the speech of friends and relatives, and they hear stories and other material read to them. Unfortunately, as you know, some children hear a lot more language than others. Hart and Risley (1995, 2003), for example, found that by age 3 children reared in poverty had heard up to 30 million fewer words than their middle class counterparts, and children who do not speak English as their native language hear extremely few English words before going to school. However, whether they have been read to before school a lot or a little, students profit greatly from being read to in school—at all grade levels.

Almost everyone, adults as well as children, loves to be read to, and learns a lot of words from the experience. Students will learn a lot more vocabulary from being read to if we occasionally focus their attention on words. For example, it is useful to ask students to listen for and keep a journal of new words they hear as you're reading to them. It is also useful to identify particularly adroit uses of words in what you are reading aloud and point these out to students, and to sometimes ask students to use these words in their speech or writing. Of course, simply reading to children is also worthwhile. As teachers, we should frequently read to students, model our enthusiasm for reading, and do everything we can to help students enjoy these experiences. Reading to children has been shown to be particularly effective, however, when it is coupled with discussion and when children are actively involved and responding to the books or other reading selections being shared.

Speech is the other language mode that children begin mastering well before entering school. Most children utter their first word at about age 1. By the time they enter first grade, most children are actively using several thousand words in their conversations, and once in school their speaking vocabularies will continue to grow by several thousand words each year. This growth will come from many sources, but a lot of it will come from classroom talk, something you have control over. Middle-school students particularly need to engage in real discussions—give and take conversations in which young learners have many opportunities to discuss topics of interest in an open, positive, and supportive climate. Such discussions are valuable for all students, but they are also particularly valuable for students with vocabularies that are smaller than those of their peers. In summing up the major message of their longitudinal study showing the huge and ever-widening gap between the vocabularies of middle class children and many children reared in poverty, Hart and Risley (1995) note that "the most important difference among families was in the amount of talking that went on."

Classroom discussions are also an extremely important instrument of vocabulary growth for English-language learners. Particularly if students do not speak much English out of school, they need many opportunities to speak English *in* school. This does not mean that classroom discussion is unimportant for students with large and sophisticated vocabularies. Anything we can do to promote real discussions in which students do their best to communicate, listen to each other, and learn how to understand and be understood by their classmates from various linguistic and social backgrounds will help all students to build their vocabularies. And, as we will point out in the section of this chapter on Word Consciousness, if we can get students interested in the words used in discussions— the words they use, the words others use, words that help them get their points across and those that don't—class discussions will foster even more vocabulary growth.

Reading is a language mode that some children begin to acquire before entering school but that most children don't become very adept at until they are in school. Of course, once students can read, they should be reading as much as possible in a variety of materials. As we have stressed throughout this book, wide reading is important for a host of reasons, but it is particularly important to vocabulary growth. If students learn to read something like 3,000 to 4,000 words each year, it is clear that most of the words they learn are not taught directly. With a 180-day school year, teaching 3,000 to 4,000 words would require teaching approximately 20 words each and every school day. Obviously, this does not happen. Instead, students learn many of the words that make up their vocabularies from their reading (Anderson, 1996). Thus, if we can substantially increase the amount of reading students do, we can markedly increase their vocabularies. Moreover, wide reading will foster automaticity, provide knowledge about a variety of topics and literary forms, and leave students with a habit that will make them lifelong readers.

By the time they arrive at middle school, many students are very competent readers and many others are relatively competent readers. Unfortunately, many middle-school students, including many students who are competent readers, do very little reading, and some do almost none. Allington (1977) summed up the situation nicely in his memorable plea for students doing more reading—"If they don't read much, how they ever gonna get good?" The answer is clearly that they are not. Moreover, as Allington (2001) and a number of others have noted, a substantial amount of the reading students do needs to be easy enough that they can understand and enjoy what they are reading rather than struggling to decode it. Obviously, if the selections students are reading do not contain any new vocabulary, the students will not learn any new words from reading it. Not quite as obviously, if the selections contain too many unknown words, students will not understand enough of what they are reading to infer the meanings of the unfamiliar words. The goal is to motivate students to do lots of reading, to help them select a lot of texts that are interesting and informative but do not contain an undue proportion of unknown words, to encourage them to sometimes select texts that presents challenging vocabulary as well as other challenges, and, as we discussed in Chapter 4, to scaffold their efforts when dealing with more challenging texts.

Writing is a language mode that some children begin to acquire before entering school but that virtually no children become adept at without many years of instruction and practice. Although some students are adept writers by the time they enter the middle grades, most are not. As we now know but somehow did not know a few years ago, writing is a powerful ally and aide to reading. Students at all grade levels need to engage frequently in activities in which reading and writing are paired, and some of these paired activities should focus on words. The stage of the writing process at which students edit and hone their writing provides you and your students with excellent opportunities to look for just the right words to effectively convey their thoughts and to discuss the importance of word choice and how one chooses just the right word for a particular context.

Pause and Reflect 8.1

Since you are reading this book, you are in all probability either a teacher or someone preparing to be a teacher. It is almost certain that you have had a number of rich and varied language experiences, since such experiences are necessary to getting where you are. Think back on the rich and varied language experiences you have had both in school and out of school during your own middle-school years. ■

Teaching Individual Words

Here, we first discuss the various word-learning tasks students face and ways of identifying words to teach. Then, we discuss teaching procedures for each of these word-learning tasks. Since new words come up in all content areas and since learning the vocabulary of a domain is crucial to understanding the domain itself, all teachers are involved in teaching the vocabulary of their subjects.

The Word-Learning Tasks Students Face

All word-learning tasks are not the same. They differ substantially, depending on such matters as whether the words are in students' oral vocabularies, how much students already know about the words to be taught, the complexity of the concepts represented by the words, and how well you want them to learn the words. Here, we consider five tasks students face in learning words. Note that the type of learning required and the difficulty of the learning are quite different from task to task.

Learning a Basic Oral Vocabulary. Most children will have already acquired a basic oral vocabulary long before they reach the middle grades. However, some children raised in poverty and some English-language learners enter the middle grades with meager oral vocabularies. For such children, building a basic oral vocabulary of the most frequent English words is of utmost importance.

Learning to Read Known Words. Learning to read words that are already in their oral vocabularies is the major word-learning task faced by beginning readers, but by the time they enter middle school most students will be able to read almost all of the words in their oral vocabularies. However, the task of learning to read the words in their oral vocabularies still remains a challenge for many less able readers and for some English-language learners.

Learning New Words Representing Known Concepts. A third word-learning task students face is learning to read words which are in neither their oral nor their reading vocabularies but for which they have an available concept. For example, the word *excel* would be unknown to a number of sixth graders, but almost all sixth graders know what it means to do exceptionally well at something. All students continue to learn words of this sort throughout their years in school. This, of course, is a major learning task for English-language learners, who have many concepts for which they do not have English words.

Learning New Words Representing New Concepts. Another word-learning task students face, and a very demanding one, is learning to read words which are in neither their oral nor their reading vocabularies and for which they do not have an available concept. Learning the full meanings of such words as *perseverance, theme* (as a literary concept), and *volume* (as a science concept) is likely to require many middle-grade students to develop new concepts. All students continue to learn words of this sort throughout their years in school and beyond. Once again, learning new concepts will be particularly important for English-language learners. Also, students whose backgrounds differ from that of the majority culture may have internalized somewhat different concepts than those internalized by students in the majority culture. Thus, words that represent known concepts for some groups of students will represent unknown concepts for other groups.

Clarifying and Enriching the Meanings of Known Words. The last word-learning task considered here is that of clarifying and enriching the meanings of already known words. The meanings students originally attach to words are often imprecise and only become fully specified over time (Carey, 1978). For example, some middle-grade students might not recognize any difference between the meanings of *brief* and *concise,* not know whether *condominium* and *town house* are synonyms, or not realize that although the term *virtuoso* is most frequently applied to those who play musical instruments, it can also be applied to those who show exceptional ability in other pursuits. Although students will naturally expand and enrich the meanings of the words they know as they repeatedly meet them in new and slightly different contexts, some more direct approaches are definitely warranted.

Pause and Reflect 8.2

In this section, we have briefly described five word learning tasks. Each of them requires different sorts of learning. In a later section of the chapter, we will describe instructional procedures appropriate for each of them. However, considering how the instruction for these various tasks might differ would be a useful constructivist activity before you consider the procedures we describe. It would be useful to do this with a classmate and then, after you have discussed your response, to actually write it out. Writing out the response will give you an opportunity to really think it through. ■

Identifying Vocabulary to Teach

Once you have considered the word-learning tasks students face, you still have the task of selecting specific words to teach. In this section of the chapter, we recommend a two-step process in which you first get some idea of which words are likely to be unknown to your students and then follow several criteria for selecting the words to teach.

Three sources are useful for identifying words to teach—word lists, selections your students are reading or listening to, and the students themselves. Word lists are particularly useful for identifying a basic oral vocabulary you may want to teach to students who have not already developed such a vocabulary. One widely used and easily obtained list is Fry's list of the 1,000 words most commonly used in English (Fry, 2004). It is absolutely crucial that students master these words—initially in their oral vocabularies and then in their reading vocabularies—as soon as possible because they make up a huge percentage of the words they will come across as they read. According to Fry, the first 100 of these words account for about 50 percent of the words students will encounter in what they read and the total 1,000 of them make up about 90 percent of those they'll encounter.

The second source useful for identifying words that you might teach is the selections students are reading or listening to. This will be the major source of vocabulary for all of your students except those who have not acquired a basic vocabulary or 1,000 or so words. English, like all natural languages, consists of a small number of frequent words and a very large number of infrequent words. Once students acquire a basic vocabulary of 1,000 or so words, the number of different words you might teach is so large that frequency does not provide much of a basis for choosing just which ones to teach. Because of this, as students' vocabularies grow, using word lists becomes problematic, and for the vast majority of middle-grade students, the best option is to use your best judgment to select vocabulary from the material students are reading and listening to.

In most selections, you are likely to find more potentially useful vocabulary to teach than you have time to teach. In winnowing the number of words to teach, the answers to the four questions can be helpful.

  1. "Is understanding the word important to understanding the selection in which it appears?" If the answer is "No," then other words are probably more important to teach.

2. "Are students able to use context or structural analysis skills to discover the word's meaning?" If they can use these skills, then they should be allowed to practice them. Doing so will both help them consolidate these skills and reduce the number of words you need to teach.

3. "Can working with this word be useful in furthering students' context, structural analysis, or dictionary skills?" If the answer here is "Yes," then your working with the word can serve two purposes. It can aid students in learning the word, and it can help them acquire a strategy they can use in learning other words. You might, for example, decide to teach the word *regenerate* because students need to master the prefix *re-*.

4. "How useful is this word outside of the selection being currently taught?" The more frequently a word appears in material students will encounter, the more important it is for them to know the word. Additionally, the more frequent a word is, the greater the chances that students will retain the word once you teach it.

Finally, another very important source of information about what words to teach is the students themselves. You can identify words on word lists or in upcoming selections that you think will be difficult for your students and build simple tests to find out whether or not they are difficult. Of course, constructing such tests is time consuming and certainly not something you need to do for every selection. However, several experiences of identifying words that you think will be difficult and then checking students' performance against your expectations will sharpen your general perceptions of which words are and are not likely to cause your students problems.

In addition to testing students on potentially difficult words, you can simply ask students about which words they know. One easy way of doing this is simply dictating words or listing words on the board and having students raise their hands if they do not know a word. This approach is quick, easy, and risk free for students; it also gives students some responsibility for their word learning. Moreover, research (White, Slater, & Graves, 1989) indicates that students can be quite accurate in identifying words that they do and do not know.

Methods of Teaching Individual Words

How might you go about providing instruction for each of the five word-learning tasks described? As we have said, the instruction needed for some word-learning tasks is quite different than that for others. Note too that some of these instructional methods will promote deeper levels of word knowledge than others. For the most part, you will use these procedures to preteach words before students read a selection. Frequently, however, you will want to review the words immediately after students read the selection and from time to time after that. Also, it is important to note that you can you can teach up to half a dozen or so words before students read a selection if the words do not represent new and difficult concepts. When word do represent new and difficult concepts, you will usually be able to teach only one or two of them.

Learning a Basic Oral Vocabulary. As noted, acquiring a basic oral vocabulary of 1,000 or so words is crucial for success in school. Thus, one priority in vocabulary instruction is helping students who lack such a vocabulary to gain one. This being the case, we suggest a combination of both direct and systematic methods and more informal methods.

The most direct method entails assembling groups of words and teaching and reviewing them week by week. Ten is probably an ambitious but still reasonable number of words to teach each week, and sets of 10 or so words can be assembled, grouped solely on the basis of frequency or grouped by themes. Initial teaching, probably done on Mondays, should include defining the words, using them in context, and giving students opportunities to contribute anything they know about the words. Although the principal goal is getting the words into students' oral vocabularies, it is probably a good idea to assist students in recognizing the written versions of the word at the same time. This is the case both because students will need the words in their reading vocabularies and because having the words written down makes it much easier for you and the students to keep track of what words are being studied and learned.

After words are initially taught, students should actively rehearse and use the words in many different ways, some of which are listed here.

- Post the words and pictures depicting them around the room.
- Point out the words and briefly discuss their meanings when you are reading to students.
- Students can listen to the words and their definitions on audio tapes.
- Students can work in pairs or larger groups, teaching and testing each other on them.
- Students can draw pictures illustrating the words and share their pictures with the class.
- Students can write the new words on cards and build constantly growing individual word banks.
- Students can play games and complete puzzles with the words.
- Students can categorize the new words and relate them to other words.
- Students can engage in any of a number of other activities that give them opportunities to hear the words and associate them with their meanings.

At the end of the week, give a quiz on the words for that week and be sure students get feedback on how well they are learning them. Finally, over time students need to review and rehearse the words in many different ways, with your referring to them when they appear in something you are reading orally, when they come up in discussion, and when they come up in any reading students do.

We would also use less formal methods to teach a basic vocabulary. One of these would be to pay particular attention to this key vocabulary during oral reading. In doing so you can:

- Alert students to what you are trying to do—help them learn a basic vocabulary of words they will hear, see, and use often.
- Point out instances of frequent words you think students may not know as you are reading to them.
- Ask students to listen for words they don't know and ask you about any words they don't know or aren't sure of as you read.

Other informal activities would include just about anything you can think of to remind students of the words and give them opportunities to hear, see, and manipulate them. The following suggestions come from Morrow (1993). Many of them assume that students are studying a particular theme—in this case, *winter*. Others can be used with or without a theme.

- Hold discussions about the theme—*winter*.
- Ask students to name all the words they know about *winter*.
- Put up pictures of *winter*.
- Have students bring things from home related to *winter*.
- Do a science or art activity related to *winter*.
- Make some *winter* food, or do a skit about *winter*.
- Discuss related concepts, such as weather.
- Take a field trip—out into the cold.
- Read stories about *winter*, have some student tell personal stories about *winter*, and have other students retell those stories.
- Have students bring in their favorite words about *winter*, share them, and post them around the room.
- Periodically take time to share with the class what you have been doing with these *winter* words and get their responses on what they particularly like and what they might do differently with other words or groups of words.

One reading authority, Elley (1996), coined the term *book floods* to describe programs in which children were literally flooded with books to read. These programs were very successful. What Morrow describes might be called a *word flood*. It is likely to be an extremely valuable part of helping students learn a basic listening (and reading) vocabulary.

Learning to Read Known Words.   As is the case with learning a basic oral vocabulary, learning to read known words is a vocabulary learning task only some of your students face. Most average and above-average middle-grade students can already read all or most of the words in their oral vocabularies. But for those who can't, learning to read the words in their oral vocabularies is extremely important, because these are the words they will encounter most frequently in their reading. In learning to read known words, the basic task for the student is to associate what is unknown, the written word, with what is already known, the spoken word. To establish the association between the written and spoken forms of a word, the student needs to see the word at the same time that it is pronounced, and once the association is established, it needs to be rehearsed and strengthened so that the relationship becomes automatic. We have listed these steps below to emphasize just how straightforward the process is.

1. See the word.
2. Hear the word as it is seen.
3. Rehearse that association again and again.

Of course, there are a number of ways in which each of these three steps can be accomplished. Students can see the word on the board, on a computer screen, or in a book that they are reading or that you are reading to them. They can see the

Even upper grade students will profit from vocabulary instruction.

word paired with a picture on the bulletin board. They can hear the word when you say it, when another student says it, or when a voice simulator on a computer says it. And they can rehearse the association by seeing the word and pronouncing it a number of times, writing it, and playing games that require them to recognize printed versions of it. However, wide reading in materials which contain many repetitions of the words and which are enjoyable and easily read by students is by far the best way to empower students to automatically and effortlessly recognize these words whenever they see them.

Finally, one very important point to remember when teaching these words is that there is no need to teach their meanings. These are words students already know and understand when they hear them; they simply cannot read them. Time spent teaching students the meaning of words they already know is time wasted.

Teaching New Words Representing Known Concepts.   The methods just discussed are used primarily with less proficient readers; those discussed here are for average and above-average readers. For the most part, new words representing known concepts will be ones you select as potentially difficult from upcoming readings and preteach to students. There are many ways of teaching new words representing known concepts. Here, we describe three approaches that have been shown to be particularly useful. As you will see, each of them requires different amounts of teacher time, different amounts of class time, and different amounts of students' time and effort; and they are likely to yield different results. Each of them, however, is very appropriate for introducing a small number of potentially challenging words.

Context Plus Use of the Dictionary.   This requires little teacher preparation time, but a fair amount of class time. The purpose is to provide students with a basic understanding of a word's meaning and give them practice in using the dictionary. Here is the procedure:

- In a handout, computer file, or on the chalkboard, give students a word in context. For example, *impromptu:*
- The class was not very pleased to received the *impromptu* writing assignment instead of free reading time.
- Have students read the word and context-rich sentence, then look up the meaning of the word in a dictionary.
- Discuss the word and its meaning.

Definition Plus Rich Context. This requires a fair amount of teacher preparation time, but very little class time. The purpose is to provide students with a basic understanding of a word's meaning and give them practice in reading dictionary entries. Here is the procedure:

- Provide students with both a definition of a word and a rich context. For example,
  plausible (PLA zi bul)—believable
  Although Zack's answer was *plausible,* it was not correct and clearly indicated he knew very little about Greek history.
- Have students read the definition and context-rich sentence.
- Discuss the word and its meaning.

Context-Relationship Procedure. This requires quite a bit of teacher preparation. However, presenting words in this way takes only about a minute per word, and we have repeatedly found that students remember quite rich meanings for words taught in this fashion. The purpose of this technique is to provide students with a basic understanding of a word's meaning and give them practice in using context to determine a word's meaning. Here is the procedure: Create a brief paragraph that uses the target word three or four times. Then, follow the paragraph with a multiple-choice item that checks students' understanding of the word. A sample paragraph and multiple-choice item and the steps for presenting each word are shown below.

Conveying

The after-dinner speaker was successful in *conveying* her main theme to the audience. Almost everyone understood her message, and most agreed with her. *Conveying* has a more specific meaning that telling. *Conveying* means that a person is getting her or his ideas across well.

Conveying means

_____ A. putting parts together.
_____ B. communicating a message.
_____ C. hiding important information.

Here are the steps the teacher follows:

1. Explain the purpose of the procedure.
2. Pronounce the word to be taught.
3. Read the paragraph in which the word appears.
4. Read the possible definitions, and ask students to choose the best one.

5. Pause to give students time to check a definition, give them the correct answer, and answer any questions they have.
6. Read the word and its definition a final time.

Teaching New Words Representing New Concepts. Teaching new words representing new and potentially difficult concepts is a challenging task, and one of the main things to realize about teaching new and potentially difficult concepts is that it is going to take time. Another thing to realize about teaching new and difficult concepts is that students from different cultural and language backgrounds will have different stores of words. Thus, what is new and difficult for some students may be familiar and not difficult for others. The following method developed by Frayer (Frayer, Frederick, & Klausmeier, 1969) illustrates one very effective method to use in helping students gain knowledge of new words which represent new concepts. It also illustrates the fact that it is likely to take a good deal of time to teach a new concept. As we have noted, when teaching new and difficult concepts before students read a selection, you will usually have time to teach only one of two of them.

The Frayer Method for Teaching New Words Representing New Concepts. The purpose of this method is to introduce eighth-grade students to the new word and concept; in this example, *temerity*. Here is the procedure:

- Define the new concept, giving its necessary attributes.

  Temerity is a characteristic of a person. A person demonstrates *temerity* when he or she exercises reckless boldness, ignoring serious dangers.

- Distinguish between the new concept and similar but different concepts with which it might be mistaken.

  Temerity differs from *foolishness* in that *temerity* necessarily involves some element of danger. *Temerity* also differs from *foolishness* in that the deed that demonstrates *temerity* needs to be somewhat admirable. It is usually the case that the danger involved is physical; however, the danger need not be physical.

- Give examples of the concept, and explain why they are examples.

  A person who wrestles a bear would be demonstrating *temerity* because there is some element of danger and the practice could be admired.

  The cliff *divers* of Acapulco demonstrate *temerity* because what they do is definitely dangerous and the divers are admired by many for their bravery.

- Give nonexamples of the concept, and explain why they are nonexamples.

  Someone who fishes for marlin with a fly rod is not demonstrating *temerity* because there is no danger involved.

  Someone who drives after drinking too much is not demonstrating *temerity* because there is nothing admirable here.

- Present students with examples and non examples, ask them to identify which are and are not instances of the concept and to state why; give them feedback.

  Riding a motorcycle on the freeway without a helmet (nonexample)

  Crossing the Pacific in a one-person sailboat (example)

  Eating a whole watermelon (nonexample)

Standing on the wing of a stunt plane in mid-air (example)

- Have students present their own examples and nonexamples of the concept, have them discuss why they are examples or nonexamples, and give them feedback.

Teaching concepts using the Frayer method takes a good deal of your time and a good deal of students' time. The method also requires a good deal of thought on the part of both you and your students. However, for important concepts, the fruits of the labor are well worth the effort, for with this method students can gain a new idea, another lens through which they can interpret the world. The two methods discussed in the next section—semantic mapping and semantic feature analysis—can also be used for teaching new concepts. Although they are generally not as powerful as the Frayer method and require learners to have some information about the new concepts, they often take considerably less time than the Frayer method.

Clarifying and Enriching the Meanings of Known Words. Semantic mapping and semantic feature analysis are two well-researched and widely used methods of clarifying and enriching the meanings of known words. These methods, both developed by Johnson (Johnson & Pearson, 1984; Heimlich & Pittelman, 1986; Pittelman, Heimlich, Berglund, & French, 1991), are also useful in preteaching unknown words to improve students' comprehension of a selection. They serve the purpose well because they focus not just on the words being taught but also on related words and on the part the words play in the selection. As we just mentioned, these two methods can also be used to teach *new* concepts—if the concepts are not too difficult and if students already have at least some information related to them.

Semantic Mapping. Semantic mapping makes use of a graphic organizer in which lines connect a central concept to related ideas and events. Shown in Figure 8.1 is a semantic map for the word *tenement.* You and your students might create a map such as this before or after reading a social studies chapter on urban housing.

The purpose of semantic mapping is to enrich and clarify students' existing knowledge of a concept by having them identify categories of ideas and events that relate to that concept. The procedure is as follows:

- Put a word representing a central concept, such as *tenement,* on the chalkboard.
- Have students form groups, brainstorming a list of as many words related to the central concept as they can think of.
- Write students' words on the chalkboard grouped in broad categories.
- Have students name the categories and perhaps suggest additional ones.
- Discuss with students the central concept, the other words, the categories, and their interrelationships.

Semantic Feature Analysis. This procedure employs a grid, such as the sample grid shown in Figure 8.2, which is a slightly modified version of one provided by Pittelman and her colleagues (Pittelman et al., 1991).

The purpose of this procedure is to enrich and clarify students' existing knowledge of a concept by having them identify words that belong to a category. In this case, students in a seventh-grade social studies class have been studying Early Civilizations and are using semantic feature analysis as a review that will help them compare and contrast critical terms. The procedure is as follows:

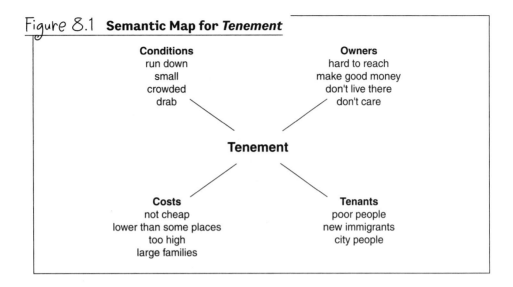

Figure 8.1 **Semantic Map for *Tenement***

- Select a category, in this case, Early Civilizations.
- With students' help, list critical words that fall into this category.
- With students help, list the features that words in the category might have. For example, some of the features for Early Civilizations might be agriculture, democratic, builders, traders, and the like.
- Determine the feature of some words. Put a + when a word has a certain feature, a – when one does not, and a ? when the class is not sure whether or not a word has a particular feature. Work with students in adding and discussing some of the plusses, minuses, and question marks indicating that each word does, does not, or may share each feature listed.
- Add more words and features. Work with students to extend the grid and more precisely define words. For example, adding the feature *theater,* meaning the civilization had a theater, might allow students to distinguish between Roman and Viking civilizations.
- Have students complete the grid. They can do this independently, in groups, or as a whole class.
- Examine and discuss the completed grid. This discussion is often the most interesting and revealing activity. For example, you would want to point out that the Greek civilization was like the Roman civilization in many ways, but differed in the very important feature that one was a democracy while the other was a monarchy. As part of the discussion, encourage students to add additional words and features to the grid.

As with many instructional activities, gradually lessen your role when your students are working with semantic feature analysis, over time. Initially, you may need to do much of the work. Later, you can give the students grids with some terms and some attributes and ask them to add to both the list of related words and the list of attributes and then to fill in the pluses and minuses. Still later, after students become proficient in working with partially completed grids you supply, they can create grids for sets of related words they suggest.

Figure 8.2 Semantic Feature Analysis Chart for Early Civilizations

Early Civilizations / Features	educated	monotheism	slavery	democratic	monarchy	naval power	baths	architecture	builders	traders	theater
Roman	+	–	+	–	+	?	+	+	+	+	+
Egyptian	+	–	+	–	+	+	+	+	+	+	–
Viking	–	–	+	–	+	+	–	–	–	?	–
Greek	+	–	+	+	–	?	+	–	+	+	+
Frank	–	–	+	–	+	–	–	+	–	–	–
Assyrian	+	–	+	–	+	–	+	–	+	–	–
Anglo-Saxon	–	–	+	–	+	+	–	+	–	–	–
Byzantine	+	+	+	–	+	–	+	+	+	+	+

Teaching Idea 8.1
Creating Materials for Teaching Individual Words

Identify a group of middle-grade students. Select one word that is likely to be in their oral vocabularies but that they probably don't recognize in print, one that is a new label for a known concept, one that represents a new concept, and one that they probably know but for which you would like to give them a fuller understanding. Choose an instructional procedure described in the chapter for teaching each word, create any materials you will need to teach them, and then explain just how you would go about teaching each of them. If you have a few classmates available who could serve as students, an excellent option would be for you to role play the teaching rather than simply explain how you would do it.

In this section of the chapter, we have described a number of approaches to teaching individual words. We recommend them strongly. They are powerful procedures, and they provide you with appropriate ways of dealing with the various learning tasks different words present to middle-grade students. Teaching Idea 8.1 can guide you through this process.

Teaching Students Word-Learning Strategies

As noted at the beginning of this chapter, students learn something like 3,000 to 4,000 words each year, many more words than could be directly taught. Thus, even when instruction in individual words is as frequent and rich as one could possibly make it, students need to learn much of their vocabulary independently. Here, we consider three strategies that students need to become independent word learners: using context, using word parts, and using the dictionary. Although the instruction for these three strategies differs considerably, in each case we follow the explicit instruction model we described in Chapter 5. In addition to considering how to teach word-learning strategies, it is important to consider who will teach them. We believe it is very important that certain classes—probably reading or language arts class—be designated as places where the strategies are initially taught. However, we believe that it is equally vital for students to practice the strategies and be encouraged and reinforced in their efforts to do so in all classrooms!

Using Context Cues to Unlock the Meanings of Unknown Words

We learn most of the words we know from meeting them in context. No other explanation can account for students' learning 3,000 to 4,000 words each year. At the same time, it is important to realize that gleaning a word's meaning from written contexts is often a challenging task and that time spent increasing students' ability to learn words from context is time very well spent. In addition to following the explicit instruction model, the instruction we suggest for using context clues—the words, phrases, and sentences that surround an unknown word and provide clues to its meaning—includes two steps. First, you present a well-planned unit on context cues. Second, over time, you repeatedly remind students of the value of using context to learn word meanings, encourage them to use context, and give them opportunities to use context and get feedback on their success in doing so.

Step One: An Introductory Unit on Using Context.   Begin work on context with a 3- to 4-day unit. This concentrated effort is necessary to get students off to a solid start. Tell students what you and they will be to be working on, why being really good at using context clues to infer word meanings is important, and when and where they are likely to employ their skills in using context.

Next, put several sentences containing unknown words and nonsense words and some fairly rich context on the board or overhead and talk through the cues that context provides to the words' meanings. Include some nonsense words so you can be certain students deal with at least some unfamiliar words.

> *The buttery and salty smell of the* zeemee *filled the movie theater lobby, and Sara's mouth began to water.*
> "Let's see. *Zeemee* smells buttery and salty, you get it in a movie theater, and smelling it makes Sara's mouth water. That's easy. It's popcorn."
>
> *Rusty* scowled *angrily at Mary and then stamped out of the room. "I'm never coming back!" he shouted as he left.*
> "Hum. *Scowled* is something Rusty did at Mary. He was angry, and he scowled just before he stamped out of the room, and then he shouted at Mary. I'm not sure what *scowled* means, but it must have something to do with showing anger. Maybe it means the same thing as *shouted,* or maybe sit means *sticking out your tongue,* or maybe it means *giving a mean look.* I'm still not sure what scowled means, but I think it's related to anger, that it's a way of showing anger. (Goerss, Beck, & McKeown, 1999)

After discussing several examples, continue your introductory remarks, telling students that they are likely to use context often and that using context should generally be the first thing they do when they come to an unknown word.

Next, introduce the basic facts students need to know about context cues. These should be initially presented on an overhead or the board, and they should also be put on a chart that is prominently displayed.

- Most words are learned from context.
- Sometimes, context clearly tells us a word's meaning, but sometimes it only hints at it.
- Context cues include words, phrases, and sentences that give us hints about the unknown word.
- Cues can come before or after the unknown word.
- Cues are usually in the same sentence but sometimes they are in other sentences or paragraphs.

Don't have students memorize these points, but do discuss them, clear up any confusion, and give examples where appropriate. Also, tell students that eventually you do want them to learn these facts about context.

This would conclude the first day of the context unit. On the following day, present students with the procedure for using context shown below. Again, present the procedure on an overhead or the board and also put the steps on a chart so that they can be left up and referred to from time to time. Tell students that it is important for them to learn the steps of the procedure, and have them write out the steps and work in pairs to learn them.

- Identify the unknown word.
- Look for words that give hints about what it means.
- Read the sentence with the unknown word. If you need more cues, read the sentences before and after the one with the word.
- Infer the unknown word's meaning based on what you have found in the context.

Now comes a crucial part of the instruction. It consists of you modeling the procedure and then gradually transferring the task of using the procedure to students so that in time students can use the procedure independently.

Your first attempt at modeling would be very similar to what you did with the examples used in introducing the concept of context cues. However, slow down a bit here, emphasizing the steps you are going through. Begin by putting a sentence containing an unknown word and some rich context on the board. Then, model the procedure, asking students to follow along and record the cues on paper as you put them on the board.

> *As Tom stepped out of the tent, the* moist *grass soaked his shoes and he wondered if it had rained.*
> "First, I find the word I don't know. It's *moist.*
> Second, I look for cues to its meaning in the sentence:
>> The grass is moist.
>> It soaks Tom's shoes.
>> Tom thinks it rained.
>> Rain makes things wet.

Once the cues have been listed, synthesize them to infer the unknown word's meaning.

> "Third, I try to put it all together and get a meaning for *moist.*
> Let's see. The moist grass soaks Tom's shoes, which means they got wet.
> Tom thinks it rained which would make the grass wet. *Moist* must mean wet.
> And, fourth, I'll try my meaning in the sentence to see how it works. 'As Tom stepped out of the tent, the wet grass soaked his shoes and he wondered if it had rained.' That makes sense, so I think *moist* probably means 'wet.'"

After this, use the procedure with additional sentences, gradually letting students do more and more of the task. With the next sentence, for example, volunteer some cues and let students volunteer others. Then, let students volunteer some of the cues and have them try to put the cues together to get a meaning for the unknown word. Next, still working from the board, have students volunteer all of the cues and attempt to add them up to get a meaning.

Finally, give students some sentences as seatwork. At first, have students work on these in pairs; later, they can work on them independently. In both cases, review the work as a group activity, praising students when they were correct, trying to figure out what went wrong and how it could be avoided in the future when they were incorrect, and reteaching as necessary.

The process of your modeling, getting responses from student volunteers as you work at the board, having students practice using context in pairs and independently, and discussing their work and reteaching as necessary should continue over several days. Conclude this concentrated instruction once you think students have internalized the basic procedure.

Step Two: Further Work with Context. After this introductory unit, most work with context should take place when students need to figure out unknown words in their reading. As noted, further work should include your repeatedly reminding students of the value of using context to learn word meanings, encouraging them to use context, and giving them opportunities to use context and get feedback on their success in doing so. Of course, you might at some later point teach another unit on context, either as a review or with longer and more difficult contexts. Whether or not you teach another extended unit on context, this further work with context is vital. It is only through your nurturing students' proficiency with context, periodic incidental instruction in context, and some additional instruction, that you can ensure that students maintain and extend their ability to use context.

Using Word Parts to Unlock the Meanings of Unknown Words

The word parts to which we are referring are prefixes, suffixes, and roots. As the heading indicates, here we are concerned with students using these elements to infer word meanings, not to decode words. As is the case with teaching context, we would use explicit instruction in teaching these elements. We would also use a two-part procedure—introducing the element in a unit and then following up that initial instruction with additional instruction, reviews, and reminders over time. Because we have just described some detailed procedures for teaching context, we do not provide a similar description of the instruction here. What we do provide is a description of these elements, how you identify those to teach, and which students are likely to profit from instruction.

Prefixes. Prefixes represent the simplest case. There are a small number of prefixes, many of them are used in a substantial number of words, they appear at the beginnings of words so they are easy for students to spot, and they tend to have a clear lexical meaning that changes the meaning of the root word to which they are attached. White and his colleagues (White, Sowell, & Yanagihara, 1989) have identified the 20 most frequent prefixes, and we have listed these in Figure 8.3. These are the prefixes students need to know.

Almost all middle-grade students will know some of these prefixes and some will know all of them, so you will need to test your students on their prefix knowl-

Figure 8.3   **Twenty Most Frequent Prefixes**

Prefix	Words with the Prefix
un-	782
re-	401
in-, im-, ir-, il-, 'not'	313
dis-	216
en-, em-	132
non-	126
in-, im-, 'in or into'	105
over- 'too much'	98
mis-	83
sub-	80
pre-	79
inter-	77
fore-	76
de-	71
trans-	47
super-	43
semi-	39
anti-	33
mid-	33
under-	25
TOTAL	2,959

Modified from White, Sowell, and Yanagihara (1989).

edge and then teach as appropriate. We suggest that you teach half a dozen or so prefixes in your initial unit and then additional ones, if there are additional ones your students don't know, in subsequent units. If you want a very detailed description of such instruction, one of us (Graves, 2004) has provided one.

Suffixes.   Suffixes represent a more complex case than prefixes in several ways. There are two quite different kinds of suffixes—inflectional suffixes and derivational suffixes. Inflectional suffixes (for example, *-s* and *-ed*) serve grammatical functions such as number and tense. Derivational suffixes (for example, *-ible* and *-less*) signal actual meaning changes; *-ible* means susceptible or capable, and *-less* means without. Since suffixes come at the end of words, so they are not as readily apparent as prefixes. Also, suffixes tend to be difficult to explain to students. Moreover, virtually all middle-grade students who are native speakers of English will already use and understand all English inflectional suffixes. For these reasons, we do not recommend teaching suffixes to native English speakers.

The situation is different for many English-language learners. Many of them will not be adept at using or understanding English suffixes, and it makes good sense to teach them the most frequent ones. White and his colleagues have also identified the

Figure 8.4 **Twenty Most Frequent Suffixes**

Prefix	Words with the Prefix
-s, -es	673
-ed	435
-ing	303
-ly	144
-er, -or (agentive)	95
-ion, -tion, -ation, ition	76
-ible, -able	33
-al, ial	30
-y	27
-ness	26
-ity, -ty	23
-ment	21
-ic	18
-ous, -eous, -ious	18
-en	15
-er (comparative)	15
-ive, -ative, -itive	15
-ful	14
-less	14
-est	12
TOTAL	2,167

Modified from White, Sowell, and Yanagihara (1989).

20 most frequent suffixes, and we have listed those in Figure 8.4. These are the suffixes that English-language learners most need to know. We suggest that you test your English-language learners on these suffixes and then systematically teach those that they don't know.

Using the Dictionary to Identify or Clarify Word Meanings

As Miller and Gildea (1987) have convincingly demonstrated, children frequently have difficulty using the dictionary to define unknown words. For example, after finding the phrase "eat out" in the definition of *erode*, one student showed her confusion in using the definition by composing the sentence "Our family erodes a lot." Another student showed similar confusion after looking up the meaning of *meticulous* and finding the phrase "very careful" in its definition. Her sentence employing the new word read "I was meticulous about falling off the cliff." Obviously, these students found at least some dictionary definitions considerably less than helpful. Perhaps this should not be surprising. Students often receive instruction in alphabetizing, in using guide words, and in using pronunciation keys. However, instruction usually does not go much beyond this, and such instruction is not sufficient for teaching students to effectively work with a tool that they will use throughout

Figure 8.5 **Guidelines for Looking Up Word Meanings in the Dictionary**

- When reading a definition, be sure to read all of it, not just part of it.
- Remember that many words have more than one meaning.
- Be sure to check all the definitions the dictionary gives for a word, not just one or two of them.
- Decide which definition makes sense in the context in which the word is used.
- Often, the dictionary works best when you already have some idea of a word's meaning. This makes the dictionary useful for checking a word you want to use in your writing or a speech you are giving.

their schooling and that most adults continue to use almost daily after completing school.

Many students need help in learning to use the dictionary effectively, and as with teaching the use of context cues and word parts, explicit instruction is a powerful approach to use. Begin by telling students that you are going to be working on using the dictionary to define words, and tell them that spending some time learning to use the dictionary is worthwhile because using the dictionary sometimes isn't as simple as it seems. Then, put some guidelines like those shown in Figure 8.5 on a bulletin board, and leave them up over the upcoming weeks. Don't have students memorize these guidelines, but talk through them, further explaining them as necessary.

The remainder of the procedure continues to parallel that used with context and word parts. Do some modeling; demonstrate how you would look up the meaning of an unknown word. Think aloud, sharing your thinking with students as you come across the unknown word in a text. Show students how you look through the dictionary and find the word, find the definition that seems to fit, consider all of that definition, and then mentally check to see if the meaning you chose makes sense in the context in which the unknown word occurred. Then, gradually, let students take over the procedure and model it for you and for each other. Finally, encourage students to use the procedure when they come across unknown or vaguely known words in context, and from time to time give them opportunities to model their thinking as they use the dictionary so that you can check their proficiency and give them feedback and further instruction as needed.

In addition to learning this general approach to using a dictionary, students need to learn some things about the particular dictionary they use—what the entries for individual words contain and how they are arranged, what aids to its use the dictionary provides, and what features beyond the basic word list the dictionary includes. Much of the important information appears in the front matter of the dictionaries themselves. However, it is very seldom read, and simply asking students to read it is hardly sufficient instruction. Thus, explicit instruction in how to use specific dictionaries is useful.

In this section of the chapter, we have discussed three word-learning strategies—using context, using word parts, and using the dictionary. In deciding which strategies to teach and how long to spend on them, you will first need to find out how

Teaching Idea 8.2
Examining Various Dictionaries

Stop by the curriculum materials library at your university or a local public library, and examine the different levels of dictionaries that they have. Note, for example, how dictionaries for younger students have fewer words, define words more simply, and are generally easier to use and therefore more appropriate for younger readers. Identify a particular middle-grade, and select a dictionary appropriate for that grade. Now make a list of what you need to teach students to use this dictionary effectively, and jot down some notes about how you would teach the things on your list.

skilled your students already are at using them. Once you discover this, spend enough time on each strategy you teach that students become proficient in using it, without spending so much time that students become bored with a strategy. Note that students certainly do not need to learn all of these strategies in a single year. Start where they are, and devote what seems to be a reasonable amount of time to one or more of them. Teaching Idea 8.2 can guide you in preparing for work with dictionaries. If it is possible to coordinate activities with teachers at other grade levels so that a strategy gets initially taught at a particular grade and then reviewed at other grades, that is an excellent arrangement.

Pause and Reflect 8.3

To get a feeling for the extent to which context reveals word meanings, get together with a classmate and arrange for each of you to independently select one or more passages of college-level material that you might read. Identify and white out some difficult words in each of the passages, and then get back together and discuss how and to what extent you can infer the deleted words' meanings from context. ■

Fostering Word Consciousness

Here, we describe our fourth and final approach to helping students build rich and powerful vocabularies—fostering word consciousness. As defined by its most prominent advocates (Anderson & Nagy, 1992; Beck, McKeown, & Omanson, 1987; Graves & Watts, 2002), word consciousness is a disposition toward words that is both cognitive and affective. The student who is word conscious knows a lot of words, and she knows them well. Equally importantly, she is interested in words, and she gains enjoyment and satisfaction from using them well and from seeing or hearing them used well by others. She finds words intriguing, recognizes adroit word usage when she encounters it, uses words skillfully herself, is on the lookout for new and precise words, and is responsive to the nuances of word meanings. She is also well aware of the power of words and realizes that they can be used to foster clarity and understanding or to obscure and obfuscate matters.

Complimenting students when they use sophisticated and apt vocabulary will help to foster their interest in words.

Fostering such attitudes is absolutely crucial and it is something to be achieved across all the years of schooling, but it is a particularly fruitful approach with active and energetic middle-school students. There are myriad ways of developing and nurturing such positive attitudes. Those we highlight here are modeling, recognizing, and encouraging adept diction; promoting word play; and providing intensive and expressive instruction.

Modeling, Recognizing, and Encouraging Adept Diction

Modeling adept diction, recognizing skillful diction in the texts students are reading, and constantly encouraging students to employ adept diction in their own speech and writing are starting points in building word consciousness. As with teaching in general, modeling is critical. Specifically, it is vital to model both enthusiasm for and proficiency in adept word usage.

Consider, for example, the difference between asking a student to close the door because it is *not quite closed* and asking him to close the door because it is *ajar* or the difference between describing the color in a student's painting as *reddish purple* as opposed to *mauve*. When students hear unfamiliar words used to describe concepts they are familiar with and care about, they become curious about the world of words. In addition, they learn—from experience—that word choice possibilities are immense and varied. As their "word worlds" open up, so too do the wider worlds in which they live.

Another opportunity to model, recognize, and encourage adept diction is to use the word-of-the-day approach. Allocating time each day to examine a new word can be effective with students of all ages. The word can be teacher-selected or student-selected and might be chosen from books, magazine articles, or newspapers, or from heard contexts such as appropriate television programs, discussions, and other teachers. It often works well to begin with teacher-selected words and to present the word and its meaning, including both definitional and contextual information, an explanation of why it was selected, and examples of how it relates to the lives of one or more members of the class. When appropriate, and particularly for English-language learners, adding relevant pictures, gestures, concrete objects, and drama increases students' enthusiasm and understanding. Further, a period for student questions and comments allows for the type of deep processing necessary for effective word learning.

Once the responsibility for word selection has been shifted to students, motivation usually increases, as students enjoy finding new words in their worlds. Students can select words in small groups, pairs, or individually and are then responsible for teaching the word to the class. Word-of-the-day activities help students to internalize a sense of word consciousness and associate this sense with both intellectual and emotional responses.

Word-of-the-day activities also encourage students to notice and appreciate the sheer volume of words that surround them, and the uniqueness of individual words. Students can also be encouraged to notice particular words and types of words in their everyday lives. It is particularly useful, for example, for Spanish-speaking students to be on the lookout for cognates, since something like 20 percent of English words have Spanish cognates.

In addition to collecting words that relate to instructional topics, students can collect words related to themes of interest to them. For example, students might enjoy collecting words related to athletics such as *agile, flexible, muscular,* and *brawny,* or words relating to fear, such as *phantom, apparition,* and *specter.*

Good authors, of course, employ appropriate and often colorful words in their writing, and it makes good sense to occasionally point out particularly felicitous or interesting word choices. For example, if a class of fifth graders were reading the chapter on D-Day in Joy Hakim's award-winning history text *War, Peace, and All That Jazz* (1995), a teacher might point out that Hakim chose to use the word *armada* in the sentence "The largest armada ever assembled appeared off the French coast," and ask why *armada* might be a more powerful word than *fleet,* supplying the answer that *armada* refers specifically to a fleet of warships rather than to any sort of fleet, if none of the students supplied an answer.

Or, if a group of seventh-grade students were reading and discussing Russell Freedman's *Eleanor Roosevelt: A Life of Discovery* (1993), a teacher might give special attention to these lines, "Franklin remembered Eleanor as a skinny girl in a *hopeless* party dress. Now she was wearing a stylish outfit from Paris." How, the teacher might ask, could a party dress could be *hopeless*? Why has Freedman chosen this particular word to describe Eleanor's dress? Of course, with only this fragment of context, one is forced to do a lot of inferring, but it seems likely that Eleanor herself, and not just the dress, seemed rather hopeless to Franklin at the time.

Scott and her colleagues (1996) have studied vocabulary as a vehicle for connecting reading and writing. Within the context of literature discussion groups, they assign one student the role of word hunter, whose job it is to look for particularly interesting uses of language in the literature read by the group. This student might, for example, draw the group's attention to Sharon Creech's use of the word *lunatic* in *Walk Two Moons* (1994) to describe a mysterious stranger. Why doesn't the author use *mentally ill* or *weirdo*? How does the author's word choice relate to the character who first uses the word to describe the mysterious fellow? Such discussions can lead students to more thoughtful word choices in their own writing.

Another way Scott suggests to encourage adept diction in students' writing and speaking is to scaffold their use of new words. They might construct sensory webs for words likely to be useful in their writing or for words they have read and would like to understand more fully. The lines leading from the word itself outward provide places for students to fill in what the word smells like, tastes like, looks like, sounds like, and feels like. For example, fourth graders might construct a sensory web showing that *anger* smells like "hot burning coals," looks like "broken glass on the pavement," tastes like "dry sand in the desert," sounds like "fingernails screeching on the blackboard," and feels like "a cold wind gripping you all over." As we have already noted, visuals can be particularly helpful for English-language learners.

Promoting Word Play

Words can simultaneously feel good on the tongue, sound good to the ear, and incite a riot of laughter in the belly. Verbal phenomena such as homographs, idioms, clichés, and puns offer myriad opportunities for investigating language; and word play books to entice middle-grade students are widely available.

Homographs. A large proportion of English words have more than one meaning. These homographs allow for a variety of games, including the following one, taken from Richard Lederer's *Get Thee To a Punnery* (1988). In each of the lines below, students insert a word that means the same as the word or phrase at either end; the number of blanks indicates the number of letters in the missing word.

> summit __ __ __ spinning toy
> hole __ __ __ fruit stone
> nation __ __ __ __ __ __ rural area

Having students complete such puzzles can be fun and entertaining, but having them create such items can be even more valuable. As with many word-play activities, making up items of this sort is well within the reach of many middle-grade students and provides an active, creative, and rewarding learning experience.

Idioms, Clichés, and Puns. Students are often fascinated by idioms such as "A bird in the hand is worth two in the bush" and "Don't count your chickens until they're hatched." Representing as they do the language of particular groups, idioms reflect particular periods of time, particular regions of the country, and particular cultures. Students can enjoy drawing or dramatizing the literal meanings of idioms such as "Don't look a gift horse in the mouth," "Roll with the punches," and "food for thought" and contrasting them with their figurative meanings.

Clichés are often thought of as being unimaginative and trite. But in fact they are actually examples of language use that have endured over time, expressing familiar sentiments and wisdom that are timeless. They are at once phrases that many are familiar with and expressions of shared human experience, making them accessible and important forms of language for students to experience. You can kindle students' word awareness by being "down to earth" with them, warning them about "jumping out of the frying pan into the fire," and repeatedly playing around with phrases such as these "until the cows come home."

Like clichés, puns are memorable and often quite clever. Advertisers often use them in songs and jingles, and newspapers often use puns in headlines. For example, the day after the Minnesota Vikings' star kicker muffed a short field goal that led to the team's ouster from the playoffs, the local paper ran the headline "Kicked Out!" Collecting or creating puns, cliché's and idioms can be both educational and a lot of fun for middle-grade students, and is particularly valuable for English-language learners, who are likely to find these figures of speech a challenge and to need help in understanding them.

Word Play Books and Books in Which Words Play a Central Role. Word play books are very popular, and as a consequence a typical branch library is likely to have a dozen or so of them. Those we have found for just plain fun include Herb Kohl's *A Book of Puzzlements: Play and Invention with Language* (1981), Lorraine Hopping Egan and Lorraine Jean Hopping's *Best-Ever Vocabulary & Word Study Games* (2001), Imogene Forte and her colleague's *ESL Vocabulary and Word Usage: Games, Puzzles, and Inventive Exercises* (2001), and our favorite, Richard Lederer's *Pun and Games* (1996). Children's literature in which words play a central role—for example, Andrew Clements' *Frindle* (1996), Monalissa Degross's *Donavan's Word Jar* (1994), and Norton Juster's *The Phantom Toll Booth* (1961)—are terrific for focusing students' attention on words. For more books that celebrate words, see Laura Hornik's "A Celebration of Words" (2000), an annotated list of word play books and other books focusing on words.

Providing Intensive and Expressive Instruction

Some very interesting and highly effective activities that can foster word consciousness have been developed and carefully researched by Beck and McKeown (1983) and by Duin and Graves (1988). The activities are quite similar, except that Beck and McKeown's goal was full and deep understanding of words while Duin's goal was full and deep understanding of words coupled with children's using the words in writing. Developing and presenting these activities involves several steps. The first step is to select a small set of words that are semantically related. For example, a set used by Beck and McKeown—*rival, hermit, novice, virtuoso, accomplice, miser, tyrant,* and *philanthropist*—contained words that refer to *people*; and a set used by Duin—*advocate, capability, configuration, criteria, disarray, envision, feasible, habitable, module, quest, retrieve,* and *tether*—contained words that can be used in talking about *space exploration*.

Teaching Idea 8.3
Constructing an Activity for Fostering Word Consciousness

Get together with a classmate, identify a group of students, and brainstorm a set of brief and upbeat activities you might employ over a semester in fostering their word consciousness.

Describe one of those activities in some detail. Finally, critique your activity. What are its strong points? What are its weak points? How can it be improved?

The next step, the central part of the instruction, is to have students work extensively and intensively with the words, spending perhaps half an hour a day over a period of a week with them, and engaging in a dozen or so diverse activities with them—really getting to know them, discovering their shades of meaning and the various ways in which they can be used, and realizing what interesting companions words can be. Beck and McKeown's activities, for example, included defining the words, asking students to use them in sentences, and asking students to respond to words like *virtuoso* and *miser* with thumbs up or thumbs down to signify approval or disapproval. Their activities also included asking which of three actions an *accomplice* would be most likely to engage in—robbing a bank by him- or herself, stealing some candy, or driving a getaway car; and asked such questions as "Could a *virtuoso* be a *rival*? Could a *virtuoso* be a *novice*? and Could a *philanthropist* be a *miser*?" Duin's activities also began with defining the words and asking students to use them in sentences. Her other activities included asking students to discuss how *feasible* space travel might soon be, asking them how a space station could *accommodate* handicapped persons, and asking them to write brief essays called "Space Shorts" in which they used the words in dealing with such topics as the foods that might be available in space.

The third step, which is used only if the goal includes students' using the words in their writing, is to have students write more extensive essays using as many of the taught words as possible, playing with them and exploring their possibilities.

Finally, we would conclude with a fourth step—that of directly discussing with students the word choices they make, why they make those choices, and how adroit use of words makes our speech and writing more precise, more memorable, and more interesting. See Teaching Idea 8.3 as a start-up activity.

Concluding Remarks

Students face an extremely large task in mastering the vocabulary they need to succeed in school and in their lives outside of school. Competent students will have vocabularies in the range of 30,000 words by the time they complete eighth grade. It is crucial that we provide them with a robust vocabulary program to assist them with this formidable task. A robust program should include at least four components: (1) frequent, extensive, and varied language experiences, (2) instruction in individual words, (3) instruction in strategies for learning words independently—that is, instruction in using context clues, word parts, and the dictionary, (4) and word consciousness activities. For additional information on each of these components, we suggest *The Vocabulary Book* (Graves, 2006).

Obviously, the task of teaching vocabulary is a large one. However, no one teacher is expected to be singularly responsible for vocabulary instruction. Teachers in all classes must work together to ensure that their students develop the broad and rich vocabularies they need. You can choose which word-learning task is most important at a particular point in your class, which level of word knowledge you expect students to achieve with particular words, what teaching procedure or procedures will be most appropriate for the words in a particular selection your students are reading, and what specific words you wish to teach. Moreover, as suggested earlier, not every teacher needs to take major responsibility for teaching students to use context, use the dictionary, and the like. You and the other teachers in your school can work together to decide who is responsible for these various teaching tasks.

Rich and powerful vocabularies are, of course, an important part of becoming fully literate. Students who have achieved full literacy have vocabularies that enable them to be precise and even colorful in their own speech and writing, to recognize and appreciate the skillful use of words in the literary selections they read, and to understand the sometimes subtle and often crucial meanings of words in the informational reading they do.

■ EXTENDING LEARNING

1. As we have emphasized, given the very large number of words that students must learn, wide reading is one of the best vehicles for developing vocabulary. Your ability to promote wide reading among your students will depend heavily on your getting the right books into their hands. As one step toward becoming more skilled in selecting books for middle-grade students, imagine a particular grade level in grades 4–8 and a group of students, and brainstorm possible topics that would interest this group. Then, using bibliographies, the web, library card catalogs, electronic data bases, and the advice of a librarian, select half a dozen books on this topic that are likely to be of interest to your students. If the group of students you are considering includes less skilled readers or English-language learners, be sure to include some books appropriate for these children.

2. Identify a particular middle grade and group of students to whom you might teach vocabulary. If at all possible, this should be actual group of students that you can really teach. If you do have a group of students to work with, talk to their teacher and ask him to select half a dozen or so words that he would like his students to learn. If not, select a set of words yourself. Next, identify one of the procedures presented in the chapter that is appropriate for teaching these words, develop whatever materials you need to teach with those procedures, and prepare to do the teaching. If you haven't taught much before, it would be a good idea to rehearse with a classmate. Finally, teach the vocabulary, and then

afterwards talk to students to get their reaction to your instruction. If it isn't possible to work with a real class, simulate this experience using your university classmates as students.

3. Look back at the procedure for teaching context cues, and assume that you have already completed the first day of instruction on using context, much as it is described in the chapter. Assume further that you did some modeling of your using context cues, and that students seemed to be picking up on the technique, but you think some further modeling would be useful. Select two sentences containing difficult words and some cues to the words' meanings, much like the sentence we used with *moist*. Then, create a lesson plan for modeling your use of context to puzzle out the words' meanings. Because this is your first attempt with this procedure, actually write out the script of what you would say, just as we did. Finally, teach your excerpt from a unit on context cues with some of your university classmates playing the role of students.

■ BOOKS FOR MIDDLE-GRADE READERS

Clements, A. (1996). *Frindle.* New York: Simon & Schuster.

Creech, S. (1994). *Walk two moons.* New York: HarperCollins.

DeGross, M. (1994). *Donovan's word jar.* New York: HarperCollins.

Egan, L. H., & Hopping, L. J. (2001). *Best ever vocabulary & word study games.* New York, Scholastic.

Forte, I., & Pangle, M. A. (2001). *ESL vocabulary and word usage: Games, puzzles, and inventive exercises.* New York: Inventive Publications.

Freedman, R. (1993). *Eleanor Roosevelt: A life of discovery.* New York: Scholastic.

Hakim, J. (1995). *War, peace, and all that jazz.* New York: Oxford University Press.

Kohl, H. (1981). *A book of puzzlements: Play and invention with language.* New York: Schocken Books.

Lederer, R. (1988). *Get thee to a punnery.* Charleston, SC: Wyrick & Co.

Lederer, R. (1996). *Pun and games.* Chicago: Chicago Review Press.

Juster, N. (1961). *The phantom toll booth.* New York: Knopf.

chapter

9

Assessment

Teachers who watch students as they engage in classroom activities know a lot about their students' strengths and weaknesses.

In one corner of the room a group of students is talking about a book that they are reading. Ton, their teacher, is watching and listening, making notes on a form that he has on his clipboard. Most of the other students are in one of three other small groups, also discussing the book they are reading. A small number of students are sitting at their desks, writing in their response journals, while others are filling out a questionnaire that asks about their reading habits out of school. Ton gets up and moves over to another small group, clipping a clean observation form onto his board.

Later that week Ton has finished observing all of the small discussion groups, everyone has filled out the questionnaire, and, as always, everyone has been writing in their response journals. Today, each small group finishes their discussion—their last for this particular book—with a 5-minute self-evaluation of the effectiveness of their group. After talking together about the questions on the form Ton gave them, individual students fill it out and hand it in.

Although it might not look like it at first glance, these students were all participating in assessment. They were writing in response journals, which Ton collects every Friday and reads over the weekend, making notes of what he sees his students doing, what they seem to be having trouble with, and anything else that he wants to keep track of. They were also providing him with information about their reading habits outside of school so that he will know what he needs to do in school to promote independent reading. They were being formally evaluated by Ton as he watched them work in small discussion groups, and they engaged in self-evaluation as they considered the effectiveness of those groups. All of this "authentic" assessment information helps Ton plan his instruction to meet the needs of his students.

Assessment permeates all aspects of good teaching and is constant across a school day and year. Assessment, the careful observation or measurement of students' performance, is *the* essential element that allows reflective, responsive instruction. The kind of assessment that positively affects instruction is different from the evaluation of student progress through standardized tests, offering a different kind of information that is more useful to teachers and leads to better instruction.

In this chapter we examine various facets of the assessment of reading and literary practices and response. First, we discuss standardized tests, their role in education, and how to prepare students to take them. Then we present various assessment opportunities that allow teachers to pinpoint the strengths and weaknesses of their students. We then turn to ways to help students learn to assess their own progress, and ways to document that progress. We close with a discussion of how to assess the effectiveness of your own teaching.

Pause and Reflect 9.1

Think about the tests you have taken over your career as a student. How did it make you feel to go into a room filled with other students and perform the testing task in a specified amount of time? How did it make you feel to know that you couldn't ask any questions? That people were watching to make sure that no one was cheating? Was this in any way a learning experience? ∎

Beyond Standardized Tests

For years, teachers have relied on their own observations and their self-constructed tests and other assessment tasks to help them know whether their students were learning. The kind of assessment we find the most useful is often called *authentic assessment,* to call attention to its grounded-in-practice nature. We teach, however, in a system that embraces standardized tests and therefore it is necessary to understand, not only how to incorporate authentic assessment in your classroom, but also how to think about the standardized tests that become the data through which administrators and the general public make inferences about the success or failure of schools and individual teachers and students.

Norm-Referenced Standardized Tests

Norm-referenced tests such as the Iowa Test of Basic Skills, the Scholastic Aptitude Test, or the American College Testing Program, which you may have taken before applying for college, provide a way of describing student performance relative to the performance of other students who took the same test. Norm-referenced scores such as grade-equivalent scores and percentile ranks reflect this comparison between the test taker's score and the score of students in the *norm* group—a group of students whose scores are used as a reference point. The results of such tests are reported in several ways, two of which are grade-equivalent scores and percentile ranks.

Grade equivalent scores describe the average performance of students at various grade levels. A student obtaining a grade equivalent score of 5.9, for example, has scored as well on the test as did the average student in the norm group taking the test in the ninth month of fifth grade. Unfortunately, grade-equivalent scores are not nearly as precise an indicator as they appear to be and are often misinterpreted. Percentile ranks are more easily interpreted. *Percentile ranks* describe the relative position of the test taker compared with students in the norm group. A student scoring at the fiftieth percentile, for example, has performed equal to or better than 50 percent of the students at his or her grade level in the norm group, and a student scoring at the seventy-fifth percentile has performed equal to or better than 75 percent of these students.

There are many factors to consider when evaluating scores on norm-referenced tests, and it is important not to overemphasize the value of such tests. Their primary merit lies in the fact that they can usually be given to large groups of students at one time and can give you a general idea of how a student is performing relative to other students. However, you must also keep in mind that norm-referenced tests measure decontextualized skills—skills as used in a testing situation rather than in standard practice in the classroom—in a stressful, high-stakes context, and they often suppress student performance. The most important thing to remember is that the scores are only helpful if the test is a valid test of, for example, reading ability or literary knowledge, and if the students in the norming group are similar to your students.

Validity is the extent to which a test actually measures what it purports to measure. For example, while most norm-referenced reading tests have a vocabulary section, some consist of only a vocabulary test requiring students to match words with their definitions. Because reading involves the comprehension of phrases, sentences, and larger chunks of extended discourse, a test of vocabulary in isolation is a valid test of word knowledge but not of reading performance as a whole.

Norm groups consist of those students on which the norm-referenced scores are based. This group of students should be as similar to your students as possible. If, for example, you are teaching in a suburban school district and your students represent several ethnicities, the tests you give should have been normed on a group that includes suburban students and multi-ethnic students. If you are teaching in a rural school and all of your students are African American and the test you give was normed on a group of white students in an urban area, the resulting scores will be difficult to interpret. In addition, U.S. tests are generally normed on students whose native language is English. Thus, the performance of an English-language learner student on such a test would be difficult to interpret.

Finally, norm-referenced tests are *summative*, in that they purport to measure the impact of instruction at a point in time that usually makes it impossible to alter that instruction. If instruction has not been successful, it is up to the next year's teacher to bring students up to grade level . . . but they won't know if they've been successful until the end of the year, when it is again too late to alter instruction. It is no wonder that both teachers and students often are frustrated by this process.

Nevertheless, norm-referenced tests are, for better or for worse, an important aspect of education today. Norm-referenced tests may be used to determine whether a student is eligible for special services, such as additional help from a reading specialist. Administrators are often, and it can be argued, justly, concerned with how students in their schools fare compared to students in other schools. Public officials are often concerned with how students in the areas they represent compare to other students across the country. On a national level, those who set educational policy are often concerned with how U.S. students perform relative to students in other countries. All of this impacts the classroom teacher, as these scores often become the standard by which others measure an individual teacher's success. Given the limitations of norm-referenced tests, this is problematic.

Further, as students progress across the grades, their scores on norm-referenced tests increasingly impact their lives. In the middle and high school years, prospects for college and jobs increasingly depend on a student's ability to do well on norm-referenced tests. Because of this, it is important that teachers know how to help middle-grade students become strategic and successful test takers. We discuss how to do this later in this chapter.

Criterion-Referenced Standardized Tests

Criterion-referenced tests focus on how well students perform specific tasks rather than on how their performance compares to that of other students. These tests use the idea of a cutoff score, or a criterion, set by the test makers, your school district, or you. Students scoring at or above this point are said to be proficient in the particular facet of reading or language arts tested, while student scoring below this point are said to require further development in order to reach proficiency. Thus, a criterion-referenced test accompanying a reading series might include a passage followed by five comprehension questions. Someone, either the test makers or the school district, sets a goal of 80 percent accuracy, meaning that students must answer at least four of the questions correctly in order to demonstrate the criterion of proficiency specified.

Generally, audiences such as parents, principals, and educational policy makers find commercially produced norm-referenced and criterion-referenced tests more helpful than do teachers. These kinds of tests can reveal general facts about achievement and provide information on groups of students. In most cases, however, they do not provide information that is specific enough to aid in the planning of instructional goals, methods, and materials for individual students. Further, since they are not designed to match the instructional emphasis of a specific school or district, they are not necessarily good measures of what students are learning on a day-to-day basis. Finally, there is some concern that these measures may not be sensitive to small increments in growth over time, making it difficult to determine how students who struggle are progressing.

Despite the shortcomings of standardized tests, they are part and parcel of education in the twenty-first century. They affect you, the teacher, and your students. Because of this, it is important to do what you can to help your students become confident and strategic test takers.

Preparing Students for Standardized Tests. One of the biggest problems with getting students ready to take standardized tests is the amount of time spent doing so. It is important to remember that if you are teaching students how to be strategic, thoughtful readers then you are also teaching them how to do well on standardized tests. You can, however, include in your teaching some strategic preparation for the process of testing, as you help your students understand the purpose of the tests and the procedures they need to follow when taking it. Calkins, Montgomery, Falk, and Santman's (1998) *A Teacher's Guild to Standardized Reading Tests* provides suggestions you will find very helpful.

Even though individual student scores rarely affect individual students, middle-grade students know that the better they are at taking these tests, the easier it will be for them to succeed in high school and beyond. These students have gone to school long enough to know that attitudes toward students whose scores are high are different from attitudes towards students whose scores are low. Even if you tell them that the scores won't even be reported for months, they may still feel apprehensive, or perhaps even antagonistic. Be honest with them, telling them what's at stake. Everyone in a class, a school, and a school system is, in some way, affected by standardized test scores. Because of this, it is important to take these tests seriously, but to not worry too much about them.

One way to help assuage your students' worry is to teach them how to be strategic test takers. Standardized tests provide a script of what you can say during their administration. You can't repeat instructions, explain them, or answer questions. You can't even reassure your students. But you can teach them how to listen carefully and give them practice in following oral instructions, an ability that will maintain its usefulness well beyond standardized test time. You can also help students learn to read test passages and respond to test questions by giving them sample items that provide practice of particular test-taking strategies. Help them learn to work under time pressure by giving them only a certain amount of time to finish a passage and questions. Then talk with them as a group about the experience. What

Teaching Idea 9.1
Teaching the Test as a Genre

Many teachers in the middle grades spend some time during the school year helping students learn about the various genres in literature. Each genre has particular content, conventions, or constraints that allow us to identify it as a particular genre. When students learn these characteristics it helps them be able to make sense of what they read in each genre. For example, they wouldn't expect science fiction to be realistic, but they would expect it to be logical.

In many ways the text in standardized tests—brief reading passages and followup questions—is itself a genre of reading not found anywhere else. Students who have learned to ap-proach reading particular genres in particular ways can easily understand that certain reading practices will be most effective when working with a test genre. Use passages from old tests or practice items and ask students to note the characteristics of the texts. After you have recorded these characteristics, work with your students to suggest strategies for successful completion of the reading task that a standardized test presents. A bit of practice on similar passages using these strategies can help students become more confident about taking standardized tests.

was confusing? What was difficult? What was successful? Teaching Idea 9.1 gives you an example of a strategy that many middle-grade teachers have found effective as they prepare students for standardized tests.

General tips for test-taking are also both appropriate and helpful. If a test does not penalize incorrect choices, tell students to "finish the test," even if they aren't sure of the answers. If they're uncertain, they should pick what they think is the best answer and go on. An alternative is for students to mark those answers that they are not sure of and then go back over them after they have completed the test. Teach your students to manage their stress by rolling their shoulders, putting their pencils down and flexing their hands, or closing their eyes and visualizing something pleasant.

Getting ready to take standardized tests by discussing the reasons for the testing and by learning about effective procedures and strategies for test taking will help students build on the sound reading practices that you have been teaching throughout the school year. Even though standardized tests don't help you, as a teacher, understand what or how your individual students are learning, you can make preparing for these tests an opportunity for learning test-taking skills that will stand your students in good stead as they progress through school. Just don't take too much class time to do so!

Authentic Assessment

The measures that, compositely, are often called *informal* or *authentic* assessment are much more useful for making instructional decisions. Although not as securely established in the politics of U.S. education, they are the most important kind of assessment practice if your goal is to make instruction responsive to the needs of your students. Assessment practices that are part of the regular life of the classroom, with

Standardized tests can be less stressful if teachers help students learn how to be strategic test takers.

teachers and students engaged in assessing progress in meaningful contexts and in a useful and timely fashion, is authentic assessment. This is assessment that influences instruction, and that offers teachers the opportunity to examine student progress so that they can make informed decisions about instruction across the course of a school year. This kind of assessment also offers meaningful opportunities for students to assess themselves, set goals, and monitor their own progress. Further, authentic assessment is especially important when working with English-language learners (Bernhardt & Kamil, 1998).

Authentic assessment is an on-going process. Teachers assess students' learning on a day-by-day and, sometimes, a moment-by-moment basis. For example, as you talk to your students, you may scan the group and make a mental note of whether each student appears to be engaged in the lesson. If you see a look of confusion, you will probably restate what you just said or invite questions. This almost invisible ongoing assessment of the learning situation allows you to modify your instruction in order to maximize student learning.

Of course, observation is only one of several types of assessment. Assessment takes many forms, as we describe below, and the type of assessment used in any given situation is determined by the purpose of that assessment—that is, what it is you are trying to learn about a student or group of students. If you are trying to learn whether students are comprehending instruction, you might observe their facial expressions and body language or ask them a question. If you are trying to learn about students' reading habits and preferences, you might give them a questionnaire or talk with them individually. If you are trying to learn about students' comprehension of or response to the texts they are reading you might want to talk with them, give them a paper-and-pencil test, or set a task for them to do that will allow you to assess their comprehension in action. If you are trying to learn about the amount of reading students are doing, you might want to ask them to keep some kind of record and then collect those records as evidence. Once you decide what information you are after, your purposes for assessment, you can decide how to go about collecting that information.

Whereas norm-referenced and criterion-referenced assessment is done for the sake of informing people outside of the classroom about students' performance and has little or no direct influence on instruction, most of the time the authentic assessment practices that you use will be inextricably linked with instruction. Information gleaned from various assessments will inform your teaching, and your teaching will inform your decisions about the types and amounts of assessments to conduct, as authentic assessment both reflects and influences classroom practice. Specifically, authentic assessment can help you to: (1) determine how quickly and in what ways your students are progressing as readers; (2) identify students who are not making adequate progress and pinpoint specific areas of difficulty for these students; (3) identify students who have mastered particular aspects of reading and determine ways to continue to challenge them; (4) evaluate the effectiveness of your instruction and plan future instruction that meets the needs and utilizes the strengths of your students; and (5) evaluate your overall effectiveness as a teacher.

Reflective, responsive teachers have many ways to do this. Several techniques are described in the following section; all of them are merely examples of what you can do as you develop the assessments that allow you to monitor your specific students in your particular classroom setting. But first you need to determine the purpose for your assessment. What is it that you need to know?

Assessing Student Performance

There are many purposes for assessment, many questions about student performance that teachers need to ask. Likewise, there are many ways to approach assessment, and what works for one teacher with one particular class will not necessarily work for others. There are, however, some general ways of organizing assessment that help frame effective assessment. These include regularly scheduled, formal observation, informal observation of students as they engage in classroom activities, collecting student work, and talking with students.

What Needs Assessing?

Recently, the two largest professional organizations in literacy, the International Reading Association and the National Council of Teachers of English, collaborated to develop Standards for the English Language Arts (1996). Other organizations, such as the National Science Teachers Association and the National Council of Social Studies have developed standards for their specific fields. The English-language standards call for the ability to comprehend, interpret, evaluate, appreciate, research, and reflect on the ideas and information gleaned from print. They call for the development of the high levels of literacy needed for full participation in today's world. The English-language standards are a good place to begin when thinking about what you want to assess in your students. Below are some basic questions that you might want to ask about your students. Following that, we give examples of different ways you can obtain the information that you are looking for.

To understand your students as readers, look for evidence that answers the following general questions:

- Does the student read and enjoy reading?
- Does the student understand what he or she reads?
- Does the student think and share thoughts about his or her reading?
- Does the student apply ideas gleaned from reading to the real world?
- Does the student talk with others to add to his or her understanding?
- Does the student understand how texts work?
- Does the student understand his or her own role in the reading process?

More specific questions regarding reading would include the following:

- To what extent does the student self-check and self-correct?
- How fluently does the student read?
- What is the student's silent reading rate?
- How large is the student's vocabulary?
- What sort of vocabulary building skills does he or she have?

These and other important questions can be answered in a variety of ways. Below we discuss formal and informal observation, student products or artifacts, and talking with students as important ways of obtaining the information you need. We then follow this with examples of combining multiple assessment strategies to find out what you need to know.

Formal Observations

Formal observations involve setting an interesting task for students and evaluating their performance on that task. This observation process looks a lot like regular classroom procedures, but in this instance teachers are formally evaluating their students' performance and students know that this is happening. Observations might occur while students are reading, doing oral reports, meeting in small groups to talk about text, or engaging in any literacy activity that is important in the classroom. These assessments occur throughout the year, and sample from the wide variety of tasks that occur in the classroom. They differ from other types of observation in that these are scheduled, students know that they are being observed, and teachers generally use a checklist, observation guide, or some kind of formal procedure so that their observations are relatively standard across groups and across time.

The first step in constructing a schedule for formal observations is to decide what it is that you want to watch your students doing. The purpose will reflect what you value in your classroom, as the formal nature of these observations require preparation and a commitment of time. For example, if you are teaching using literature discussion groups, you will probably want to formally observe how those groups operate, noting what aspects of text are discussed and how your students interact in those groups. If you ask students to practice certain comprehension strategies, then you will want to document how and when they do that. If you want to know how students read orally and to assess their comprehension abilities, then you might want to schedule time to do informal reading inventories with each student.

Once you have decided what you want to observe, then you will develop some systematic procedures that will allow you to document student behavior. Before we describe some examples of such procedures, it is important to think about the skill of being a good observer.

Observing Carefully. People constantly observe and assess. We make sense of our lives through our observations of the stream of events and behaviors that occur. What we observe, however, is always influenced by our presence as an observer as well as who we are, what we have experienced, and what we expect to see. This holds true for teachers observing students in the classroom. What we see is never objective, as it is always a combination of what is there to observe and how we look at it. For example, a seventh-grade student comes into your classroom, and you look at him. He has multiple piercings on his head, you can see the edge of a tattoo just below his t-shirt sleeve, and his clothes are all black. You think you see a student who is potential trouble. Actually, he might be a very bright, articulate, kind person, but the image that you have created takes in the way he looks and makes a value judgment. You think you see trouble, when what you actually see is a young man dressed in black with multiple piercings and a tattoo.

To become an effective observer you need to try to identify personal biases and control them as best you can. All teachers have ideas of what they like and don't like in students, what they expect from students from certain families, or how they feel about individual children. If you get to know your students as well as we hope you do, then you can't help but develop these biases. Because of this, it is important to strive to distinguish between what you *observe* and what you *infer*. If, for example, you observe your class during your time in the library, you might see two students sitting by a window, books in hand, gazing out of the window. You think to yourself: "Ah, Mary is thinking about her book. And look at Bob, he's daydreaming again." You're observing the same behavior in both students, but your biases are affecting what you think you are seeing. You observation is that both Mary and Bob are holding books and looking out of the window. That's what is happening. While the inference that Mary is thinking and Bob is daydreaming may be a correct inference, it is important to understand that it is an inference, not observed behavior, and is based on the teacher's perception of the individual students. It is only over time and across many observations and situations that the teacher can be sure that the inferences he or she is making about students are, in fact, sound.

With that in mind, it becomes clear that a valid assessment of a student's progress in the classroom is possible only with multiple pieces of information, including observations that are as unbiased as possible. Structured observation guides and formal assessment procedures such as those discussed below help teachers maintain a measure of objectivity.

There are many ongoing events in a classroom that can be formally observed and assessed. Scheduling time to sit and watch particular classroom events or practices offers teachers the opportunity to assess student behaviors within the context of classroom practice. This kind of assessment is, unlike taking norm-referenced or criterion-referenced tests, *contextualized*—it takes place within the naturally occurring routines of the classroom. To do this well, teachers first decide which events to observe by thinking about what they want to know about their students, their classroom practices, and the effectiveness of their instruction. They then select appropriate behaviors to watch for, a selection based on their knowledge of the content or processes that are part of the event they are observing. From this they create an observation guide on which to take notes. The guide allows more time for actually observing what is going on and the generation of comparable data across groups and students. Below we present examples of common classroom events and suggest items for an observation guide or specific procedures to follow.

Observing Discussion Group Interaction. The formal observation of the functioning of the discussion groups in your classroom is an important tool for determining the effectiveness of those groups. Observation of discussion groups allows you to assess the behaviors of a group as a whole and those of individual students within the group. For example, an observation guide might include the following items suggested by Strickland, Galda, and Cullinan (2004), with space for making notes between each item.

- What is the context? (participants, physical setting, book, topic, or task)
- What types of discussion behavior do you observe? Possibilities include:
  - turn taking
  - listening to others
  - responding to others' comments
  - staying on topic
  - supporting statements with specific examples from text
  - politeness as group member
  - contributions as group member

Looking for these behaviors will help you assess a group's performance or an individual's performance. This list can also be adapted to become a self-assessment tool for groups or individual students.

Assessing the Content of Literature Discussion. The content of a literature discussion, whether in a group, with a peer or between teacher and student is something else that can be observed and recorded. Below is a basic list of things to listen for during literature discussions (Strickland, Galda, & Cullinan, 2004) that can be adapted to suit the needs and abilities of groups of students as well as the dimensions of a particular text.

- understands the gist of the story
- recalls plot sequence

- understands plot structure
- considers genre demands such as setting
- considers characters':
  - motivation
  - interaction
  - growth
  - development (author's technique)
- considers theme
- considers style
- comments on author's word choice
- sentence structure
- evaluates categorically
- evaluates analytically
- generalizes

A simple page with these items running down the left-hand side creates an instrument that allows you to focus on these items; alternatives to this focus abound, depending on what you want to know about what your students say about the books they read.

Assessing the Content of Discussions of Nonfiction Texts. There are also things that you can listen for when students are discussing a nonfiction text, whether in the English language arts classroom or another content area classroom. Some things you might want to note include the following:

- Do students link new information to what they already know?
- Do students go beyond reproducing information to discuss broad ideas and concepts?
- Do students understand the difference between fact and opinion?
- Do students refer to the author's qualifications and use of resources?
- Do students use appropriate, discipline-specific terminology that is present in the text?
- Do students make use of the illustrations (pictures, graphs, diagrams, etc.) as they build meaning?
- Do students make use of the organizational features of the text (table of contents, index, glossary, etc.) as they refer to the text to find specific information to support their statements?

Observing Oral Reporting Skills and Content. Students' skill at oral presentations can also be observed as they are giving oral reports to the class or a small group. This allows you to keep track of students' developing competencies in formal oral language use. Items on an observation guide or checklist for oral reports might include the following:

- orders information that is accurate
- considers audience knowledge and experience
- offers new, interesting information that is accurate
- well-constructed, logical

Reading proficiency is easily assessed through a one-on-one Informal Reading Inventory.

- adapts language to audience needs
- times presentation to include questions
- speaks clearly
- evenly paced
- attends to audience for feedback

Other items can be added to the guide as needed.

Assessing Oral Reading and Comprehension: Informal Reading Inventories. Informal reading inventories (IRIs), a commonly used tool, help teachers determine the reading proficiency of their students. They consist of passages that a student reads orally to a teacher. They can be used to assess both the appropriateness of specific texts for individual students as well as to investigate areas of strength and weakness for individual students. Informal reading inventories allow you to check student development in such areas as oral reading (fluency, decoding strategies, and types of oral reading errors), reading comprehension (literal and inferential), sight vocabulary, reading rate, and behaviors such as finger pointing and holding the text too close. IRIs are effective in both English language arts and content-area classrooms, and provide important data about reading proficiency as that relates to the material being used to teach any content, for any reader. A teacher-made IRI is a perfect tool to assess how English-language learners are processing the texts they encounter in the classroom.

The particular IRI described here is teacher-made and individually administered. In order to avoid confusion, we should point out that this version of an IRI differs in some ways from conventional IRIs, which have been described in detail by Marjorie Johnson and her colleagues (1987). To make your own IRI, first select a text. Selecting a text that you might actually use with the student will maximize the applicability of the assessment. This text can be a portion of a book for adolescents or a portion of the textbook that you use. After making your selection, follow the steps outlined here.

• Select two passages that seem representative of the book as a whole in terms of sentence length, vocabulary, prior knowledge required, and so on. A 200- to 250-word passage is appropriate for most middle-grade readers.

• Make sure the student feels at ease, then introduce the passage by saying something such as, "I'm going to have you read this paragraph about whales to me and then I'd like you to tell me what you read about."

• As the student is reading, follow along with a duplicate copy. Circle words that the student has difficulty with or omits during reading, noting in the margin any mispronunciations or substitutions of one word for another. In addition, note any significant behaviors exhibited by the reader, such as lack of expression during reading, finger pointing, holding the text close to the eyes, and markedly slow or markedly rapid rate.

• After the passage has been read, check comprehension by asking the student to retell what he has read. Initially, ask the student to respond without looking back at the passage. However, if he needs to look back in order to give a satisfactory retelling, let him do so. Characterize the retelling using simple descriptions such as "complete, coherent, and shows good understanding," "somewhat sketchy but showing basic understanding" or "sketchy and not showing much understanding." You might also want to ask a question or two, perhaps an inferential question and an application question, and record the student's success with those. Additionally, your notes should indicate whether the student needed to look back to retell the passage.

• If you are uncertain about the student's competency with this and similar texts, you can repeat the IRI with the second passage.

In addition to providing you with information on the student's oral reading, reading comprehension, sight vocabulary, and reading rate, an informal reading inventory will give you a good sense of whether the reading material from which the passages were taken and similar selections are appropriate for the student.

Identifying the level of students' competence with a particular selection—and, therefore, with other selections much like the one used—is useful when you consider matching students with texts of any kind.

• *Independent level.* Material is at a student's independent level when he can read it with fluency and ease, can effectively retell a short passage, and can answer inferential and application questions on the passage. This level of material is suitable for independent reading in the classroom and for reading outside of school.

- *Instructional level:* Material is at a student's instructional level when he can read it but occasionally stumbles over words, can retell some of a short passage but may have to reread to give a fairly detailed retelling, and seems to find answering inferential and application questions challenging. This level of material is appropriate for lessons in which you will aid the student; that is, this level of material is appropriate for classroom instruction in which you would provide some of the types of assistance we describe in Chapters 4 and 5.

- *Frustration level.* Material is at a student's frustration level when he reads it somewhat haltingly, pausing or stumbling over 10 percent or more of the words. Another sign that material is at a student's frustration level comes if he can retell little of it, has to reread to retell it, or is confused in his retelling. Still another sign comes if the student cannot answer inferential or application questions. If the inventory reveals any of these characteristics, the material used in the inventory and probably other similar material is too difficult for the student and not something that you want to encourage him to read in or out of school.

In addition to creating your own IRIs for the purposes of selecting appropriate materials for specific students, understanding how students are processing the textbooks that you use, or spot-checking reading progress throughout the year, you may wish to use a published IRI to measure growth from the beginning of the year to the end. There are several good IRIs on the market including the *Qualitative Reading Inventory—II* by Lauren Leslie and Joanne Caldwell (1995).

Assessing Silent Reading Rates. Knowing the silent reading rates of your students is both easy and important. It is important because how much reading you assign needs to be dictated by students' reading rate. In particular, you want to be sure that you do not assign reading that would take much more time than you allot in class or much more time that can reasonably be expected for homework. The question is also important because very low rates may suggest a general lack of reading proficiency.

Checking silent reading rates can be done as a class. We suggest that you choose two selections that students typically read in your class, one of which is fairly easy and one a bit challenging, and both of them long enough that students will *not* complete them in 5 minutes. If a textbook is the primary reading material that you use, select from that. Next, make up three or four simple comprehension questions on each selection. After this, tell students that you want to get an idea of their reading rate, that it is not a race and they should read as they usually do, and let them know that they will be asked to answer a few questions after they read the passage. Then, start them all reading at the beginning of the selection at the same time, and stop them at the end of 5 minutes and ask them to put a pencil mark where they finished. As soon as students have marked their finishing points, ask your three or four questions and let students jot down their answers. After students have completed both the easier and the more challenging selections, either you or the students can then tally the words read per minute, and this is what goes in your record. The comprehension questions were included just to let students know that they did need to read

Teaching Idea 9.2
Assessing Vocabulary and Vocabulary Building Skills

When assessing vocabulary and vocabulary-building skills, four items—each of which is assessed somewhat differently—are worth considering: oral vocabulary, reading vocabulary, use of context cues, and knowledge of word parts.

First, you can classify students' oral vocabularies as average, smaller than average, or larger than average simply on the basis of the oral language you hear them use. Second, you can classify students' reading vocabularies based on the vocabulary section of a norm-referenced test they have taken and the word knowledge they display as they read in class. Estimates of both oral and reading vocabulary are particularly important for English-language learners, who may have relatively small English vocabularies and who may need extensive opportunities to build their oral or reading vocabularies. At the same time, it is crucial that you avoid deeming a student incapable of increasing his standard English vocabulary or of having below-average intelligence because his vocabulary consists largely of words from another language or from a nonstandard dialect of English.

Third, you can check students' abilities to use context cues to determine the meanings of unknown words by having them read orally from a text containing some challenging words. When they come across a word they do not know, ask them to try and use context to figure out its meaning. The data you record here can be a simple statement about students' proficiencies. For example, you might note that a particular student is "Generally able to use context cues when reading easy materials but can make almost no use of them when reading difficult material." Assessing students' knowledge of word parts can be done in the same way.

for understanding, and students' scores on these do not need to be recorded. Of course, checking rate several times will increase the accuracy of your estimates. Like IRIs, assessment of silent reading rates is important in both English language arts and other content area classrooms, and provides essential information for effectively working with all readers, including English-language learners.

Formal observations of students using a guide or a standard assessment procedure allow you to make sound judgments about students' progress. Additionally, creating observation guides or checklists makes it possible to have a fairly systematic way to assess a multitude of behaviors. You can create guides that focus on any behavior you want to assess. Observing your students using a guide or a standard procedure on a regularly scheduled basis will allow you to make sound judgments about students' progress. These observations can also be supplemented with anecdotal evidence from your more informal observations. Indeed, most teachers employ both formal and informal techniques, as described in Teaching Idea 9.2.

Informal Observations

Another source of information is the observational notes, or anecdotes, that teachers compile as they routinely observe what students are doing in the classroom. Part of being a reflective, responsive teacher is watching students to determine what they can do well and what they are having trouble doing. Effective teachers watch their students and know their social, emotional, and cognitive strengths and weaknesses. They know which students work well together and which do not. They notice how their students work on the tasks they have set. They recognize student achievements, both large and small. And they realize when their teaching has not been effective and they need to try a different approach. These informal observations can serve as assessments to be acted on immediately, or can become material for constructing a record of how students engage in classroom practices.

Teachers who observe their students can easily and efficiently keep anecdotal records of what they see. Some teachers clip sheets of large address labels—the kind that have 10 or fewer on a sheet—on a clipboard and carry it with them as they watch their students work or walk around the room to drop in on small groups. These labels are a perfect size to take brief notes about important student behavior. A date and a jotted note on a label can then be transferred to a piece of paper in a student's file. These informal observations can then be read at any point in time and the information can be summarized and added to more formal assessments to present a more complete picture of individual students' behavior.

You can observe virtually anything using this technique. If you want students to respond to what they read in a variety of ways, then you will want to watch them respond to see what they do. If you are interested in understanding what your students do as they engage in independent reading, you might want to jot notes as you watch how students select books for independent reading, how they use books to get information, or how they use reference aids, such as tables of contents, indexes, and glossaries. Look for and record how students share ideas and information from the books they are reading with you and their peers. Notice how they attempt to apply ideas from their reading to new learning situations. Note the comprehension strategies that you notice students using. Observe how students enter the classroom and settle into their work, whether or not they seem to be engaged in the tasks that you set, or whether or not they are contributing members of the class during discussions or other whole-class activities. While you could, if you wanted to, make a more systematic, formal observation guide, anecdotal notes are also appropriate in many situations. Still, it's important to keep in mind the distinction between observed behavior and inferences. Some teachers mark their inferences by putting them in the form of questions, or underlining the part of their notes that is inferential. For example, the teacher observing Mary and Bob that we described earlier might write the following on one label:

> Mary is sitting in the back of the library with *The Other Side of Truth* (Naidoo) in her hand. Is she thinking of the book?

And on another label, the following:

> Bob is sitting in the back of the library with *Jason's Gold* (Hobbs) in his lap, <u>daydreaming.</u>

Anecdotal information from informal observations combined with the more formal, systematic observations that you engage in are important components of a total picture of the accomplishments and instructional needs of your students. So, too, is a record of products and other artifacts that students produce.

Student Artifacts

There are several types of artifacts that you will want to include in any assessment of student progress. These include formal instruments such as questionnaires and teacher-made tests as well as a variety of student products.

Formal Assessment Instruments. Two commonly used types of formal assessment instruments are questionnaires that teachers give to students to assess reading attitudes, interests, or practices and teacher-made tests that assess the content they hope students are learning.

Reading Practices, Interests, and Attitude Questionnaires. There are a number of commercially prepared surveys that you can use to assess student interest in and attitude towards reading, such as Tunnell, Calder, and Justen's (1988) reading attitude survey, or the more recent McKenna, Kear, and Ellsworth (1995) national survey. It is also easy to create your own questionnaires that can help you tap reading practices, interests, and attitudes. Some questions you might want to ask middle-grade students include the following:

- Do you like to read? Why?
- Are you a good reader? Why?
- What does a good reader do?
- What are you reading now?
- Where and when do you like to read? Why?
- Have you ever read a book more than once? What made you do this?
- What kinds of books do you like to read? Why?
- Do you have a favorite book? What is it? Why is it your favorite?
- Do you have a favorite author? Who is it? Why is this author your favorite?
- How do you choose the books that you read?
- Where do you get the books that you read?
- Who else likes to read the same kinds of books that you like?
- What one word would you use to describe how you feel about reading?

You can, of course, add other questions that you might want answers to. Note that the questions above cover attitudes, practices, and interests. Not all students would want to answer this many questions at one time, so forming several smaller questionnaires is advisable.

Teacher-Made Tests. Teachers have, probably from the beginning of time, constructed their own tests to determine whether their students were learning the content being taught. These tests can tap students' literal comprehension, inferential comprehension, or ability to make judgments about texts. They can determine students' knowledge of how literature works in terms of understanding the setting, plot, character development, thematic structure, and style. They can measure students' vocabulary, grammatical, and spelling knowledge, albeit in a decontextualized fashion. In many ways a teacher-made test functions as a criterion-referenced test, in that teachers set certain criteria to determine a score, and that score indicates the depth and quality

Teaching Idea 9.3
Checklist for Response Journals

Name _____   Date _____

- [ ] Includes title
- [ ] Includes author
- [ ] Retells
- [ ] Descriptive summary
- [ ] Evaluative summary

Makes personal connection
- [ ] With character
- [ ] With event
- [ ] With setting
- [ ] With other books

Notices author's craft in
- [ ] Setting
- [ ] Characterization
- [ ] Plot
- [ ] Style
- [ ] Theme
- [ ] Makes inferences
- [ ] Considers theme

of students' knowledge. While too many tests stifle students' motivation and enthusiasm, some testing does provide another useful data source for assessing students' progress.

Student Products. The products that students produce during the course of a school year, such as reading records, response journals and logs, projects, and written and visual responses to their reading—including essays, poems, character sketches, drawings, paintings, and computer-made representations of response—are also important sources of information for assessment. A record of what students have read over a period of time tells you the amount, variety, content, and pace of their independent reading. Response journals or logs tell you how they react to what they read, giving you a window into the depth and breadth of their literary understanding, their use of reading strategies, and the connections that they make with what they read. Teaching Idea 9.3 presents an example of a teacher-created checklist that helps keep track of individual students' response strategies. Response journals can also give you a very sound indication of students' engagement with their reading. Response projects offer the same kind of information.

These and other varieties of student work and student-generated records and plans allow teachers and students to determine how far students have come in reaching the goals that they and their teacher have set. Combined with formal assessments and informal observations, student-generated artifacts help teachers make decisions about instruction. Add to this compilation the information that you can obtain through talking with your students in both formal and informal situations and you have a thorough and balanced assessment practice. Talking with students not only provides additional information for you, the teacher, to use to assess

Teaching Idea 9.4
A Quick Check of Oral Fluency

Fluent oral reading is usually an indication of understanding, while lack of fluent reading can indicate a variety of difficulties that may be interfering with understanding. With older and more able students, a check on fluency is not absolutely necessary, but most often your classroom will contain a wide range of reading abilities, so it is best to ask everyone to read orally early in the year, with rechecks of struggling readers at intervals. This is easily done during a book conference when it is quite natural to ask a student to read a favorite passage, but you also need to ask them to read a paragraph or so in a grade-appropriate text (perhaps something from an old basal reading series). After you have heard them read, jot down a brief descriptive comment, such as, "Orally reads grade-level material fluently and with few errors." Remember that a few miscues are not a cause for alarm, especially if they do not affect meaning.

student progress and your own effectiveness, but also provides the perfect opportunity to help students learn to assess their own progress.

Talking with Students

Conferences. Sitting down and talking with your students is a great way to get to know each student, helps students develop their oral language skills, helps students learn how to talk with each other, and is an important opportunity for assessment. Conferences between teacher and student are most frequently about students' literacy practices, students' literacy products, and students' progress.

Talking with Students About Practices and Products. Many teachers strive to hold regularly scheduled conferences with their students because they see these conferences as an important part of a student's literacy development. Conferences often focus on either reading or writing and serve simultaneously as a source of information about individual students' progress and as an opportunity for instruction.

Talking with students about their reading practices and processes is an effective way to discover students' reading preferences and behavior. Coupled with observation and data from instruments such as attitude surveys, informal reading inventories, and response logs, talking with individuals can serve to round out the picture of individual readers. Conferences also allow teachers to check on their inferences and perceptions gathered through other means. Talking with students about specific books they are reading helps teachers understand the level of engagement and motivation that students are bringing to the task of reading. These conferences are also an opportunity to ask students to read aloud to you as a brief check of their oral reading fluency, as described in Teaching Idea 9.4. When that reading sample is followed by a brief discussion, it is also an opportunity to assess students' comprehension. And, along with those assessments, talking with students about the

Figure 9.1 **Whole-Class Conference Record**

Name	Date	Book	Notes	New Goal

books they are reading also allows you to share your enthusiasm about specific titles, reading, and books in general. Often, the opportunity to talk with a teacher one-on-one about a book is the first conversation about books with an adult that students have.

Many times you will have read the book or passage that the student is reading, but not always. It's important to develop a list of standard questions that can further the book discussion between you and your students, much like those below.

- Tell me about what you're reading.
- How did you decide to read this book?
- Are you confused by anything? What?
- Does this book remind you of anything else you've read? What?
- If you could talk with the author, what would you ask?
- Have you read anything else by this author?
- Who else in the class might enjoy this book? Why?
- Did the book remind you of anyone or anything that you know?
- What would you have done (when discussing a character's action)?
- How do you think [the main character] felt?
- What do you think will happen next?
- Do you think this story could really happen?
- Did you learn anything new from this piece of nonfiction?
- Did the graphs/figures/illustrations help you understand the information?
- What was the most important part of this book?

While some teachers designate a particular spot for conferences, many simply roam the room, dropping in on students for a brief chat, clipboard in hand for easy note taking. You can construct a simple form for conference notes for individual students, or keep track of the whole class on a form that is similar to the one in Figure 9.1.

Combining Assessment Strategies

We have talked about assessment in terms of formal and informal observation and assessment, teacher-generated questionnaires and tests, student products, and conferences. In the real world of the classroom, most purposes for assessment call for a combination of information sources and procedures, much like the following scenario in which the teacher, Anna, is concerned with assessing her students' use of self-checking and self-correcting strategies as they read.

> Anna knew that assessing the extent to which her students self-checked and self-corrected would involve several steps, and she constructed a plan that would allow her to create an accurate picture of each student's behavior. First, she looked for signs in her students' oral and written work that they were not self-checking or self-correcting; she looked for statements and answers showing that they had misinterpreted parts of what they had read. Second, she talked to her students, trying to determine whether they understood the general notion of self-checking and self-correcting. Some of them did, but several did not. Finally, she asked those students that she was still uncertain of to be aware of points in their reading that caused them confusion and to jot down notes about their confusions and attempts to remedy them. She then looked to see which students noticed confusion and had a plan to remedy it, and which did not.
>
> Anna then recorded who did monitor and self-correct when necessary and who did not. As she worked with those students who did not monitor and self-correct, she identified the specific areas of self-monitoring and self-correcting her students needed assistance with. This helped her create small, temporary groups for specific instruction in this area. It also allowed her to be able to include students with good self-monitoring skills in groups when these skills would be necessary for successful group work.

In this example, the teacher informally observes her students, assesses their work products, sets some a formal task to complete, and then observes those students having difficulty until she can pinpoint the specific areas in which they need assistance. She has used her repertoire of assessment strategies to inform her instruction. Her reflective, responsive attitude means that her students have the opportunity to learn what they need to know.

Encouraging Student Self-Evaluation

Students who monitor and assess their progress are more engaged in learning than are students who do not. They are more likely to adjust what they are doing in order to achieve their goals than are students who see assessment as merely imposed from without, something that they can't do much about. Just as we discuss in Chapter 2, students who take responsibility for their own performance are more motivated to learn.

Pause and Reflect 9.2

Think about your own self-assessment and goal setting. Consider, for example, the experience of this particular course. What are the goals that you have set for yourself? Go beyond wanting a good grade and think about what you want to learn and be able to do. How will you be able to assess your progress toward these goals? ■

Talking with Students about Progress

Sitting down with individual students to discuss their progress at regular intervals across the school year is an important part of assessment. In these conferences, you and the student discuss together the student's performance and progress. It is not simply a time for you to tell students what your assessment is, but to talk with them about what they have been doing as learners. You might focus on a particular product, such as an essay or a reading test, or look across several pieces of your student's work, you own observation notes, and your student's self-evaluation.

In getting ready for a conference about student progress, students and teachers need to develop, together, some criteria for assessment. Sometimes this will be general, whole-class goals, such as completing assignments, working together supportively, and the like. These general goals are usually supplemented by specific, individual goals, such as a student reading books in a new and unfamiliar genre, or reading a certain number of minutes a day, or raising their score on a test of comprehension. Whatever the goal, both teacher and student prepare for the conference by looking at and thinking about the data that they have gathered regarding the student's progress. Sometimes teachers also develop a self-evaluation form that allows students to summarize their progress, similar to the form in Figure 9.2.

Figure 9.2 Self-Evaluation of Progress

Name _____   Date _____

My goal was to: _____
_____
_____

How I accomplished that goal was: _____
_____
_____
_____

I am most proud of: _____

My rating (1–5): _____   Reason: _____
_____

Stopping by to discuss work with individual students is a good way to keep track of their progress.

Student Collection of Self-Assessment Data

Conferences are one important tool for encouraging student self-evaluation, but almost everything that we discuss in this chapter can be structured so that students can, along with you, assess their progress. If you construct a form for observing a particular behavior, share the form with your students and encourage or require that they, too, observe themselves and their peers. If you have a rubric with which you grade papers, give that rubric to students so that they can check their paper against it either before or after turning it in for a grade. If your students spend a lot of time in small groups, you will want both individual students to assess their own performance and the group to assess how well they work together, using a form that you and the students create together.

Helping Students Understanding Their Own Needs

Students need to think about, to become metacognitive about, their reading. They need to realize the strengths and weaknesses that they have so that they can build on their strengths and try to remedy their weaknesses. If, for example, a student realizes that he is not very adept at using context to glean word meanings but is adept at using the dictionary, then he can make a conscious decision to get out the dictionary when encountering an unknown word. Similarly, if a student knows that a single reading of a poem is not likely to leave her with enough understanding to be able to talk about the poem in small-group discussion, she will schedule her time so that she can read and think about the poem several times.

Your role in helping students become increasingly aware of their strengths and weaknesses is threefold. First, let them know the importance of their becoming metacognitive, of becoming better and better at realizing which reading tasks they do well and which ones they need to become more proficient at. Second, share the assessment information you gather with students frequently and in a way that indicates that you and your students are joint participants in fostering their literacy. Praise them for what they do well, point out areas in which they can improve, and congratulate them when they do improve. Finally, let students know that each of them is capable of becoming an independent and metacognitive reader who can assess his own proficiency and improve his skills, knowledge, and strategies where necessary.

Asking middle-grade students to assess their own progress forces them to accept a significant amount of responsibility for their own actions. It also helps them to set goals and work toward them, an important skill in life outside of the classroom as well as inside. And it allows them to take pride in their work.

Documenting Student Progress

Ongoing, authentic assessment helps you document your students' progress in a way that is meaningful to your students, their parents, and yourself. Having records of students' efforts, behaviors, products, and processes allows everyone to notice what individual students do well. Often, grades mask all but performance on tests or regular submission of completed homework. At the very least, you will want to keep a file on each student into which you can put work samples, your notes from informal observations, and records of formal assessments. When you want to know where your students are in their progress, this folder will tell you much more than a few grades noted on a class grade sheet. Even more useful are portfolios that are constructed by you and your students.

Portfolios

"Portfolio assessment," according to Gillespie, Ford, Gillespie, and Leavell (1996), "is a purposeful, multidimensional process of collecting evidence that illustrates a student's accomplishments, efforts, and progress over time" (p. 487). Documenting student progress with portfolios provides a much more complete picture of what students can do in the context of the classroom. As part of helping students assess their own progress, make them active participants in creating their own portfolios and allow them easy access to their portfolios. Building a portfolio allows students the opportunity to look at their work, your assessments, and their own self-assessments and assemble a display of what they know and can do. The evidence contained in a portfolio is selected by you, by the student, and jointly. Criteria for selection are generated by both you and your students. Criteria for evaluation of the portfolio as a whole are also generated jointly, with students an integral part of the selection and evaluation process from the beginning. This makes portfolios not only an important tool for documenting student progress but also an effective tool for teaching students to be metacognitive about their reading development.

Once the portfolio has been assembled, evaluating it with you and even explaining their portfolio to their parents helps students see what they have accomplished in a way that a grade on a report card simply does not. In many schools, teachers use one or more of the regularly scheduled parent nights or parent–teacher conferences as a time for their students to sit down with their parents and explain their portfolio and its evaluation. This is an important experience for both students and parents, as they effectively change roles because the student, in this case, is the expert.

Keeping Track of the Whole Class

Portfolios are wonderful records of individual student achievement, but are not useful in providing day-to-day information about your class as a whole. Many effective teachers choose to create charts that help them keep track of student progress in each class. By listing the names of your students down the left-hand column of a chart and the knowledge, skills, strategies, and attitudes that you are focusing on across the top, you can create a grid such as that shown in Figure 9.3. You might use the letter *S* to denote *satisfactory* and *N* to denote *needs improvement* in each of the categories. Or, you might simply use checks, or pluses and minuses, to indicate students' mastery in particular areas. Such a chart is particularly handy when making grouping decisions for specific assignments and is also a constant reminder of the skills, strategies, attitudes, and knowledge that you are trying to help your students develop. As the year progresses, the items across the top will change as students progress. Thus the chart can serve as a reminder to move on as well.

Assessing the Effectiveness of Your Teaching

In addition to teachers assessing students' performance and students assessing their own performance, another kind of assessment is important in a responsive classroom. To be an effective teacher, you need to constantly assess your own performance, or engage in reflection on your teaching. We all too often hear comments such as, "I taught this but they didn't learn it." We argue that if they didn't learn it, then you didn't teach it, as teaching isn't completed until learning takes place. Using student assessment data as a way to evaluate your own performance means that you understand the connection between effective teaching and student progress.

You need to repeatedly reflect on your instruction, students' responses to your instruction, and how you can improve your instruction so that your students' performance improves. This makes teaching exciting and challenging. Every year is different. Every class is different. Every student is different, on a daily basis. What you have done in the past may or may not work in the present, or the future. Your challenge is to build on your successes while you modify your approach, based on the information that assessing your students' progress provides you.

Figure 9.3 **Class Assessment Chart**

Students	Read Frequently	Enjoy Reading	Share Reading	Apply Reading	Comprehend Well	Self-Correct	Read Fluently	Rate Adequate	Use Word Recognition Strategies	Use Vocabulary Building Skills	Adequate Vocabulary	Show Awareness of Author's Craft

The classroom is an ever-changing mosaic of students, activities, goals, attitudes, and texts that you arrange and rearrange in order to constantly increase each student's success at becoming an able and avid reader. There is no perfect prescription for teaching anything that you can discover and continue to use throughout your teaching career. Instead, each day, each week, and each new class present new opportunities for reflecting on what went well, what did not go as well, and what you can do to make your classroom an increasingly effective environment in which each student can develop his reading proficiency to the greatest extent possible. It is precisely this challenge that makes teaching an art—and a most interesting profession.

Concluding Remarks

Standardized tests are part of the landscape of U.S. education but actually tell teachers little that is useful in their quest to construct the most effective learning environment possible. More useful information comes from a process of ongoing, authentic assessment practices that are grounded in the practices evident in the English language arts and other content-area classrooms. Authentic assessments take the form of formal observations and assessment, informal reading inventories, informal observations of target activities, teacher-generated questionnaires and tests, and teacher–student conferences. They are coupled with a systematic effort to help students develop their skills at self-assessment. Often, these various assessments become the basis for the joint construction of portfolios, an effective way of documenting student progress. Portfolios are effective ways of demonstrating progress to students and parents. They also allow you to reflect on your own teaching by giving you information about how well all of your students are able to do the instructional tasks that you set for them. This information is crucial if you are to be an effective teacher.

In conclusion, keep the following (based on Kibby, 1995) in mind as you structure your own assessment process and practice.

- Authentic assessment is an ongoing process.
- The primary purpose of classroom assessment is to support and give direction to your instruction.
- Assessment is really the process of answering questions, and your choice of type of assessment will depend on the question that you want to answer.
- Assessment should reveal strengths as well as weaknesses.
- Multiple sources of information, gathered over time and representative of authentic classroom experiences, lead to the most accurate documentation of student progress.
- Students should take an active part in assessing their progress and setting future goals.
- Assessment of student progress allows teachers to assess their own effectiveness and plan instruction.

EXTENDED LEARNING

1. Join others to form a small group, focused on a specific grade level. Consider the reading skills, competencies, and attitudes that you might assess at this grade level and write a prioritized list in which you identify those items you consider most important to assess and those of lesser importance. Then write a brief rationale for the importance of each item. Also, make a note of any other sources you would like to consult before finalizing your list.

2. Working from the list of assessments that your group constructed, select three to five of the most important and three to five of the least important items and list ways that you might approach assessment. Then, think about the limited amount of time you will have and devise an efficient and balanced assessment plan.

3. Examine some assignments from published teaching materials in your field and determine what you can learn about student performance from those assignments. Then try to redesign the assignment to make it a better assessment instrument.

4. Create a list of guidelines to follow when assessing students. Use these guidelines to critique the assessment practices in the class you are currently taking or teaching.

BOOKS FOR MIDDLE-GRADE READERS

Hobbs, W. (1999). *Jason's gold*. New York: Morrow.
Naidoo, B. (2000). *The Other Side of Truth*. New York: HarperCollins.

Organizing Classrooms to Promote Reading and Responding

Gathering together to talk about books gives students and teachers the opportunity to share their ideas.

It's difficult to see the teacher in room 28 because her desk is shoved into a corner and piled with books, paper, writing implements, folders, and a pot of flowers. Student desks are in clusters of six, but not every chair is filled, as many of these seventh graders are on the rug on the floor in the corner that is defined by overflowing book shelves. Today the students are working in their small groups, talking about a book that they are reading as a class. They've just finished writing a quick, 10-minute response to what they read during the first half-hour today and now they're hearing what others have to say. The conversation is spirited, and sometimes a little loud. Sarah, their teacher, is sitting with one of the groups, listening to what they have to say. She's been moving from group to group in the past 10 minutes, and has dropped in on almost all of them by the end of the 15-minute discussion time. When the timer rings, all students wrap up their conversations and go back to their desks. Sarah has about 15 minutes to talk with her students about what they've said in small groups, what questions have arisen, and how they might want to approach their reading for tomorrow. Tonight they'll take their books home and read and respond to a chapter in preparation for the discussion that will open class tomorrow. Once that discussion is over, there'll be a significant amount of time for Sarah to work with her students on the skill of visualizing as they read. She's got some interesting response options available for them that will push them to visualize the setting, characters, and action in the novel.

Sarah's colleague, Jeff, a social studies teacher, is working with his seventh graders on summarizing. They have been reading several nonfiction texts on the South Pole, and today they are preparing to read Jennifer Armstrong's *Shipwreck at the Bottom of the World: The Extraordinary True Story of Shackleton and the Endurance,* a nonfiction depiction of the 1915 expedition to Antarctica, the "most hostile place in the world." Jeff wants his students to be able to distinguish between more and less important information, and to feel confident in summarizing the important information succinctly. While they read Armstrong's book, they will be able to see how she combines expository and narrative structures to create a memorable piece of nonfiction. Even though Jeff and Sarah have very different goals and different texts, Jeff's classroom looks a lot like Sarah's as students are working together in groups on the tasks that he has set for the day, moving between reading, individual work, group discussion, and whole-class instruction.

Sarah and Jeff's classrooms are busy places, and their students are thoroughly engaged in learning about the world through reading while also learning about how to read with comprehension and engagement. Sarah teaches literature and Jeff teaches social studies, but both teach reading.

In this chapter we present four ways of structuring effective instruction, all of which are widely used in English language arts classrooms, while we also pay attention to how these structures might link to other content-area practices. We then look at effective literacy instruction in action in four different classrooms: a traditional self-contained class, a general language arts class, a science class, and an English class.

Pause and Reflect 10.1

Jeff and Sarah's classes move among whole-class, small-group, and individual work. Think about other classrooms you have seen. How would you characterize their organizational structures? How do they compare to Jeff and Sarah's? ■

Creating Effective Instruction

There are many ways to structure a curriculum to support engaged, responsive, strategic readers. The instructional goals and plans of many successful teachers focus on reading skills and strategies that, in English language arts classrooms, are augmented by a robust independent reading and read-aloud program. Or, in the case of other content areas, the reading skills and strategies instruction is embedded in a focus on the content. Many other successful teachers structure their curriculum thematically, exploring important ideas across time using a variety of texts and embedding their reading and literary or other content-area instruction within this thematic organization. Some English language arts teachers select texts according to genre, focusing on reading strategies and literary properties as related to each genre, helping students learn about both reading and writing within particular genre constraints. Some teachers are lucky enough to be able to team with a colleague from a different discipline, and there are many examples of successful curricula that link, for example, the books read in English language arts classes with the ideas presented in a social studies/ history class. Other teachers work with a basal reading series or a textbook that their districts have adopted, using the selections that those texts supply to teach the lessons that their students need to learn, but supplementing this material, which is minimal, with other texts that will intrigue their students and further their curriculum. Still other teachers focus specifically on fostering higher-order thinking and teaching a few topics in depth so that students understand them fully and can apply what they learn in school to their lives outside of school. However the curriculum is organized, there are certain features that help create engaging classrooms anywhere.

As we discuss in earlier chapters, an effective classroom is filled with material that students will find compelling and that will both support and stretch their reading and content area skills. A successful environment also develops a supportive community of readers who have time to read, time to explore their individual responses, and time to talk with peers about books. This kind of classroom organization also includes time for teaching—for carefully selected lessons and demonstrations, and for whole-class discussions. Ample time gives teachers flexibility, allows them to make cross-curricular connections, delve more deeply into an interesting text, or follow the students' interests with additional material. With the components of appropriate instruction, good books, supportive community, and ample time, middle-grade readers will thrive.

All effective teachers think about comprehension strategies, vocabulary, higher-level thinking, and teaching for understanding as they set their instructional goals. Exactly what they teach will, of course, vary according to the instructional needs of their students and, to an extent, the demands of the curriculum that has been set for their school districts. A fifth-grade teacher, for example, may work within a curriculum that is focused on reading rather than literature. An eighth-grade teacher may work within a literature curriculum that is structured by a literature textbook. A science teacher may use a textbook and appropriate nonfiction and embed instruction on the use of specific reading strategies within units of content. Of course, all of those teachers can, as we suggest in this book, strive to teach their students appropriate and useful strategies for reading and understanding a wide variety of texts and thinking critically about what they are reading.

Organizational Patterns

Organizing instruction into a daily or weekly schedule, or across grading periods, depends on the parameters of the school day. Jeff and Sarah worked within a 75-minute time period, but teachers' schedules can range from a 50-minute class period 5 days a week, as in many seventh- and eighth-grade classes, to larger blocks of time that are either consistent or vary by days, to a whole day with a fifth- or sixth-grade class. Large blocks of time are, certainly, more conducive to teaching in an integrated, student-centered manner. That said, whatever the schedule, effective teachers manage to include time for what is important: helping their students become engaged, effective, critical readers and thinkers.

Here we present some organizational structures that have been developed in the past two decades—reading workshop, literature circles, and book clubs—as well as a traditional organization pattern that you can adapt to fit your schedule and curriculum. We then go on to describe different teachers working within different structures, each of them successful. Whatever the structure, students can become engaged, strategic readers, learn to monitor themselves as readers, learn about literature, and learn how to read to learn in middle-grade classrooms.

Reading Workshop. A popular structure with English language arts teachers, reading workshop was described and popularized by Atwell in her 1987 edition of *In the Middle*, and has been revised in her second edition, published in 1998. Currently, Atwell's reading workshop consists of a 90-minute block of time 4 days a week in which she teaches both reading and writing. Each block consists of time to read and discuss a poem, a reading/writing mini-lesson delivered by the teacher, independent writing and conferring, a read-aloud, 15 to 20 minutes of independent reading, and homework of at least another half-hour of reading. Whereas her early workshops relied entirely on books that students chose for themselves, she now mixes those books with assigned literature that pushes students in new directions. As part of her workshops, she and her students write dialogue journals or letters about the books they have read. Students are asked to write a letter to the teacher at least once every 2 weeks, and to peers whenever they care to. They also write in a response log at least once a week, and there are regularly scheduled conferences between teacher and student. Finally, students maintain personal reading records, and the teacher maintains a reading record for the entire class.

Note that the workshop contains time for whole-class reading and discussion—in this case, of poetry, time for direct instruction or demonstration by the teacher, time for students to write and talk about their writing, time for reading aloud, and time for independent reading. A weakness of this workshop approach is that there is little time for small-group discussion of books, although that certainly could be built into the schedule. Instead of conversation, Atwell relies on the dialogue journals to encourage a thoughtful exchange of ideas about books. One of the strengths of this approach is that reading and writing time are integrated, both within any given workshop period and through teacher-directed instruction. A workshop structure can accommodate a thematic curriculum, a curriculum that is linked with another area, or a curriculum that focuses on fostering higher-order thinking and deep understanding, as well as other types of curricula.

Although Atwell's workshop contains opportunities for reading and writing, some teachers prefer to have separate writing and reading workshops. In a curriculum that is organized through genre study, a typical reading workshop might begin with reading a brief example of the genre being studied—perhaps an excerpt from a memoir, followed by time to respond orally. Often this read-aloud selection will be tied to the lesson or demonstration by the teacher that follows. This might include information about structure, genre constraints, and effective reading strategies for the genre. Then students might move directly into independent reading of a book in the target genre, either selected independently or assigned by the teacher. The workshop might end with students writing about or discussing what they are reading. This structure is both predictable and flexible, allowing students to be comfortable knowing what will be expected of them while at the same time allowing the teacher to introduce lessons and texts that suit his or her purpose. Other possibilities include focusing on nonfiction about specific content areas while also discussing genre characteristics of nonfiction in reading workshop, and working on nonfiction writing during writing workshop.

In *Mosaic of Thought: Teaching Comprehension in a Reader's Workshop,* Keane and Zimmermann (1997) describe how teachers across elementary and middle grades adapted their original reading workshop procedures to focus on teaching comprehension strategies. Working within the framework of both mini-lessons and individual conferences, as well as repeated teacher demonstrations of, and commentary about, comprehension strategies such as making inferences or creating images, the teachers guided their students toward an increasing metacognitive awareness of their reading processes, an increasing knowledge of the fix-up strategies they could call on when meaning broke down, and thus an increasing ability to comprehend what they read. This, in turn, led to increasing engagement and motivation, which led to more reading.

Literature Circles. Literature circles are another structure that works well for many successful teachers. This structure rests on social constructivist principles that stress the importance of others in learning, and involves students working in small groups to read and discuss literature. Literature circles provide the venue for students to discuss ideas, responses, problems, questions, and other issues that arise from their reading.

Literature circles vary in the amount of teacher direction. Some teachers allow students to select the literature they read and discuss, with groups coming together and dissolving according to student interest. Other teachers offer students an array of books from which to select, and circle groups are formed through the book selection process. How students conduct themselves in literature circles also varies, with many teachers choosing to instruct their students in the procedures of cooperative group work (Johnson, Johnson, & Holubec, 1994) and assigning students roles that are suggested by cooperative learning procedures. Other teachers find this too restricting and opt instead for a collaborative group model in which students learn specific lessons about how to work together but are allowed to put them into practice in their own way. Rather than assuming assigned roles, students in collaborative groups assume roles as needed to work together successfully. The presence or absence of a teacher is yet another way that literature circles can vary. Many teachers begin the year by being present during circle discussions and then gradually move away from participation. Others make literature circles completely student-directed. If the groups are student-directed, they might even decide on their own schedule, although many teachers give their students a schedule to work within. Literature circles can span a few days or several weeks, depending on the text being read.

Using literature circles within a curriculum organized around themes might involve the classroom teacher presenting several sets of books that are closely related thematically. For example, there might be five sets of six books each that all have a theme of freedom. The teacher gives a book talk on each of the six titles, and literature circles are formed depending on student interest in a particular title. Once the groups have their books, the teacher might lead a discussion of the theme that they will be exploring. Sometimes the teacher will read aloud from another book that treats the same theme so there is some whole-class experience surrounding the individual literature circles. Exploration of the theme continues as individual circles read, think about, write about, and discuss their books. The thematic study usually culminates with a project in which each circle presents its experience to the rest of the class. Themes and books can easily be related to topics being studied in the content areas, as well. See Teaching Idea 10.1 for one example: an author study.

While literature circles can include a number of opportunities for writing, they do not necessarily involve students in writing about their own topics at their own pace, nor do they involve writing conferences. However, they can certainly be combined with a writing workshop, during which teachers might make connections between student writing and the literature they are reading. For an excellent presentation of writing workshop, see Calkins' *The Art of Teaching Writing* (1994).

Book Club. Book Club contains many of the essential elements of a workshop, and looks very much like literature circles, but is organized in a more centralized manner. Developed by McMahon and Raphael with their colleagues Goatley and Pardo (1997), Book Club is thoroughly grounded in cognitive psychology, social constructivism, and transactional theory, which we describe in Chapter 1. Book Club usually begins with a whole-class mini-lesson, followed by time for independent reading, then time for writing, and then student-led discussion in small book clubs, consisting of a group of four to six students that is stable across the reading of a particular book. Book club discussions are usually followed by a whole class period of sharing.

The books that students read and discuss are either assigned by the teacher or, as in one version of literature circles, selected by students from a larger set of books that the teacher has already identified. Sometimes the whole class reads one book; at other times each group might be reading different books that relate thematically to each other or are by the same author. The books that are selected support the coherent exploration of a theme across a unit of time ranging from a grading period

Teaching Idea 10.1
Author Study

Select an author your students enjoy, one who writes well and is worth studying. Ask students to gather facts about the author, comments from the author, and a complete bibliography of books. Most of this information can be found on the web, as many authors have their own web sites. If an author's web site is not listed in his or her books, contact the publisher for information. Also, the multi-volume *Something About the Author,* found in most reference libraries, contains essays about most published writers for children and adolescents. Many authors also have autobiographies that help students understand how their lives link to their writing, what processes they use as they create their books, and what their goals are.

Then select books that exemplify what you think are outstanding characteristics of the au-

thor's work. This should be linked to ideas that you are focusing on in your writing instruction. For example, Karen Hesse is known for her ability to create a strong *voice* in her characters. If your students are reading her work and are also thinking about voice in their own writing, an author study of Hesse would be appropriate. Other sources of information include reviews of the author's work as well as any interviews the author might have given. Some authors, such as Katherine Paterson, Jane Yolen, and others have also written about writing, and their insights into their craft are quite invaluable.

Combining the information about the author, a careful reading of the author's work, and a consideration of the author's craft will help your students learn to read with discernment and write with skill.

to a year. As we discuss in Chapter 6, these thematic explorations consider big questions, ideas that matter intensely to young readers, and ideas that serve to link readings together. They might also be linked to other curricular areas, such as social studies. These books are meaty, the kinds of books that engage adolescent readers, as described in Chapter 3. One possibility for linking reading and social studies to study historical themes is presented in Teaching Idea 10.2.

Most Book Club teachers begin their sessions with a demonstration or mini-lesson that speaks directly to what they want their students to learn—a literary device that they want their students to notice, a comprehension strategy that they want their students to employ, or a concept that they want students to grapple with. Through direct explanation and modeling, the teacher helps the students learn what they need to know. The structure of Book Club allows them to practice what they are learning in the meaningful context of their reading, which immediately follows the whole-class instruction.

The Book Club structure includes regularly scheduled time for independent reading following the whole-class instruction. Sometimes the teacher reads aloud while students follow along, and students also are free to read in pairs or to listen to books on tape if they need the extra support. At other times students might read silently. Reading time is always followed by a time for students to think about what they have read. This thinking is prompted by the need to write something in their response logs. As they progress across the school year, students gradually learn a number of ways to respond to their reading. Much of this learning comes from the

Teaching Idea 10.2
Linking English and Social Studies through Theme: Cultural Perceptions of History

By selecting books for middle-grade readers that present different perspectives on historical events, you can help students understand that one's point of view shapes how one sees the world. For example, if you link your language arts class to the American history class that your students are taking, you might want to have them read Jane Yolen's *Encounter* and Michael Dorris' *Morning Girl* and *Guests* as they study the more traditional view of the "discovery" and settling of America presented in many textbooks. In this case, the concept of discovery is challenged as the Taino are depicted as human beings who welcome the European visitors who appear in their sailing ships. The idea of Thanksgiving is also broadened to include the perspective of the Native people who have been forced to share their land with European settlers. As the year progresses, books that view the American Revolution, the Civil War, and many other landmark events from varied perspectives can help your students understand how the same historic event can be perceived differently by different cultures.

prompts that teachers give them in their response logs. They may be asked to write a character description, sketch the setting, trace the plot, find interesting words, or question the author, among many, many other tasks. Over time they learn the possibilities for response, and frequently students become increasingly responsible for how they respond in writing.

Reading with comprehension and then writing about a book allows students to be contributing members of the small, peer-discussion groups known as book clubs. As with literature circles, these discussions allow students to clarify understandings, solve problems, and share responses with others. They provide students with the opportunity to develop some of the positive attitudes toward their own response and the responses of others discussed in Chapter 6. These discussion groups serve as a powerful motivating force, as students develop responsibility toward and interest in the conversations that they have in their groups. As they talk, the teacher moves about the room and takes notes on what is occurring. These notes often prompt what happens in the final segment of instruction, whole-class share, in which the teacher helps each group share their ideas, or clarifies misconceptions, poses new questions to think about, or even teaches a spontaneous lesson that it is clear the students need. This might take the form of another mini-lesson in which the teacher either delivers instruction or demonstrates some skill or strategy that he or she has noticed that students are ready to learn.

One of the strengths of Book Club is the structure: Independent reading time is always followed by time to think and write about what has been read, and this is always followed by time to talk with peers. The social nature of the book club discussions highlights the importance of peers as resources for clearing up confusions, providing alternative explanations and responses, and offering an audience for students to explore their individual responses and tentative ideas in a safe atmosphere. Structured time for teaching, both before and after the reading, writing, and discussion components, allows teachers to help students learn what they need to know.

Effective teachers plan cohesive units of study.

Like literature circles, Book Club does not contain a time for working through the writing process on a piece that is self-selected, but it can certainly precede, follow, or alternate with a writing workshop. Book Club does, however, ask students to write in response to what they read, and to write in many different ways, and the reading log prompts can be coordinated with goals for the writing curriculum. Further, in many cases the groups work on a culminating project, and this often involves a significant amount of writing.

Traditional Organization. In many middle-school classrooms, the basic structure does not follow a specific plan such as those described above but rather a more traditional organization. Since traditionally organized classes do not follow a specific plan, they take a variety of forms. Often, however, a traditionally organized class takes on a unit or project-based format. For a period of time ranging anywhere from a week to a month, the class centers on a particular unit. Examples of these units might include a novel study, a science or social studies research project, an intense study of a comprehension strategy, or the writing of a paper in a certain format or genre. By balancing these units across the year, the teacher offers the various components of a comprehensive literacy program.

Teaching Idea 10.3
Linking Vocabulary and Reading

As you talk about books with your students, demonstrate how you notice interesting words by verbalizing your pleasure in wonderful words. You can help students notice words by simply commenting, as you read aloud or discuss books, when a word is the precise word needed, strongly conveys meaning, is melodious, or particularly effective. Attention paid to important words in all content areas is an essential component of effective reading instruction. You can ask students to find words that they don't know the meaning of or that they have noticed in their reading, write the words down, look up their definitions, and come prepared to share their words with the class. You might also require some information on part of speech, root words, or affixes, if appropriate. If students each look for one word each week, you can have as many words to learn as there are students in your class. You might supplement the words that students notice with those that you want them to learn, whether it be for understanding content or learning about language. When these words come from the reading that students are doing, vocabulary instruction is linked to reading fluency and comprehension.

This unit-based structure reflects the traditions of both the secondary high school English class and the elementary class. Each individual unit often mimics one or the other approach, with novel units often closer to the literary criticism style of the high school, comprehension strategy units tying more to the emphasis on teaching reading in the elementary school, and project units tying directly to the integrated instruction model in many self-contained elementary classrooms. Units on writing frequently straddle the borders of the two traditions, offering explicit instruction on using particular formats, but focusing on fostering increasingly complex content and including peer revision and critique on a more independent basis than in the elementary grades.

In determining the order of the units throughout the year, the teacher may use a thematic or genre-oriented organizational emphasis, but more frequently the units are ordered so that they provide a logical sequence of skills or strategies over the course of the year. For example, a teacher might present a sequence of comprehension strategies, beginning with making inferences, moving to determining what is important, and concluding with summarizing. Frequently, language arts teachers attempt to coordinate units with topics being studied in the other subject areas. It is not uncommon to see teachers scheduling first the key texts and related units that can relate to particular content in the social studies class—for example reading *My Brother Sam is Dead*, by James and Christopher Collier, while students are studying the Revolutionary War in their history classes. After these initial units are scheduled, the other units are placed in the best-fitting order. While units and emphasis change from month to month, most traditionally organized classrooms offer a few ongoing activities throughout the year. These typically include a reading log assigned as daily homework, regular grammar assignments, short lessons on literary elements, some isolated vocabulary work, and, occasionally, comprehension strategy instruction. Reading logs and grammar assignments frequently seem unconnected to the larger projects. However, vocabulary work may be contextualized in the larger units, as described in Teaching Idea 10.3.

Figure 10.1 **A Typical Traditional Schedule**

10:00–10:05	Completed log for the previous night's reading/homework
10:05–10:20	Instruction on particular skills
10:20–10:40	Individual or small group work on the current unit
10:40–10:50	Large group sharing and coordination of the unit work and homework assignment

A fairly typical 50-minute period in a traditionally organized classroom might look like the schedule that appears in Figure 10.1.

Occasionally, a unit in a traditionally organized classroom may be used for a Book Club project, may present a condensed version of a readers' workshop, or may incorporate the use of literature circles. However, using these structures in a single unit is very different from using the Book Club or literature circles structures throughout the entire school year. In a traditional classroom, the structures are only temporary and are used for the specific purpose of the unit. One example of this might be using literature circles with books related to a particular social studies theme, to expose students to more texts than they could read individually in a short period of time.

Whatever the structures you choose to frame your curriculum, you will have to do extensive teaching for your students to learn how to operate within the structures that you have put in place. The beginning of the year is usually marked by many lessons on procedures, as students learn to negotiate the curriculum and structures you have set. Students need to know what they are expected to do, when they are expected to do it, and how they are expected to act. For example, as we noted in Chapter 6, it takes time for students to learn how to participate in peer-led discussion groups.

As the year continues, students become increasingly independent and able to manage the work of the classroom on their own. This frees up your time to hold conferences with students about their reading and writing, and to observe and assess students' interaction skills and their reading performance and literary understanding, as discussed in Chapter 9. In a very real sense you "teach yourself out of a job," but instead of having nothing to do, you simply have more time to do what you *need* to do—be a reflective and responsive teacher.

These three specific structures—reading workshop, literature circles, and Book Club—as well as more traditional patterns of organization, have all been used successfully by many teachers. Other teachers have taken elements of these structures and put them together in a way that works for their students within the context of their school and their community. The best way to understand the particular choices that all teachers have to make as they teach is to look closely at several teachers in action.

Pause and Reflect 10.2

Which of the four patterns for organizing instruction appeals to you the most? Why? What are the strengths that you can build on within this structure? What are the weaknesses? ■

Effective Instruction in Action

We said in the beginning of this book that adolescence and the middle grades are marked by variability. Perhaps the only constant across this period is that of difference. As it is true of students, it is also true of successful teachers. Different teachers select different structures for their classrooms, based on their own preferences, the needs and strengths of the students, and the context in which they teach. Middle-grade teachers work in many different settings. They may have a self-contained classroom, affording them the opportunity to work with students for large blocks of time. They may have many students for shorter periods of time. They may be called a fifth/sixth-grade teacher, a reading teacher, a language arts teacher, a science teacher, or an English teacher. Whatever their job title and however the day is structured, they do share the commonalities of sound instructional principles that we describe throughout this book. They are:

- focusing on academically relevant tasks
- employing active teaching
- fostering active learning
- distinguishing between instruction and practice
- providing for sufficient and timely feedback
- teaching for transfer

Effective teachers work with these principles to achieve their goals through instruction that reflects constructivist and socio-cultural perspectives. The approaches they use include the following:

- scaffolding
- the Gradual Release of Responsibility model
- direct explanation
- contextualizing, reviewing, and practicing what is learned
- teaching for understanding
- building on the social nature of learning

David Carberry's Fifth/Sixth-Grade Self-Contained Class. David has been teaching fifth and sixth grade at Oak Grove Intermediate School for more than 10 years. The school includes grades 4 through 6 and is in a middle-income suburb of a major Midwestern city. Most of the children at the school are European American, with small numbers of Asian Americans, American Indians, and African Americans across the grades.

David works in a team with three other teachers to make program, curriculum, and scheduling decisions. The four classrooms on the team each contain approximately 15 fifth-grade students and 15 sixth-grade students, with the fifth-grade students staying with the same teacher for their sixth-grade year. One of the challenges that David and his team face is the extreme differences in reading ability across their fifth- and sixth-grade students. He and his team have devised a plan for organizing their curriculum that emphasizes reading and writing instruction throughout the school day.

Figure 10.2 **David Carberry's Daily Schedule**

9:00	Homeroom
9:00	Daily Oral Language, Sustained Silent Reading, Journals
9:20	Morning Meeting
9:30	Language Arts Block
11:00	Mathematics
12:00	Lunch and Recess
12:30	Physical Education and Music
1:30	Thematics: Social Studies, Science, Art, Health
3:00	Homeroom and Assignment Logs

David and his team decided that having a homeroom that included a large block of time for students to be together with the same teacher was important for their students. This allowed them to integrate reading, writing, listening, and speaking within the block. They also decided that a thematic organization, centering instruction across the curriculum on a broad idea, was important. Finally, they identified reading comprehension strategies that they could teach throughout the year that were applicable across the curriculum and the range of reading abilities they had to work with. A typical daily schedule in David's class looks like the schedule in Figure 10.2.

David's students are with him each morning from 9 until 11, after which they separate into grade-level groups for mathematics, music, and physical education. Following their homeroom/language arts period, heterogeneous groups made up of students from all four classes move from teacher to teacher according to the teacher's content-area specialty, and then return to their homeroom for an end-of-day wrap up.

The team works together to decide what to teach. Using the district goals and objectives, they look for ways to weave their teaching into explorations of three broad themes over the course of a year. They then identify activities and instruction that will allow them to meet district goals and objectives. And they attempt to thematically integrate science, social studies, health, and art, as much as possible. Sometimes music and physical education can be integrated as well, as when the music teacher created a score for a play that David's homeroom was creating.

This thematic integration is supported by what the students are doing in their language arts block. Additionally, David has learned over the years to select a small number of comprehension strategies, perhaps three, to teach his students. He stresses that they can and should use the strategies in their independent reading, their assigned reading, and their content-area reading. His teaching is recursive, in that he initially teaches the strategies using direct explanation, as we discuss in Chapter 5, and then returns to them during the course of the year.

This four-teacher team has created an integrated day for their fifth- and sixth-grade students. They have managed to provide a large chunk of time for students to engage in language arts activities, have integrated the language arts with each other and across the curriculum, and have created a thematic structure that allows students to connect their learning across domains. No wonder their students thrive.

Jessie Escobar's Seventh-Grade Language Arts Class. Jessie Escobar has been teaching for 3 years in a large southern state, in a rural school surrounded by farms. Many of her students ride the school bus for up to an hour to get to Polk Middle School, which houses grades 6 through 8 for the whole county. Many of them are from families with incomes that hover around the poverty level. There aren't a lot of extras in the homes they come from, and their parents work constantly to keep their children clothed and fed. Some parents see school as a luxury. Others see it as the best and perhaps only opportunity for their children to get ahead. Some students find school an oasis. Others find it irrelevant. About a fifth of the students in this school are the children of migrant workers, and they come and go as their families follow the crops. Most of these students and several others who are not from migrant families are English-language learners, with Spanish as their first language. Jessie Escobar's school looks and is very different from David Carberry's school, yet many of their instructional strategies, curricular goals, and classroom procedures are the same.

At Polk Middle School the entire school has adopted a block schedule to allow the core curriculum areas ample, connected time for instruction. Although this makes for a somewhat complicated schedule, the teachers appreciate the long periods that they have—two for reading/language arts and one each for science, social studies, and mathematics. The extra time allows them the same flexibility that it allowed David Carberry and his colleagues. Another resource in this school is the two teachers for English as a Second Language (ESL); their expertise is added to the English/language arts instruction in an inclusion model. Rather than have students leave their regular class to go for ESL instruction, the ESL teachers come to them on a rotating schedule.

Jessie, with five classes to teach and one preparatory period each day, has decided to focus on reading during the fall semester, integrating language study, composition, literature, and oral language activities within this focus. Her students span a wide range of abilities, so she has set up some temporary, small instructional groups that will enable her to work on developing fluency with those who need it. Her whole-class lessons are initially a mix of procedural lessons, in which she helps students learn how to work within the structures of the classroom, but by the end of the first week she begins to introduce her planned sequence of comprehension lessons. Because her students are, for the most part, not avid readers, she also reads aloud every day, in every class, while students follow along; fortunately, the school has class sets of several paperbacks that students enjoy. The oral reading gives students extra time with print and the experience of hearing (and seeing) a book read fluently. She also makes time to do book talks once a week, usually on Thursdays at the end of the read-aloud period, hoping to introduce her students to the books she has in her classroom library in a way that will entice students to read them.

Her weekly schedule for reading and language arts appears in Figure 10.3.

This schedule works well. After the first week in which she has been reading aloud from Gary Paulsen's *Hatchet*, a big favorite even for those who are familiar

Figure 10.3 **Jessie Escobar's Schedule**

MWF

Read-aloud/brief discussion *(10–15 minutes)*
Procedural or comprehension lesson *(10–15 minutes)*
Independent practice *(15–20 minutes)*
Whole class discussion/debriefing *(10 minutes)*

TuTh

Read-aloud/brief discussion *(10–15 minutes)*
Comprehension lesson *(15–20 minutes)*
Independent practice *(15–20 minutes)*
Writing workshop and lesson *(30–45 minutes)*
Writing lesson *(15 minutes)*

with it, Jessie notices that most of the students are getting to class on time and quickly settling into their desks so that they can hear her read. The book is doing what the bell couldn't: getting her students' attention. It also sets up the lesson that follows, in that she can often link the lesson to the story, using the content of the read-aloud as material with which to practice a particular skill or strategy. She is focusing on predicting and visualizing, two strategies that work well with this text. As she reads aloud she is sure to talk about what she is visualizing, and what she thinks will happen. Soon her students join her in describing what they see and making predictions. Brief discussions that follow the reading increase students' investment in the book as they become interested in hearing what others have to say and in sharing their own ideas. Beyond that, because her students are enjoying the book, they are more positively disposed to work on improving their reading.

In the lessons that follow, Jessie explains and demonstrates the strategies that she is focusing on. Sometimes she follows this up by setting a specific task for the whole class. Other times she breaks the class into groups and moves between groups as they put into practice what they are learning. On Tuesdays and Thursdays the ESL teacher often works with the English-language learners who are not yet reading well in English. The material students are working with might be the next section of *Hatchet*, or prepared material for practice, or their independent reading choices. Students who read fluently and finish their work early always have the option of reading or working on their writing. On Tuesdays and Thursdays, everyone has time to write. Jessie's writing lessons focus on narrative structures and author's craft, which she easily ties to Paulsen's writing.

As the year progresses Jessie continues to read aloud, adds vocabulary study, teaches other comprehension strategies, and works in many ways to promote higher-order thinking and deep understanding—and she reteaches, when necessary. During her lessons and read-aloud time she also introduces knowledge about literature, looking at different genres and their characteristics as well as how authors manipulate the literary elements of plot, characterization, and theme. Style continues to be a focus in her writing lessons. Discussions of books begin to include comments about these elements. Independent practice is sometimes supplanted by

Literacy is an important part of learning in a science classroom.

small-group discussions, and she gives students an opportunity to talk about their independent reading with their classmates as well. Slowly but surely, her students begin to develop an interest in books that just might extend beyond the classroom. At least half of them are taking home books from the classroom library and she's even seen some of them reading at lunch.

Todd Roudabush's Seventh-Grade Science Class. For 5 years, Todd Roudabush has taught seventh-grade science in a junior high school (grades 7 through 9) in a large, suburban district near Minneapolis. Todd's school has focused on literacy instruction across the curriculum, and he has had training on how to implement specific literacy strategies. Because he is a reflective practitioner, Todd carefully examines how effective his instruction is in helping his seventh-grade students learn the content in their science textbooks. It seems clear that the systematic instruction in comprehension strategies, tied to specific content in the textbook, helps his students learn science.

Todd introduces an appropriate strategy at the beginning of each unit. Students might study the organization within a chapter before reading it or get instruction in determining the main idea, or summarizing, or distinguishing between fact and opinion. He often creates Interactive Reading Guides (Vacca & Vacca, 1993) for specific chapters. These guides offer tasks for individuals, pairs, small groups, and the whole class to complete, asking for both oral and written responses. For example, in the guide on the characteristics of living things, Todd asks small groups of his students to list four living things and four nonliving things that they see every day, and later to brainstorm and list the stimuli they encounter in a given day, then share these lists with the whole class. Individually, students read and write about the chapter. Before they read each section, students make predictions regarding statements that Todd gave them, and then share their predictions with a partner before reading individually.

Todd knows that accessing prior knowledge—asking students to either discuss or write about the content *before* they read—is important. It allows him to understand their misconceptions about the topic and address those. He also recognizes the importance of social interaction, and finds that tasks that offer social opportunities, such as paired and small-group work, are most effective. He thinks these tasks have increased the time his students work with the ideas in the text and have allowed them to learn from one another. He also tries to help his students connect the material they encounter in the textbook to their own lives—thus the brainstorming tasks described above. He also asks his students to keep a journal throughout the year, and the journal entries allow him to track his students' growing understandings—as well as their misconceptions—and adjust his instruction accordingly. In Todd's science class, literacy is the key to learning science.

Aletha Pearson's Eighth-Grade English Class. Aletha Pearson teaches eighth-grade English at Pierce Junior High, a large, urban school that houses seventh and eighth grades. She has five, 50-minute classes a day, one of which is full of high-achieving students who are clearly on their way to college. The other four are a heterogeneous mix of abilities, behaviors, and attitudes. She uses different texts but many of the same instructional strategies in all of her classes. She's been an English teacher for 5 years, and has been taking courses and reading about literacy teaching to help her meet the challenges she faces in her English classes. In one of her courses she was introduced to Book Club, and last year she structured her curriculum in that way.

Aletha would tell you that the Book Club structure has allowed her to meet the instructional needs of her students and to teach the curriculum that she is responsible for. Although each of her five classes is structured in a similar manner—mini-lesson, reading, writing, small-group discussion, whole-class share—the amount of time spent on each element, the materials she uses, and the content of her lessons change with each class. For example, her advanced class really doesn't need much time to read during school; they are all recreational, if not avid, readers. They also all read well above grade level and their comprehension is excellent. Because of this, there is more time for them to discuss the literature they are reading as homework. A typical class with these students begins with Aletha presenting some historical context, or theoretical stance, or literary lesson to her students (15 minutes), the students skimming through what they had read the night before (5 minutes), and responding in their literature logs (5 minutes) to specific questions that she has given them. They then move into discussion groups and spend 20 minutes talking about their reading. In the last 5 minutes of class Aletha pulls the class back together to consider ideas, questions, and concerns. Aletha is careful to structure her lessons and her directions for response logs and small-group discussion so that her students learn the lessons about literature that her district requires her to teach. She is also able to help them learn about themselves as responsive readers by demonstrating her own examination of herself as a reader and asking her students to explore why they respond as they do. She does this 3 days a week, with the other 2 days devoted to writing, vocabulary, and language instruction. Last year she taught literature on Monday, Wednesday, and Friday, and taught composition, vocabulary, and language on Tuesday and Thursday. This year she's experimenting, teaching literature Monday, Tuesday, and Wednesday and the rest on Thursday and Friday.

Aletha's other classes have a greater range of reading abilities and motivation, and she is careful to give her students time to read in class. She begins with a 15-minute lesson focused on literature or comprehension strategy instruction, gives them 15 minutes to read, then 5 minutes to write in response to prompts in their literature log. A 10-minute discussion period is followed by 5 minutes of whole-class discussion. Again, she alternates between teaching literature and composition, vocabulary, and language instruction. She is fortunate to be able to supplement the literature text with adolescent literature and makes extensive use of short stories that pique her students' interest.

Now that she has used Book Club for a year, she is beginning to realize ways to weave these curricular demands together. Her composition lessons almost always use examples from the literature that students are reading. Students are required to bring three new and intriguing words from their reading to share with classmates during vocabulary instruction, and a class word bank is taking shape. Instruction in grammar, spelling, and mechanics is anchored in the understanding that writers use these conventions to get their ideas across to their readers, and Aletha often points out interesting grammatical structures or punctuation in the literature they read, prompting students to notice for themselves.

For Aletha, Book Club gave her a predictable structure that her students could work within, and enough flexibility that she could tailor the timing and the content to suit her students' instructional needs. Like all good teachers, she's constantly assessing her students' progress and her own teaching, and making changes as she encounters new challenges.

Pause and Reflect 10.3

Think about David, Jessie, Todd, and Aletha as teachers. What important principles do they put into practice? ∎

Concluding Remarks

There are many ways to structure a reading/language arts/English curriculum and many ways to incorporate the teaching of literacy into the other content areas. The structure of any given classroom reflects the preferences of the teacher, the strengths and needs of the students, the demands of the curriculum, and the schedule that a teacher has to work within. In all cases, effective structures reflect a teacher's best effort to meet the needs of students within a particular educational community. In all cases, the focus is on how students learn best rather than on a pre-existing program that creates a teacher-proof, one-size-fits-all curriculum. Effective teachers understand how to create a literate environment that encourages and supports students as they hone their literacy skills, while at the same time they use these skills to learn subject matter. To create such an environment requires repeated demonstrations of literacy in action, time for literate practices within the classroom, choices about materials that are intriguing, and purposeful activities that lead students to a greater understanding of content and increasing facility in reading and writing. Students in the middle grades are learning how to read more effectively and critically; they are also learning how to read to learn—in science, mathematics, social studies, and English.

Working with students in the middle grades may present special challenges, but it also affords special rewards. Middle-grade students are, indeed, on the brink of many things (Hynds, 1997). It is our privilege to help them along their way toward a literate life.

◾ EXTENDING LEARNING

1. Visit two classrooms with different organizational structures and write descriptions of each. Then share these descriptions in a small group, discussing what you observed in light of the instructional principles and theoretical perspectives presented in this text. Alternatively, describe your own classroom and compare it with the classroom of a teacher in a different school or district.
2. In small groups select a book that describes either workshop, literature circles, Book Club, or content-area reading instruction in action. Assign chapters, read, and take notes. Then construct a group presentation so you can share your information with classmates.
3. Find out all you can about the local school system's standards requirements, how the curriculum is structured, and how the school day is typically organized. Then argue for a particular organizational structure based on your assessment of the system.

◾ BOOKS FOR MIDDLE-GRADE READERS

Armstrong, J. (1999). *Shipwreck at the bottom of the world: The extraordinary true story of Shackleton and the Endurance.* New York: Random House.
Collier, J. L., & Collier, C. (1974). *My brother Sam is dead.* New York: Macmillan.

References

Adams, M., & Bruce, B. (1982). Background knowledge and reading comprehension. In J. A. Langer & T. M. Smith-Burke (Eds.), *Reader meets author: Bridging the gap* (pp. 2–25). Newark, DE: International Reading Association.

Aebersold, J. A., & Field, M. L. (1997). *From reader to reading teacher: Issues and strategies for second language classrooms.* Cambridge, United Kingdom: Cambridge University Press.

Allington, R. (1984). Oral reading. In D. Pearson, R. Barr, M. L. Kamil, & P. B. Mosenthal (Eds.), *Handbook of reading research* (Vol. 1, pp. 829–864). New York: Longman.

Allington, R. L. (1977). If they don't read much, how they ever gonna get good? *Journal of Reading, 21,* 57–61.

Allington, R. L. (1983). The reading instruction provided readers of different abilities. *Elementary School Journal, 83,* 548–559.

Allington, R. L. (1994). The schools we have. The schools we need. *The Reading Teacher, 48,* 14–29.

Allington, R. L. (2001). *What really matters for struggling readers: Designing research-based programs.* New York: Longman.

Almasi, J. F. (2003). *Teaching strategic processes in reading.* New York: The Guilford Press.

Alvermann, D., & Moore, D. W. (1991). Secondary school reading. In R. Barr, M. L. Kamill, P. Mosenthal, & P. D. Pearson (Eds.), *Handbook of reading research* (Vol. 2, pp. 951–983). White Plains, NY: Longman.

Alvermann, D. E. (2000). Classroom talk about texts: Is it dear, cheap, or a bargain at any price? In B. M. Taylor, M. F. Graves, & P. van den Broek (Eds.), *Reading for meaning: Fostering comprehension in the middle grades* (pp. 136–151). New York: Teachers College Press.

Ames, C. (1992). Classroom: Goal, structures, and student motivation. *Journal of Educational Psychology, 84,* 261–271.

Anderson, L. W., & Krathwohl, D. R. (2001). *A taxonomy for learning, teaching, and assessing: A revision of Bloom's Taxonomy of Educational Objectives.* New York: Longman.

Anderson, R. C. (1984). Role of the reader's schema in comprehension, learning, and memory. In C. R. Anderson, J. Osborn, & J. R. Tierney (Eds.), *Learning to read in American schools* (pp. 243–258). Hillsdale, NJ: Lawrence Erlbaum.

Anderson, R. C., & Armbruster, B. B. (1990). Some maxims for learning and instruction. *Teachers College Record, 91,* 396–408.

Anderson, R. C., Hiebert, E. H., Scott, J. A., & Wilkinson, I. A. G. (1985). *Becoming a nation of readers: The report of the Commission on Reading.* Washington, DC: The National Institute of Education.

Anderson, R. C., & Nagy, W. E. (1992, winter). The vocabulary conundrum. *American Educator, 16*(4), 44–47.

Anderson, R. C., Wilson, P., & Fielding, L. (1988). Growth in reading and how children spend their time outside of school. *Reading Research Quarterly, 23*, 285–303.

Anglin, J. M. (1993). Vocabulary development: A morphological analysis. *Monographs of the Society for Research in Child Development, 58*(10), Serial No. 238.

Applebee, A. N., & Langer, J. L. (1983). Reading and writing as natural language activities. *Language Arts, 60*(2), 68–175.

Appleman, D. (2004). *Critical encounters in high school English: Teaching literary theory to adolescents.* New York: Teachers College Press and National Council of Teachers of English.

Aronson, E., Blaney, N., Stephan, C., Sikes, J., & Snapp, M. (1978). *The jigsaw classroom.* Newbury Park, CA: Sage.

Aronson, E., & Patnoe, S. (1997). *The jigsaw classroom* (2nd ed.). New York: HarperCollins.

Atwell, N. (1987). *In the middle: New understandings about writing, reading, and learning.* Portsmouth, NH: Heinemann.

Avery, P. A., & Graves, M. F. (1997). Scaffolding young learners' reading of social studies text. *Social Studies and the Young Learner, 9*(4), 10–14.

Bamford, R. A., & Kristo, J. V. (Eds.). (1998). *Making facts come alive: Choosing quality nonfiction literature K–8.* Norwood, MA: Christopher Gordon.

Banks, J. A. (1996). Multicultural education and curriculum transformation. *Journal of Negro Education, 64*(4), 390–400.

Beach, R. (1997). Students' resistance to engagement in responding to multicultural literature. In T. Rogers & A. O. Soter (Eds.), *Reading across cultures: Teaching literature in a diverse society* (pp. 69–94). New York: Teachers College Press.

Bean, T. W., Valerio, P. C., & Stevens, L. (1999). Content area literacy instruction. In L. B. Gambrell, L. M. Morrow, S. Newman, & M. Pressley (Eds.), *Best practices in literacy instruction* (pp. 175–192). New York: The Guilford Press.

Beck, I. L., & McKeown, M. G. (1983). Learning words well: A program to enhance vocabulary and comprehension. *The Reading Teacher, 36*, 622–625.

Beck, I. L., McKeown, M. G., & Omanson, R. C. (1987). The effects and uses of diverse vocabulary instructional techniques. In M. G. McKeown & M. E. Curtis (Eds.), *The nature of vocabulary acquisition* (pp. 147–163). Hillsdale, NJ: Erlbaum.

Beck, I. L., McKeown, M. G., Hamilton, R., & Kucan, L. (2001). *Questioning the author: An approach for enhancing student engagement with text.* Newark, DE: International Reading Association.

Becker, W. (1977). Teaching reading and language to the disadvantaged: What we have learned from field research. *Harvard Educational Review, 47*, 518–543.

Benton, M., & Fox, G. (1985). *Teaching literature: Nine to fourteen.* Oxford, GB: Oxford University Press.

Bernhardt, E. B., & Kamil, M. L. (1998). Literacy instruction for non-native speakers of English. In M. F. Graves, C. Juel, & B. B. Graves (Eds.), *Teaching reading in the 21st century* (pp. 432–475). Boston: Allyn & Bacon.

Biemiller, A. (2001). Teaching vocabulary: Early, direct, and sequential. *American Educator, 25*(1), 24–28, 47.

Bloom, B. S., Englehart, M. D., Furst, E. J., Hill, W. H., & Krathwohl, D. R. (1956). *The taxonomy of educational objectives: Handbook I: Cognitive domain.* New York: David McKay.

Blythe, T., & Associates. (1998). *The teaching for understanding guide.* San Francisco: Jossey-Bass.

Boaler, J. (2002). *Experiencing school mathematics.* Mahwah, NJ: Erlbaum.

Bogner, K., Raphael, L., & Pressley, M. (2002). How grade 1 teachers motivate literate activity by their students. *Scientific Studies in Reading, 6,* 135–165.

Bransford, J. D., Brown, A. L., & Cocking, R. R. (Eds.). (2000). *How people learn: Brain, mind, experience, and school.* Washington DC: National Academy Press.

Britton, J. (1970). *Language and learning.* New York: Penguin.

Brophy, J. (1986). Teacher influences on student achievement. *American Psychologist, 41,* 1069–1077.

Brophy, J. (1987). Socializing students' motivation to learn. In M. L. Maehr & D. A. Kleiber (Eds.), *Advances in motivation and achievement: Enhancing motivation* (Vol. 5, pp. 181–210). Greenwich, CT: JAI Press.

Brown, A. L., & Campione, J. C. (1990). Interactive learning environments and the teaching of science and mathematics. In M. Garner, J. G. Greeno, F. Reif, A. H. Schoenfeld, A. diSessa, & E. Sage (Eds.), *Toward a scientific practice of science education* (pp. 111–139). Hillsdale, NJ: Erlbaum.

Brown, A. L., & Day, J. D. (1983). Macrorules for summarizing text: The development of expertise. *Journal of Verbal Learning and Verbal Behavior, 22,* 1–14.

Brown, R., Pressley, M., Van Meter, P., & Schuder, T. (1996). A quasi-experimental validation of transactional strategies instruction with low-achieving second grade readers. *Journal of Educational Psychology, 88,* 18–37.

Buss, K., & Karnowski, L. (2000). *Reading and writing literary genres.* Newark, DE: International Reading Association.

Calfee, R. C., & Patrick, C. L. (1995). *Teach our children well: Bringing K–12 education into the 21st century.* Stanford, CA: Stanford Alumni Association.

Calkins, L. (1994). *The art of teaching writing.* Portsmouth, NH: Heinemann.

Calkins, L. M., Montgomery, K., Falk, B., & Santman, D. (1998). *A teacher's guide to standardized reading tests: Knowledge is power.* Portsmouth, NH: Heinemann.

Campbell, J. R., Hombo, C. M., & Mazzeo, J. (2000). *NAEP 1999 trends in academic progress: Three decades of student performance.* Washington, DC: Department of Education.

Carey, S. (1978). Child as word learner. In M. Halle, J. Bresnan, & G. Miller (Eds.), *Linguistic theory and psychological reality* (pp. 347–389). Cambridge, England: Cambridge University Press.

Carr, E., & Ogle, D. (1987). K-W-L Plus: A strategy for comprehension and summarization. *Journal of Reading, 30,* 626–631.

Carter, B., & Abramson, R. (1990). *Nonfiction for young adults: From delight to wisdom.* Phoenix, AZ: Onyx Press.

Cazden, C. (1988). *Classroom discourse.* Portsmouth, NH: Heinemann.

Cazden, C. B. (1992). *Whole language plus: Essays in literacy in the United States and New Zealand.* New York: Teachers College Press.

Chambliss, M. J., & Calfee, R. C. (1998). *Textbooks for learning: Nurturing children's minds.* London: Blackwell Publishers.

Clark, K. C., & Graves, M. F. (2005). Scaffolding students' comprehension of text. *The Reading Teacher, 56,* 570–580.

Cohen, E. (1994). *Designing group work: Strategies for heterogeneous classrooms.* New York: Teachers College Press.

Cooke, C. L. (2002). *The effects of scaffolding multicultural short stories on students' comprehension and attitudes.* Paper presented at the 51st Annual Meeting of the National Reading Conference, Miami, FL.

Cooper, S. (1981). Escaping into ourselves. In B. Hearn & M. Kaye (Eds.), *Celebrating children's literature* (pp. 14–23). New York: Lothrop.

Costa, A. L. (2001). *Developing minds: A resource book for teaching thinking.* Washington, DC: Association for Supervision and Curriculum Development.

Csikszentmihalyi, M. (1990). *Flow: The psychology of optimal experience.* New York: Harper & Row.

Cunningham, P. A., Hall, D. P., & Dufee, M. (1998). Nonability-grouped multilevel instruction: Eight years later. *The Reading Teacher, 51,* 652–664.

Delpit, L. (1995, December). *Other people's children.* Paper presented at the annual meeting of the National Reading Conference, New Orleans, LA.

Deshler, D. D., & Schumaker, J. B. (1993). Skills mastery by at-risk students: Not a simple matter. *Elementary School Journal, 94,* 153–167.

Developmental Studies Center. (2003). *Making meaning: Strategies that build comprehension and meaning.* Berkeley, CA: Author.

Dillon, J. T. (1984). Research on questioning and discussion. *Educational Leadership, 42*(3), 50–56.

Dole, J. A., Brown, K. J., & Trathen, W. (1996). The effects of strategy instruction on the comprehension performance of at-risk students. *Reading Research Quarterly, 31,* 62–88.

Dolezal, S. E., Welsh, L. M., Pressley, M., & Vincent, M. (2003). How do grade 3 teachers motivate their students. *Elementary School Journal, 103,* 239–267.

Donahue, P. L., Finnegan, R. J., Lutkus, A.D., Allen, N. L., & Campbell, J. R. (2001). *The nation's report card: Fourth-grade reading, 2000.* Washington, DC: Department of Education.

Donahue, P. L., Voelkl, K. E., Campbell, J. R., & Mazzeo, J. (1999). *NAEP 1998 reading report card for the nation.* Washington, DC: U.S. Department of Education.

Duffy, G. G. (2002). The case for direct explanation of strategies. In C. C. Block & M. Pressley (Eds.), *Comprehension instruction: Research-based best practices* (pp. 28–41). New York: The Guilford Press.

Duffy, G. G., Roehler, L. R., Sivan, E., Rackliffe, G., Book, C., Meloth, M., et al. (1987). Effects of explaining the reasoning associated with using reading strategies. *Reading Research Quarterly, 22,* 347–368.

Duin, A. H., & Graves, M. F. (1988). Teaching vocabulary as a writing prompt. *Journal of Reading, 22,* 204–212.

Duke, N. K., & Pearson, P. D. (2002). Effective practices for developing reading comprehension. In A. E. Farstrup & S. J. Samuels (Eds.), *What research has to say about reading instruction* (3rd ed., pp. 204–242). Newark, DE: International Reading Association.

Early, M. (1990). stages of growth in literary appreciation. *The English Journal, 49,* 161–167.

Elley, W. B. (1996). Using book floods to raise literacy levels in developing countries. In V. Greaney (Ed.), *Promoting reading in developing countries.* New York: International Reading Association.

Ennis, R. (1985). A logical basis for measuring critical thinking skills. *Educational Leadership. 43(2),* 44–48.

Ferguson, P. M., & Young, T. A. (1996). Literature talk: Dialogue improvisation and patterned conversations with second-language learners. *Language Arts, 73,* 597–600.

Fish, S. (1980). *Is there a text in this class? The authority of interpretive communities.* Cambridge, MA: Harvard University Press.

Fitzgerald, J., & Graves, M. F. (2004a). Reading supports for all. *Educational Leadership, 62*(4), 68–71.

Fitzgerald, J., & Graves, M. F. (2004b). *Scaffolding reading experiences for English-language learners.* Norwood, MA: Christopher-Gordon.

Fosnot, C. T. (1996). *Constructivism: Theory, perspectives, and practice.* New York: Teachers College Press.

Fountas, I. C., & Pinnell, G. S. (1996). *Guided reading: Good first teaching for all students.* Portsmouth, NH: Heinemann.

Frayer, D. A., Frederick, W. D., & Klausmeier, H. J. (1969). *A schema for testing the level of concept mastery.* (Working Paper No. 16). Madison: Wisconsin Research and Development Center for Cognitive Learning.

Fry, E. B. (2004). *The vocabulary teacher's book of lists.* San Francisco: Jossey-Bass.

Galda, L. (1998). Mirrors and windows: Reading as transformation. In T. Raphael & K. Au (Eds.), *Literature-based instruction: Reshaping the curriculum.* Norwood, NJ: Christopher Gordon.

Galda, L., & Cullinan, B. E. (2002). *Literature and the child* (5th ed.). Belmont, CA: Wadsworth.

Galda, L., & Cullinan, B. E. (2006). *Literature and the child* (6th ed.). Belmont, CA: Wadsworth.

Galda, L., & Guice, S. (1997). Response-based reading instruction in the elementary grades. In S. A. Stahl & D. A. Hayes (Eds.), *Instructional models in reading.* Hillsdale, NJ: Erlbaum.

Gambrell, L. B., & Almasi, J. E. (1996). *Lively discussions! Fostering engaged reading.* Newark, DE: International Reading Association.

Garner, R. (1987). *Metacognition and reading comprehension.* Norwood, NJ: Ablex.

Gergen, K. J. (1985). The social constructionist movement in modern psychology. *American Psychologist, 40,* 266–275.

Gersten, R., & Baker, S. (2000). What we know about effective instructional practices for English-language learners. *Exceptional Children, 66*(4), 454–470.

Gibbons, P. (2002). *Scaffolding language, scaffolding learning.* Portsmouth, NH: Heinemann.

Gillespie, C. S., Ford, K. L., Gillespie, R. D., & Leavell, A. G. (1996). Portfolio assessment: Some questions, some answers, some recommendations. *Journal of Adolescent and Adult Literacy, 39,* 480–491.

Goerss, B. L., Beck, I. L., & McKeown, M. G. (1999). Increasing remedial students' ability to derive word meaning from context. *Reading Psychology, 20*(2).

Goodman, K. (1986). *What's whole in whole language?* Portsmouth, NH: Heinemann.

Gordon, E. W. (2004). Closing the gap: High achievement for students of color. *Research Points, 2*(3), 1–4. Retrieved from www.aera.net/publications/?id=314.

Graves, M. F. (2004). Teaching prefixes: As good as it gets? In J. F. Baumann & E. B. Kame'enui (Eds.), *Vocabulary instruction: Research to practice* (pp. 81–99). New York: Guilford Press.

Graves, M. F. (2004). Theories and constructs that have made a significant difference in adolescent literacy—But that have the potential to produce still more positive benefits. In T. Jetton & J. A. Dole (Eds.), *Adolescent literacy research and practice* (pp. 433–452). New York: Guilford Press.

Graves, M. F. (2006). *The vocabulary book: Learning and instruction.* New York: Teachers College Press.

Graves, M. F., & Graves, B. B. (2003). *Scaffolding reading experiences to promote success* (2nd ed.). Norwood, MA: Christopher-Gordon.

Graves, M. F., Graves, B. B., & Braaten, S. (1996). Scaffolded reading experiences for inclusive classrooms. *Educational Leadership, 53*(5), 14–16.

Graves, M. F., Juel, C., & Graves, B. B. (2004). *Teaching reading in the 21st century* (3rd ed.). Boston: Allyn & Bacon.

Graves, M. F., & Watts, S. M. (2002). The Place of Word Consciousness in a Research-Based Vocabulary program. In S. J. Samuels & A. E. Farstrup (Eds.), *What research has to say about reading instruction* (3rd ed., pp. 140–165). Newark, DE: International Reading Association.

Grigg, W. W., Daane, M. C., Jin, Y., & Campbell, J. R. (2003). *The nation's report card: Reading 2002.* Washington, DC: U.S. Department of Education.

Guthrie, J., & Wigfield, A. (2000). Engagement and motivation in reading. In M. Kamil, P. Mosenthal, P. D. Pearson, & R. Barr (Eds.), *Handbook of reading research, volume III* (pp. 403–424). Mahwah, NJ: Erlbaum.

Guthrie, J. T. (2003). Concept oriented reading instruction: Practices for teaching reading for understanding. In A. P. Sweet & C. E. Snow (Eds.), *Rethinking reading comprehension* (pp. 115–140). New York: Guilford.

Hall, S. (1990). *Using picture storybooks to teach literary devices: Recommended books for children and young adults.* Phoenix, AZ: Oryx Press.

Halliday, M. A. K. (1983). *Language as social semiotic.* Baltimore: University Park Press.

Hansen, S. E. (2004). *Poetry preferences and the impact of instruction.* Unpublished M. A. thesis, University of Minnesota, Minneapolis.

Hart, B., & Risley, T. R. (1995). *Meaningful differences in the everyday experiences of young American children.* Baltimore, MD: P. H. Brookes.

Hart, B., & Risley, T. R. (2003, Spring). The early catastrophe: The 30 million word gap. *American Educator, 27*(1), 4–9.

Heard, G. (1998). *Awakening the heart: Exploring poetry in elementary and middle school.* Portsmouth, NH: Heinemann.

Heimlich, J. E., & Pittelman, S. D. (1986). *Semantic mapping: Classroom applications.* Newark, DE: International Reading Association.

Hornik, L. M. (2000). A celebration of words. *Book Links, 9*(5).

Hynds, S. (1992). Challenging questions in the teaching of literature. In J. A. Langer (Ed.), *Literature instruction: A focus on student response* (pp. 78–100). Urbana, IL: National Council of Teachers of English.

Hynds, S. (1997). *On the brink: Negotiating literature and life with adolescents.* New York: Teachers College/International Reading Association.

Institute of Educational Sciences. (2004). *Reading comprehension and reading scale-up research grants.* Washington, DC: U.S. Office of Education.

International Reading Association and the National Council of Teachers of English. (1996). *Standards for the English language arts.* Newark, DE: Author.

Ivey, G. (2001). Discovering readers in the middle level school: A few helpful clues. In A. A. Rycik & J. L. Irwin (Eds.), *What adolescents deserve: A commitment to students' literacy learning.* Newark, DE: International Reading Association.

Jimenez, R. T. (2000). Literacy lessons derived form the instruction of six Latino/Latina teachers. In B. M. Taylor, M. F. Graves, & P. van den Broek (Eds.), *Reading for meaning: Fostering comprehension in the middle grades.* New York: Teachers College Press.

Johnson, D. D., & Pearson, P. D. (1984). *Teaching reading vocabulary* (2nd ed.). New York: Holt Rinehart and Winston.

Johnson, D. W., & Johnson, R. (2002). Teaching students to resolve their own and their schoolmates' conflicts. *Counseling and Human Development, 34*(6), 1–12.

Johnson, D. W., & Johnson, R. T. (1989). *Cooperation and competition: Theory and research.* Edina, MN: Interaction Book Company.

Johnson, D. W., Johnson, R. T., & Holubec, E. J. (1994). *The new circles of learning: Cooperation in the classroom.* Alexandria, VA: Association for Supervision and Curriculum Development.

Johnson, M. S., Pikulski, J. J., & Kress, R. (1987). *Informal reading inventories.* Newark, DE: International Reading Association.

Johnston, P. H., & Winograd, P. N. (1985). Passive failure in reading. *Journal of Reading Behavior, 17,* 279–301.

Juel, C. (1990). Effects of reading group assignment on reading development in first and second grade. *Journal of Reading Behavior, 22,* 223–254.

Kamil, M., & Bernhardt, E. (2004). Literacy instruction for non native speakers of English. In F. Graves, C. Juel, & B. B. Graves (Eds.), *Teaching reading in the 21st century* (3rd ed., pp. 396–441). Boston: Allyn & Bacon.

Keane, E. O., & Zimmerman, S. (1997). *Mosaic of thought: Teaching comprehension in a reader's workshop.* Portsmouth, NH: Heinemann.

Kibby, M. W. (1995). *Practical steps for informing literacy instruction: A diagnostic decision-making model.* Newark, DE: International Reading Association.

Knapp, M. S., & Associates (1995). *Teaching for meaning in high-poverty classrooms.* New York: Teachers College Press.

LaBerge, D., & Samuels, S. J. (1974). Toward a theory of automatic information processing in reading. *Cognitive Psychology, 6,* 293–323.

Langer, J. A. (1995). *Envisioning literature: Literary understanding and literature instruction.* New York: Teachers College/International Reading Association.

Leslie, L., & Caldwell, J. (1995). *Qualitative reading inventory-II.* New York: HarperCollins.

Lewis, C. (2001). *Literary practices as social acts: Power, status, and cultural norms in the classroom.* Mahwah, NJ: Erlbaum.

Liang, L. A. (2004). *Using scaffolding to foster middle school students' comprehension of and response to short stories.* Unpublished doctoral dissertation, University of Minnesota, Minneapolis.

Livingston, M. C. (1991). *Poem-making: Ways to begin writing poetry.* New York: HarperCollins.

Maehr, M., & Midgley, C. (1996). *Transforming school cultures.* Boulder, CO: Westview Press.

Martin, B., Jr. (1992). Afterword. In B. Cullinan (Ed.), *Invitation to read: More children's literature in the reading program.* Newark, DE: International Reading Association.

Marzano, R. J. (2004). *Building background knowledge for academic achievement.* Alexandria, VA: Association for Supervision and Curriculum Development.

McCauley, J., & McCauley, D. (1992). Using choral reading to promote language learning for ESL students. *The Reading Teacher, 47,* 526–533.

McClure, A., Harrison, P., & Reed, S. (1990). *Sunrises and songs: Reading and writing poetry in an elementary classroom.* Portsmouth, NH: Heinemann.

McKenna, M. C. (2001). Development of reading attitudes. In L. Verhoeven & C. E. Snow (Eds.), *Literacy and motivation: Reading engagement in individuals and groups* (pp. 135–158). Mahwah, NJ: Erlbaum.

McKenna, M. C., Kear, D. J., & Ellsworth, R. A. (1995). Children's attitudes toward reading: A national survey. *Reading Research Quarterly, 30,* 934–956.

McKeown, M. G., & Beck, I. L. (2003). Taking advantage of read alouds to help children make sense of decontextualized language. In S. A. Stahl, A. van Kleeck, & E. B. Bauer (Eds.), *On reading books to children* (pp. 159–176). Mahwah, NJ: Erlbaum.

McMahon, S. I., Raphael, T. E., Goatley, V. J., & Pardo, L. S. (1997). *The Book Club connection: Literacy learning and classroom talk.* New York: Teachers College Press.

Mehan, H. (1979). *Learning lessons: Social organization in the classroom.* Cambridge, MA: Harvard University Press.

Meltzer, M. (1994). *Nonfiction for the classroom: Milton Meltzer on writing, history, and social responsibility.* New York: Teachers College Press.

Miller, G. A., & Gildea, P. M. (1987). How children learn words. *Scientific American, 257*(3), 94–99.

Moll, L. C. (1992). Literacy research in community and classrooms: A sociocultural approach. In R. Beach, J. L. Green, M. S. Kamil, & T. Shanahan (Eds.), *Multidisciplinary perspectives on literacy research* (pp. 211–244). Urbana, IL: National Council of Teachers of English.

Moll, L. C., & Greenberg, J. (1990). Creating zones of possibilities: Combining social contexts for instruction. In L. C. Moll (Ed.), *Vygotsky and education* (pp. 319–348). Cambridge, England: Cambridge University Press.

Morrow, L. M. (1993). *Literacy development in the early years* (2nd ed.). Boston: Allyn & Bacon.

Murphy, P. K., & Alexander, P. A. (2002). The learner centered principles. In W. D. Hawley (Ed.), *The keys to effective schools* (pp. 10–27). Thousand Oaks, CA: Corwin Press.

Nagy, W. E. (1988). *Teaching vocabulary to improve reading comprehension.* Newark, DE: International Reading Association.

Nagy, W. E., & Anderson, R. C. (1984). How many words are there in printed school English? *Reading Research Quarterly, 19,* 304–330.

Nation, I. S. P. (2001). *Learning vocabulary in another language.* Cambridge, England: Cambridge University Press.

National Center for Educational Statistics (2004). *The nation's report card: Reading highlights 2003.* Washington, DC: U.S. Department of Education.

National Council of Teachers of English. (1983). Statement on censorship and professional guidelines. *The Bulletin, 9*(1–2), 17–18.

National Council of Teachers of English. (1996). *Teaching literature in middle school: Fiction.* Urbana, IL: Author.

National Reading Panel (2000). *Report of the National Reading Panel: Teaching children to read.* (NIH Rep. No. 00–4769). Bethesda MD: National Institute of Child Health and Human Development.

National Research Council (2004). *Engaging schools: Fostering high school students' motivation to learn.* Washington, DC: National Academies Press.

Newby, T. J. (1991). Classroom motivation: Strategies of first-year teachers. *Journal of Educational Psychology, 83,* 187–194.

Newmann, F. W. (1996). *Authentic achievement: Restructuring schools for intellectual quality.* San Francisco: Jossey-Bass.

O'Flahavan, J. F. (1995). Teacher role options in peer discussions about literature. *The Reading Teacher, 48,* 354–356.

Ogle, D. (1986). K-W-L: A teaching model that develops active reading of expository text. *The Reading Teacher, 39,* 564–570.

Palincsar, A. S. (2003). Collaborative approaches to comprehension instruction. In A. P. Sweet & C. E. Snow (Eds.), *Rethinking reading comprehension* (pp. 99–114). New York: Guilford.

Palincsar, A. S., & Brown, A. L. (1984). Reciprocal teaching of comprehension fostering and monitoring activities. *Cognition and Instruction, 1,* 117–175.

Pearson, P. D. (1996). Reclaiming the center. In M. F. Graves, P. van den Broek, & B. M. Taylor (Eds.), *The first R: A right of all children* (pp. 259–274). New York: Teachers College Press.

Pearson, P. D., & Gallagher, M. (1983). The instruction of reading comprehension. *Contemporary Educational Psychology, 8,* 317–344.

Pearson, P. D., & Johnson, D. D. (1978). *Teaching reading comprehension.* New York: Holt Rinehart and Winston.

Pearson, P. D., Roehler, L. R., Dole, J. A., & Duffy, G. G. (1992). Developing expertise in reading comprehension. In S. J. Samuels & A. E. Farstrup (Eds.), *What research has to say about reading instruction* (2nd ed., pp. 145–199). Newark, DE: International Reading Association.

Perkins, D. (1992). *Smart schools: From training memories to educating minds.* New York: The Free Press.

Perkins, D. (1993, October 10–18). Making education relevant: Teaching and learning for understanding. *New Jersey Educational Association Review.*

Perkins, D., & Blythe, T. (1993). Putting understanding up front. *Educational Leadership, 51*(5), 4–7.

Perkins, D. N. (1986). *Knowledge as design.* Hillsdale, NJ: Erlbaum.

Perkins, D. N. (1994). *Knowledge as design: A handbook for critical and creative discussion across the curriculum.* Pacific Grove, CA: Critical Thinking Press and Software.

Peterson, R. & Eads, M. (1990). *Grand conversations: Literature groups in action.* New York: Scholastic.

Petty, W., Herold, C., & Stoll, E. (1967). *Knowledge about the teaching of vocabulary.* Urbana, IL: National Council of Teachers of English.

Pittelman, S. D., Heimlich, J. E., Berglund, R. L., & French, M. P. (1991). *Semantic feature analysis: Classroom applications.* Newark, DE: International Reading Association.

PLATO Learning. (2002). *Reading explorations.* Bloomington, MN: Author.

Prawat, R. S. (1989). Teaching for understanding: Three key attributes. *Teaching and Teacher Education, 5,* 315–328.

Press, F. (1984, May 30). Address presented at the Annual Commencement Convocation, School of Graduate Studies, Case Western Reserve University, Cleveland, OH.

Pressley, M. (2000). What should reading comprehension instruction be the instruction of? In M. Kamil, P. Mosenthal, P. D. Pearson, & R. Barr (Eds.), *Handbook of reading research* (Vol. 3, pp. 545–561). Mahwah, NJ: Erlbaum.

Pressley, M. (2002). Comprehension strategies instruction: A turn of the century report. In C. C. Block & M. Pressley (Eds.), *Comprehension instruction: Research-based best practices* (pp. 11–27). New York: The Guilford Press.

Pressley, M. (2002). *Reading instruction that works: The case for balanced teaching* (2nd ed.). New York: The Guilford Press.

Pressley, M., Dolezal, S. E., Raphael, L. M., Mohan, L., Roehrig, A. D., & Bogner, K. (2003). *Motivating primary grade students.* New York: Guilford Press.

Pressley, M., & El-Dinary, P. B. (1997). What we know about translating comprehension strategies instruction research into practice. *Journal of Learning Disabilities, 30,* 486–488.

Pressley, M., El-Dinary, P. B., Gaskins, I., Schuder, T., Bergman, J. L., Almasi, J., et al. (1992). Beyond direct explanation: Transactional instruction of reading comprehension strategies. *Elementary School Journal, 92,* 511–554.

Pressley, M., Harris, K. R., & Marks, M. B. (1992). But good strategy instructors are constructivists! *Educational Psychology Review, 4,* 3–31.

Pressley, M., & Woloshyn, V. (1995). *Cognitive strategy instruction that really improves children's academic performance* (2nd ed.). Cambridge, MA: Brookline Books.

Probst, R. E. (2004). *Response and analysis: Teaching literature in secondary schools.* Portsmouth, NH; Heinemann.

Purves, A. C. (1993). Toward a reevaluation of reader response and school literature. *Language Arts, 70,* 348–361.

Purves, A. C., Rogers, T., & Soter, A. O. (1990). *How porcupines make love II: Teaching a response-centered literature curriculum.* New York: Longman.

Quindlen, A. (1998). *How reading changed my life.* New York: Ballantine.

RAND Reading Study Group. (2002). *Reading for understanding: Toward an R&D program in reading comprehension.* Santa Monica, CA: Author.

Readence, J. E., Moore, D. W., & Rickelman, R. J. (2000). *Prereading activities for content area reading and learning* (3rd ed.). Newark, DE: International Reading Association.

Resnick, L. (1987). *Education and learning to think.* Washington, DC: National Academy Press.

Reutzel, D. R., Fawson, P. C., & Smith, J. A. (2003, December). *Teaching comprehension strategies using information texts.* Paper presented at the National Reading Conference, Scottsdale, AZ.

Robinson, F. P. (1946). *Effective study.* New York: Harper and Bros. (The original source of the SQ3R sequence of strategies.)

Rosenblatt, L. M. (1976). *Literature as exploration.* New York: Appleton Century.

Rosenblatt, L. M. (1978). *The reader, the text, the poem: The transactional theory of the literary work.* Carbondale: Southern Illinois University.

Rosenshine, B. (1995). Advances in research on instruction. *Journal of Educational Research, 88,* 262–268.

Rosenshine, B., & Stevens, R. (1984). Classroom instruction in reading. In D. Pearson, R. Barr, M. L. Kamil, & P. B. Mosenthal (Eds.), *Handbook of reading research* (Vol. 1, pp. 745–798). New York: Longman.

Routman, R. (2000). *Conversations.* Portsmouth, NH: Heinemann.

Rumelhart, D. E. (1977). Toward an interactive model of reading. In S. Dornic (Ed.), *Attention and performance* (Vol. 6, pp. 573–603). Hillsdale, NJ: Erlbaum.

Rumelhart, D. E. (1980). Schemata: The building blocks of cognition. In R. J. Spiro, B. C. Bruce, & W. F. Brewer (Eds.), *Theoretical issues in reading comprehension* (pp. 33–58). Hillsdale, NJ: Erlbaum.

Sales, G. C., & Graves, M. F. (2005). *Teaching reading comprehension strategies.* (U.S. Department of Education Rep. No. R3055040194). Minneapolis MN: Seward Incorporated.

Sampson, M. B., Sampson, M. R., & Linek, W. (1994/1995). Circle of questions. *The Reading Teacher, 48,* 364–365.

Schoenbach, R., Greenleaf, C., Cziko, C., & Hurwitz, L. (1999). *Reading for understanding: A guide to improving reading in middle and high school classes.* San Francisco: Jossey-Bass.

Scott, J. A., Jones, A., Blackstone, T., Cross, S., Skobel, B., & Hayes, T. (1994). *The gift of words: Creating a context for rich language use.* Manuscript prepared for a microworkshop presented at the meeting of the International Reading Association, Toronto, Canada.

Slavin, R. E. (1987). *Cooperative learning: Student teams* (2nd ed.). Washington, DC: National Education Association.

Sloan, G. D. (2003). *Give them poetry! A guide for sharing poetry with children K–8.* New York: Teachers College Press.

Something about the author. Farmington Hills, MI: Gale Research.

Soter, A. O. (1999). *Young adult literature and the new literary theories: Developing critical readers in middle school.* New York: Teachers College Press.

Stanovich, K. E. (1994). Constructivism in reading education. *The Journal of Special Education, 28,* 259–274.

Sternberg, R. J. (1998). Applying the triarchic theory of human intelligence in the classroom. In R. J. Sternberg & W. M. Williams (Eds.), *Intelligence, instruction, and assessment* (pp. 1–15). Mahwah, NJ: Erlbaum.

Sternberg, R. J., & Spear-Sperling, L. S. (1996). *Teaching for thinking.* Washington, DC: American Psychological Association.

Stewart, R. A., Paradis, E. E., Ross, B. D., & Lewis, M. J. (1996). Student voices: What works in literature-based developmental reading. *Journal of Adolescent & Adult Literacy, 39,* 468–478.

Stipek, D. (2002). *Motivation to learn. Integrating theory and practice* (4th ed.). Boston: Allyn & Bacon.

Strickland, D. S., Galda, L., & Cullinan, B. E. (2004). *Language arts: Learning and teaching.* Belmont, CA: Wadsworth.

Sum, A., Kirsch, I., & Taggart, R. (2002). *The twin challenges of mediocrity and inequality: Literacy in the U.S. from an international perspective.* Princeton, NJ: Educational Testing Service.

Sweet, A. P., & Snow, C. E. (2003). *Rethinking reading comprehension.* New York: Guilford.

Taylor, B. M., Frye, B., & Maruyama, G. M. (1990). Time spent reading and reading growth. *American Educational Research Journal, 27,* 351–362.

Taylor, B. M., Pressley, M., & Pearson, P. D. (2002). Research supported characteristics of teachers and schools that promote reading achievement. In B. M. Taylor & P. D. Pearson (Eds.), *Teaching reading: Effective schools, accomplished teachers* (pp. 361–373). Mahwah, NJ: Erlbaum.

Taylor, B. T., Pearson, P. D., Peterson, D. S., & Rodriguez, M. C. (2003). Reading growth in high-poverty classrooms. *Elementary School Journal, 104,* 3–28.

Tierney, R. J., & Cunningham, J. W. (1984). Research on teaching reading comprehension. In P. D. Pearson (Ed.), *Handbook of reading research* (pp. 609–654). White Plains, New York: Longman.

Tierney, R. J., & Readence, J. E. (2005). *Reading strategies and practices: A compendium* (6th ed.). Boston: Allyn & Bacon.

Tolkien, J. R. R. (1964). *Tree and leaf.* London: Allen and Unwin.

Tunnell, M. O., Calder, J. E., & Justen, J. E. (1988). A short form reading attitude survey. *Reading Improvement, 25*(2), 150–151.

Vacca, J. L., & Vacca, R. T. (1993). *Content area reading.* New York: HarperCollins.

Vygotsky, L. S. (1978). *Mind in society: The development of higher psychological processes.* Cambridge, MA: Harvard University Press.

Watts, S. M., & Graves, M. F. (1997). Fostering middle school students' understanding of challenging texts. *The Middle School Journal, 29,* 45–51.

Whimby, A. (1975). *Intelligence can be taught.* New York: Dutton.

White, T. G., Graves, M. F., & Slater, W. H. (1990). Growth of reading vocabulary in diverse elementary schools: Decoding and word meaning. *Journal of Educational Psychology, 82*(2), 281–290.

White, T. G., Slater, W. H., & Graves, M. F. (1989). Yes/No method of vocabulary assessment: Valid for whom and useful for what? In S. McCormick, J. Zutell, P. Scharer, & P. R. Okeefe (Eds.), *Cognitive and social perspectives for literacy research and instruction* (pp. 391–398). Chicago: National Reading Conference.

White, T. G., Sowell, J., & Yanagihara, A. (1989). Teaching elementary students to use word-part clues. *The Reading Teacher, 42,* 302–308.

Wigfield, A. (2000). Facilitating children's reading motivation. In L. Baker, M. J. Dreher, & J. T. Guthrie (Eds.), *Engaging young readers: Promoting achievement and motivation* (pp. 140–158). New York: Guilford Press.

Wiggins, G., & McTighe, J. (1998). *Understanding by design.* Alexandria, VA: Association for Supervision and Curriculum Development.

Wilhelm, J. D. (1997). *You gotta BE the book: Teaching engaged and reflective reading with adolescents.* New York: Teachers College Press.

Wiske, M. S. (Ed.). (1998). *Teaching for understanding: Linking research with practice.* San Francisco: Jossey-Bass.

Wittrock, M. (1986). Students' thought processes. In M. C. Wittrock (Ed.), *Handbook of research on teaching* (3rd ed., pp. 297–314). New York: Macmillan.

Wood, K. D., Lapp, D., & Flood, J. (1992). *Guiding readers through text: A review of study guides.* Newark, DE: International Reading Association.

Worthy, J., & McKool, S. (1996). Students who say they hate to read: The importance of opportunity, choice, and access. In D. J. Leu, C. K. Kinzer, & K. A. Hinchman (Eds.), *Literacies for the 21st century: Research and practice: Forth-sixth yearbook of the National Reading conference.* Chicago: National Reading conference.

Yopp, R. H., & Yopp, H. K. (1992). *Literature-based reading activities.* Boston: Allyn and Bacon.

Index

Photo Credits